CALLED

TO

COMMAND

★ ★ ★

A World War II Fighter Ace's Adventurous Journey

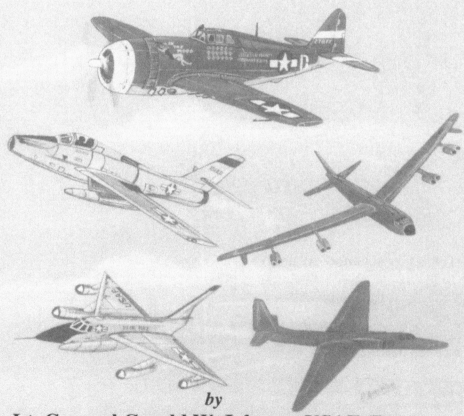

by
Lt. General Gerald W. Johnson USAF (Ret.)
with John C. McClure and Charlotte S. McClure

TURNER PUBLISHING COMPANY

Turner Publishing Staff:
Keith R. Steele, Publishing Consultant
Herbert C. Banks II, Designer

Cover art by Billy Garmon

Copyright © 1996 Gerald W. Johnson
Publishing Rights: Turner Publishing Co.
All Rights Reserved.

Writing assistance provided by John C.
McClure and Charlotte S. McClure

Library of Congress Catalog Card Number
96-60961

ISBN: 978-1-68162-358-0

TABLE OF CONTENTS

To My Grandson,
Gerald W. Johnson III

FOREWORD

This book reflects some of the major events of my life, primarily military, as I remember them. It has been written to provide interesting and informative reading and also to add to the historical record of the development of United States air power. It is my story told from my point of view. In many ways I have lived a rather unusual life. I base this on the events, experiences, responsibilities and assignments I have had compared with most of my contemporaries that I have known. My life has been filled with challenge and excitement which has continued down through the years.

Having matured during the depression years, I developed certain values having to do not only with material things but with life itself and the great gift it is to live it as we choose.

I remember as I was unpacking in the rooming house I was to stay in while attending Bryant and Stratton Business College in Louisville, Kentucky, I found a note my father had put in my bag. It said, "To be what we are and to become what we are capable of becoming is the only end of life." These words probably did not originate with my father but I have always treasured that note.

I hope the reader enjoys this book and will gain from it a better perspective of those times in which I lived. It covers three wars and the major changes that have evolved down through these fascinating years. It is serious but written with humor as to the personal experiences I remember.

Full credit is given to Charlotte and John McClure for without their help this book would not have been written. And to my dear wife, Mardi, who gave so freely of her time and energy in providing advice, guidance and understanding I owe so much.

CHAPTER 1

IN THE BEGINNING

I'm airborne. I'm alone. I'm soloing. It's a great day and a great experience. It's October 7, 1941, the first time I have had the airplane all to myself.

When reveille sounded that morning, cadets jumped from their bunks, dashed to the latrine for a quick wash and shave, rushed back to dress and make their bunks and then joined in formation to march to the dining hall. There was very little laughing and kidding that morning. Over the past week or so we had become a very somber group. After all, we were nearing eight or nine hours of flying time, many cadets had already washed out of the flying program and not one of us had soloed. This flying business for Army Air Corps students was much more difficult and serious than we had first imagined.

I needed to know how well I was flying the airplane. My instructor John Cope seemed like a fairly decent type, but he never had anything good to say about my performance—only negative comments or a bang on my knees with the control stick when the maneuver I did was not done well enough to please him.

That morning he seemed particularly grim as we walked out to the airplane, climbed in and taxied out. We took off and climbed up to altitude for a few maneuvers. Suddenly he took the control stick, rolled the plane over and dived for the airfield, landed and taxied to the ramp in front of the hangar.

I was petrified. I knew I had had it, pessimistically thinking that I would never become a pilot if my instructor didn't say those magic words to me, "The plane is all yours."

Then to my amazement he left the engine turning, climbed out and with a big grin finally said, "It's all yours."

So now it was my airplane. Even though I had been looking forward to this moment for such a long time and wondering what soloing was going to feel like, I was almost frozen on the controls.

I was thinking about my instructor who was there watching me taxi out to the runway. There wasn't all that much concrete at this primary training field at Chickasha, Oklahoma. Because of all the recent rain, the ground was soft, and we had to be very cautious to keep the wheels on the concrete because if we didn't we would be really deep in mud.

Fortunately, I managed to get to the take-off point which was on the opposite end of the field from the hangar. I got on the runway, pushed the throttle forward, heard the wonderful sound of that little engine, and felt the power as the propeller bit into the air. Even though this was a PT-19 (Fairchild Primary Trainer) with an inverted air-cooled in-line engine, it generated, for those days, a respectable 125 horsepower.

Down the runway I went. When those wheels came off the runway and I was airborne, I estimated that I should have gone past the spot where I thought my instructor stood with his eyes glued on me. Suddenly the tenseness left. I had a feeling of exhilaration that differed from any experience that I had ever had before. Finally after more than ten years of dreaming of becoming a pilot, here I was in the air with a powerful bird under my control.

Those first few minutes of flight were pure pleasure and my responses were those of complete joy. As a student in the back seat of the PT-19 there was only one double instrument available to the student - the cylinder head temperature and oil pressure. The airspeed, RPM and altimeter were taped over. This was known as flying by the seat of one's pants—Estimate your altitude, estimate your air speed. Fly by feel. It was a great way to learn to fly.

However, now that it was my airplane and I was all alone, I wanted to know how fast I was going and exactly how high I was. I didn't want to just look over the side and think I was high enough. Anyhow I didn't have these instruments, so I went ahead and flew around. My instructor told me I shouldn't stay up longer than twenty minutes. I flew around, and being alone I somehow got a much better feel of the airplane. Then it was time to return to the field and land, the critical part of the solo ride. I entered the downwind leg at the prescribed 45-

degree angle, made the turn onto the base leg at the proper spot, but due to a gusting crosswind, which gave me a tailwind, I had to immediately turn onto my final in a descending turn. I wondered what my instructor would think of that. The final approach was good, and by my correction for the crosswind, my touchdown although not in the first few feet of the runway was good. I taxied up to the hangar, and I thought, "Now comes the real test. Will John Cope be satisfied?" Sure enough, my instructor had a pair of binoculars hanging around his neck, and I knew that he had been watching me. He said some encouraging words, which included his expression of satisfaction of the way I handled the crosswind on the base leg and the final approach. To me, these comments made up for the other times when he had said very little.

This solo flight was a momentous experience for me. It was a dream come true for a young farm boy from the Midwest whose hero was a barnstorming pilot. There weren't many airplanes in the skies during the late 1920s and early 1930s. The first experiments with carrying the mail by airplane were in progress; Charles Lindbergh had flown nonstop from New York to Paris; and Wrong-way Corrigan had made his infamous adventure. In those days when I heard the sounds of an airplane engine, I immediately started searching the skies to try to see it. It was a lucky day for me when a barnstorming pilot found a satisfactory field near my home and landed. Barnstorming was a fairly common thing in those days. Pilots who had been trained during World War I and who were fortunate enough to have a small two-place airplane would travel around the country, finding small open fields near small towns and earning a few dollars by taking people up for a ride in their airplane.

I remember very well the barnstorming pilot's arrival at a field near my home in Owenton. It was a summer day. I was nine years old. I managed to get $2.00 and went to the field where he was taking people up for a short flight for that amount. I got a ride that was fascinating to me. I liked the feel of freedom, looking down on the ground, the noise of the engine, and the smell of gasoline and oil.

I spent the rest of the afternoon near the airplane and helped the pilot whenever I could and often carried cans of gasoline to the pilot when the plane needed refueling. Late in the afternoon after the crowds had dispersed the pilot removed the cowling and did a few things to the engine. He told me what he was doing and said a pilot also needed to be a mechanic because quite often the engine wasn't very reliable, it would quit; then the pilot would deadstick the airplane into the nearest field and would repair the engine himself. He then told me he had to make a short test hop and I could come with him if I desired. Little did he know how badly I wanted another flight. This time he did aerobatics. After landing I was totally convinced I was going to be a pilot.

During the Depression years life wasn't easy for most of us who were later to become fighter pilots. However, because of the hardships, sacrifices and many decisions that we learned to make at an early age, we may have become better prepared for the tough years ahead as combat fighter pilots.

I grew up on a farm in a vicinity called Pleasant Home, which was near the small town of Owenton, Kentucky, northwest of Lexington and about 20 miles from the Ohio River bordering Indiana. I was the youngest of four children—three boys and one girl. My oldest brother died as a baby. My sister Edna May was married when I was six so that left me growing up with my remaining brother Jerome, who was three-and-a-half years older than I. He seemed to be always teasing me or trying to get me into trouble with my parents. There seemed to be many reasons why we didn't get along well during those years but then maybe these experiences caused me to develop strong desires to do something worth while with my life.

My father James B. Johnson played a major role in my early development. He was a man of strict principles and strong beliefs. Although he had received very little formal education, through the sixth grade I believe, he was an intelligent man. He read a lot and stayed current in the daily happenings of the time and was always involved in politics from the local to the national scenes. Many men from some distance away would stop by our home to have conversations with my father and ask his opinions on a variety of things being considered. Regardless of what he was doing he always welcomed these visits and treated his visitors as if meeting them was the most important thing he had to do all day. I generally found some way to get close enough to overhear their conversations. Although I did not understand all they were talking about, I found it interesting. He always stressed the importance of honesty and the reasons why people should always do their very best. He frequently said, "Anything that is worth doing is worth doing right." He taught me to shoot and to hunt, always with a single shot gun. He told me, "You will never become a good shot if you know you have a second bullet to fire in case the first one misses." My father died when I was barely 20 years of age. I missed his conversations, sound judgment and good advice. My mother, Attie Reeves Johnson, always stood up for me even when I neglected writing letters to her regularly after I left home. Her family name, Reeves, I used to test German intelligence in 1944, but that story comes later.

I grew up going to the local schools in Owen County and was graduated from Owenton High School in 1937. I was elected president of my class twice and was a member of the National Honor Society for three years. I guess you could say I was a good student, especially in math. One year I was selected to represent my school in a state-wide arithmetic competition in Lexington. I won first place in the competition with students from schools from all over Kentucky.

After high school, four years in college seemed too long a time before starting to work, so I went to Bryant and Stratton Business School in Louisville. Before leaving for this school, my father took me to the best men's clothier in Owenton, Vallandingham's, and outfitted me for school: two new suits, shoes, shirts, ties, two sweaters and a hat. I got the very best quality, but I did not know at that time that Mr. Vallandingham had charged my father for much less expensive clothes than the ones I received. Such was the kind of man Mr. Vallandingham was; I had known him through all my high school years.

In Louisville I shared a room with two other very fine young men, both students at Bryant and Stratton. It was a large room and the landlady of the rooming house told us the room was for four students. A few weeks later I returned from school one afternoon to find a fourth student had joined us. He too, he said, would be a student at Bryant and Stratton. He was an interesting young man, and we talked until late that night as we tried to get to know him.

The next day when we returned from school in late afternoon we found to our utter dismay that our room had been stripped. All of our clothes and suitcases were gone. We were left with only the clothes we were wearing, which in my case was my worst suit. Although the police were notified, nothing was ever recovered. And of course, our new roommate who had joined us the night before was never seen again.

What to do? I had very little money, and I could not ask my father for more clothes. No one who has grown up subsequent to World War II can possibly imagine just how terrible those depression years were. I went to work after school and on Saturdays at the only grocery supermarket in Louisville at that time, the Atlantic and Pacific Tea Company store on Market Street. I usually worked three hours after school each day and on Saturday from six a.m. until midnight. I was paid twenty-five cents an hour, making $8.25 a week. After a couple of months my pay was raised to 28 cents an hour, which was a great boost to my morale. I was finding out what the real world was like in the fall and winter of 1937 and 1938. With this extra money I was able to buy more clothes although certainly not of the quality of those I had lost.

The Division Supervisor of this A & P store told me a new A & P Superstore was opening in Nashville, Tennessee in April 1938. If I would move there, he said, I could be the assistant to the manager for the delicatessen and bakery section of the store. And I would make considerably more money. Since I was becoming dissatisfied with Bryant and Stratton and the work schedule I was on was almost too much for me to handle, I accepted. There had to be something better, I thought.

After a few months in Nashville I began to realize I was wasting my time and getting nowhere with my life. Also I was not unmindful at that time of the gathering storm clouds over Europe and I wondered just what the future years might hold for me. One thing I had become certain of was that I must have a college education. Business school was not enough.

Although I had not had time during these past two years to think much about what seemed my unattainable goal—to be a pilot, I had not forgotten. With the help of my wonderful cousin, Martha Barksdale, at that time the registrar of Eastern Kentucky State Teachers College at Richmond, I went back to college in September 1939. Those next two years at Eastern were not easy. They seemed to drag even though I enjoyed what the college had to offer and also did some acting with the drama group, playing the role of Dr. Gibbs in Thornton Wilder's Our Town. With the war in Europe underway, Hitler sweeping across the western countries and the air battle of Britain getting started, I read and gathered all news possible about this war. Since I was enrolled in the Army Reserve Officers Training Corps (ROTC) program, I learned about the Army Aviation Cadet program of the Army Air Corps and its requirements of two years of college and passing of a very thorough physical examination. This opportunity gave me hope that I could make my dream come true. At least I had no doubt in my mind—flying was my goal.

Following the war in Europe as closely as possible and particularly the air war over Britain, I was impressed with the outstanding job the defensive fighter pilots of the Royal Air Force (RAF) were doing and could hardly wait to get started in that direction. During the latter part of my second year, I took and passed with no difficulty the required physical examination for entry into the Aviation Cadet program. Then all I had to do was finish that second year of college in early June. When June came, I was advised that I would receive notification when to report to Fort Thomas in northern Kentucky for induction.

I started to work for the state as I had done the previous summer, surveying the amount of tobacco that farmers had planted to assure they had not planted more than their authorized allotment for that year. It was interesting work and paid $10 per day. It also made my waiting time pass more quickly.

Finally I got the call. September 1 was my reporting date. I kissed my best (at that time) girl and my mother goodbye; my father had died two years earlier. I left for the beginning of the greatest, most challenging and most rewarding adventure I could have had—33 years in the United States Air Force.

After getting our immunization shots, four young men from the Kentucky-Ohio-Indiana area piled into a 1940 Chevrolet Coupe to drive the 590 miles to our primary flying school training field at Chickasha, Oklahoma, about 50 miles south of Oklahoma City. Since we had just had those shots, that was an awful ride, but at that young age, nothing was very bad, especially since we were off to the start of a long-sought adventure.

Chickasha was probably better known as the site of a girls' school. Our class of 49 young men arrived in early September 1941 at the Wilson and Bonfils Flying School, the newest air corps primary training center in Oklahoma. We found the airfield unfinished, the dormitories incomplete. Some airplanes had arrived and were in the hangars.

For two weeks, we lived in a hotel in downtown Chickasha, where we reported in to our cadet officer. We had our first meeting on the evening we arrived. All of us were assigned a room. I had a huge bed and a nice private bathroom. I woke up next morning, the telephone ringing, and a nice female voice said, "Good morning, Sir. It is time to get up." As I turned over in bed and looked around, I said to myself, "This is the life. They are going to teach me how to fly and pay me $75 per month." At that time $75 was a lot of money. I thought I was pretty lucky.

Beginning the next day, my life became very busy. Ground school was a very serious business. We spent a great amount of time with the airplane and our instructors, going over the fundamentals of flight and the specifics of this particular airplane, the PT-19. I found it interesting and fascinating. In the classroom we learned the basics of military life and the position of cadets and their responsibilities and relationship to others in the Army Air Corps. This was familiar stuff to me since I had been in ROTC in college. The study of meteorology and navigation also fascinated me. Along with all of the classroom instruction we spent a great amount of time with the drill instructor and the physical education instructor.

Although we had no upper class since we were the first class of cadets at Chickasha, the tactical officers were very observant and quick to pass out demerits. A demerit was a point or points received for not doing something or doing something wrong, i.e., making one's bunk, shining shoes, saluting, addressing or responding to an officer had to be done precisely. A demerit was redeemed by walking a given amount of time carrying a 30-06 rifle over a specified course. It almost seemed as if we were taught to drill only to be able to walk off demerits.

One of the cadets came from the mountains of Kentucky. Somehow he managed to get to Chickasha without ever learning his left foot from his right. Many of us spent a lot of time with him helping him to understand how to march and do the simple drill maneuvers required. In turn he taught us a lot about how to make moonshine without being caught by the "revenuers." It seemed that he might have had a good deal of experience in this area.

Life in general, and particularly military life, in 1941 was totally different from what it is today. What really impressed me then was the honesty and integrity of everyone in our class. Whenever anyone went out for exercise or changed clothes, he never thought of anyone walking off with anyone else's possessions. We could leave our money or our wallet or anything we had down on the bed; we didn't think about whether it was secure. The honor system worked. When we became officers later on, our word was never questioned, no one ever questioned taking our check. The degree of honor associated with a military officer in those days has, to some extent, been lost.

Next to figuring out what my instructor really wanted me to do in the airplane was to deal with my own inability to accept mediocrity. From my father came the desire to excel and willingness to put forth the necessary effort. I was the first one in my class at Chickasha to solo. I wanted to be the best. I studied hard in school and worked hard as a cadet. Still, I was always concerned that I wasn't doing well enough. The civilian instructors, experienced pilots under contract to the government, did not give us much encouragement. They were inclined to be very critical. If you did well, that was expected of you. If you did not do well, they let you know in no uncertain way. I found that flying was not difficult for me. Somehow almost from the beginning I seemed to have a feel for the airplane.

Our primary training plane was the PT-19 (Fairchild Primary Trainer). It had two open cockpits. The instructor sat in front, the student in the back. Communication was one-way only; the instructor spoke to the student through the gosport tube to each ear. However, by far the most effective communication came by the instructor's use of the control stick. He banged your knees when you did something incorrectly or when what you did didn't meet his approval.

Primary flying school was finished in early December just after the attack on Pearl Harbor and our entry into World War II. Even though we were training for war, looking back, I realize how relatively innocent and carefree we were.

We were authorized to leave the field on the Sunday of Pearl Harbor. We had been invited to several dances at Chickasha Girls' School, and had met some of the lovely young ladies. One of my good cadet friends, David Allerdice, had a Mercury sedan. On this Sunday, 7 December 1941, after church and lunch, we drove over to the school to pick up our dates. We drove around on a beautiful sunny afternoon, listening to the radio, when the program suddenly was interrupted with the announcement of the Japanese attack on Pearl Harbor—a great shock to all of us. We thought we would eventually get into the war, but we had not really thought of it as starting as it did. Shortly after this broadcast, the local radio station announced that all cadets from Chickasha Field should report back to the field as soon as possible. We drove the girls back to their school and returned to the base as soon as we could get there. The girls at Chickasha were sorry to see us leave. However, we told them not to worry for there would be a new class of cadets in a few days. And as for us, we knew there would be new girls at Randolph Field near San Antonio, Texas, who loved cadets in uniform.

When we returned to the field, we quickly put on our uniforms. At that time we were not required to wear a uniform off the field. In uniform, we went to the supply room where everyone was issued a long 38-caliber revolver and ammunition. Later in the afternoon or early evening, cadets were assigned to guard duty at different places around the flying field. I was assigned to guard one of the hangars. Carrying a 38-caliber revolver, I was driven out to the hangar and dropped off. I walked around that hangar most of that night. It was dark, I was alone and convinced that at every corner of the hangar I would find a Japanese enemy waiting for me. "What a change! What does the future hold?" All kinds of thoughts raced through my mind.

It was the next day before we began to learn anything at all about how severe the Pearl Harbor attack had been and how much damage was done. However, our cadet life changed quite a bit from that day on. We were restricted to the field; we never left it again until we departed for our respective basic flying school assignment.

For basic flying training, I was assigned to Randolph Field near San Antonio, "West Point of the Air." I flew a BT-14 (Basic Trainer) at Randolph. Again I was doing what I loved, flying. But Randolph introduced us to military tradition and discipline. Our instructors were Army officers. My instructor was Lt. Brewer, who gave me my first flight in a BT-14 on 21 December 1941. This was a considerable change from the PT-19. This airplane was large and heavier, the engine more noisy and more powerful. It had a closed canopy. It took a little getting used to but I felt I was going to like this airplane. Two of my greatest thrills were my first flight under the hood and our first night flight. The cockpit was equipped with a black canvas hood which when closed prevented any outside reference for flight orientation. One was then flying strictly with reference to the instruments. It took a lot of effort to accept that the flight instruments could really be trusted in blind flying. Although it seems strange now, we even made formation night landings, four planes abreast with our instructor leading. We just flew a tight formation position until touch down and then held this position as the instructor increased power and we took off again. It seemed that during most of my flight training I was so busy flying the airplane, staying in formation or navigating, that I had little time to just enjoy the beauty of flying. And this was particularly true during night flights. There was nothing more beautiful than flying on a moonlight night when there were just a few clouds in the sky.

Since we were the first class at Chickasha, we didn't have an upper class to instruct us in military ways and we didn't have any hazing. At Randolph the upper class knew our lack thereof and made up for any loss in that area. My loss came in poundage because of the gunner's role I so often played at mess. When we went to the dining hall, the tables were set for eight, four on either side. The cadet sitting nearest the path that the waiters used was the gunner. About four upper class and four cadets—one cadet at each meal being the gunner—sat at the table. Because meals were served family-style, the upper class helped themselves first to the food that was in bowls on the table, leaving what was left to the underclass cadets. Sometimes there was very little food left. At that point the cadet gunner had to hold up his hand to signal the waiter to bring more food. The cadet gunner couldn't eat while he was gunning. When the second helpings arrived, the upper class and the three cadets would help themselves and what was left was the gunner's portion. I had my share of being gunner. When I got through gunning at a meal, I had very little time to eat even a few bites of food before it was time to leave for class or flying duty. There was a bowl of fruit on the table, and we were allowed to take as much as we could hold in our left hand, which was rarely more than two pieces. I lost several pounds of weight during that period, but over all it was a good experience.

The upper class had a way of finding somethng wrong with everything a cadet did. The bed wasn't made right, or you didn't answer the question right, or you had a smirk on your face when you replied or something like that. You stayed in a brace, a rigid stance they called it suck in your stomach, pull in your chin. Following the war a lot of discussion about hazing took place. I am sure it was done to excess in some situations. By and large, hazing had its place in a process of discipline. We minded it at the time and we became annoyed with the individual imposing it, but pretty soon we became upper classmen ourselves and it was our responsibility to carry out the same kind of training of the under class. I suppose we got it out of our systems.

Soon graduation time arrived, and I had added 74 hours, 10 minutes to my flying time. Out of my primary class of 49 at Chickasha, 31 were graduated. Of the 18 that washed out, quite a few of them went through navigation and bombardier training. I think that rate was about average for that time, and several more were washed out in Basic training. Some members of my class had had previous flight training or had a pilot's license, they did not solo any more quickly than those of us who hadn't had flight training. And sometimes such a pilot took a superior attitude and blew it when his attitude became one of "look how I do it" rather than "do it the Army Air Corps way."

Known officially as Class 42-D, my class at Randolph completed the streamlined course in record time. More instructors, doubled flying time, a natural "up-and-at-'em" mental attitude combined to reduce sharply the regular 10-week course without sacrificing the quality of the training. This class was also the second wartime class of Aviation Cadets and Student Officers at Randolph. We were scheduled to man the fighting airships in Uncle Sam's 60,000-plane production program that President Roosevelt announced in 1942.

When my basic course was completed, I was assigned to Advanced Flight Training at Ellington Field, south of Houston, Texas. This base was among those that had both twin-engine and single-engine aircraft for students but was known as a twin-engine school. Ellington had two twin-engine airplanes. The AT-17 had a canvas skin and was rather ordinary in most ways. On the other hand, the AT-9 was a wonderful little airplane. Its skin was all metal and the engines were powerful. It flew relatively fast and touched down in landing fairly fast. It was fun to fly and I liked having another cadet along. This was the twin-engine trainer I flew most.

The AT-6 was the single engine airplane used in advanced training. This airplane was fun to fly and my advanced instructor was absolutely superior. We hit it off very well from the start, and I always thought he gave me a lot of extra attention. A frustrated fighter pilot, he wanted to leave the instruction business and to fly fighters in the war in the worst way. Whenever he could arrange it, we flew the AT-6 in formation and then split up to do simulated dog fighting and combat maneuvers. Hence I received a lot of really good single-engine training.

On 29 April 1942 I and several of my classmates with whom I later served—Walker (Bud) Mahurin, John Vogt, Joe Curtis, among others—were graduated as second lieutenants with pilot wings on our chests. I was a very proud and happy pilot.

Most of the cadets it seemed had family members or girl friends who attended the graduation ceremony and pinned on the gold 2nd lieutenant's bars or wings or both. I had neither a family member nor a girl friend present. Without previous knowledge and to my surprise when it came my turn, the beautiful young wife of my instructor stepped forward and asked if I would mind if she did the honors. Not only did I not mind, I was delighted.

After the ceremony was finished my instructor and his wife came over to me and said, "Jerry, it is about lunch time and we wonder if you would like to see the inside of the Officers Club." What a question, would I ever! I realized that more and more I was really falling in love with military life and particularly the life of a pilot.

At that time the 56th Fighter Group, formed in January 1941, was stationed at Mitchel Field, Long Island, New York. The group had a hodgepodge of older fighters such as the P-35, P-36, P-39 and P-40 and a few of the new twin-engine P-38s. It was expected that the P-38 would be its combat airplane and that is why I was sent to the 56th having just graduated from a twin-engine school. I was at Mitchel long enough to fly all the airplanes several times before being assigned to the 61st Squadron of the 56th Fighter Group and being moved to Stratford, Connecticut near Bridgeport.

Since the officer quarters at Stratford, tarpaper shacks, were not finished, we slept upstairs in a large room over the administration area of the Stratford Baptist Church. There were 22 of us on cots in this room. The bathroom was down stairs. Six lights with large frosted glass globes swung from the ceiling. Each light had a separate switch and could be turned on or off individually. Everyone slept with his 38-caliber revolver on the floor beside the cot. One night several guys came in quite late, having had a few beers. They turned on the lights and after getting into bed, one light was left on. One of our few senior captains said, "Lieutenant Schneider, put out that damned light." Lieutenant Schneider said, "Yes, Sir," picked up his 38 and shot it out.

We had been at Stratford only a few days when the squadron received its first Republic P-47 Thunderbolt. The 56th Fighter Group had been selected to receive the first of the brand new Republic Aviation Company's P-47s. It was a large airplane for a fighter, almost 14,000 pounds, powered by a 2,000 horse power Pratt and Whitney radial engine. I spent hours with that aircraft that day, just looking at it, sitting in the cockpit, walking around it and wondering what it was going to be like to fly it. Two days later I found out.

Stratford Field's longest runway was only 3,800 feet long, and there were sand dunes and beach cottages at one end of the runway. The P-47 nose was so big the only way the pilot could see how to taxi was to "ess" the airplane. On take-off I could see only the edges of the runway going by until the speed was enough for the tail wheel to come up and thereby give me forward visibility. I was not at all impressed on that first flight. I had been looking forward to the fighter I would fly and fight in—a sleek, fast and maneuverable airplane. The P-47 was heavy; it did not climb very fast and did not seem very responsive to the controls. But I found out on that first flight it could really dive and at higher speeds it was stable and responsive. During the flights that followed I began to really like this big flying jug.

The speed of sound in June 1942 was something we knew very little about, and flying faster than the speed of sound, Mach 1, I do not believe had been thought of at that time. However, we soon learned from the P-47 about compressibility. The P-47 in a dive nearly reached the speed of sound (760 mph). The controls would absolutely freeze at about 600 mph; this was known as compressibility. The pilot could not pull the stick back to come out of the dive. The first time that happened to me I was quite high, above 20,000 feet, and I had time to try several things. What finally worked was to decrease the pitch of the propeller, apply maximum throttle and lower the flaps. Needless to say, I had a lot of flap damage when I landed, but at least I came out of that situation safely.

One day a group of pilots were outside our operations tent when we heard the horrible scream of the P-47 in a dive. One of our best pilots, Lt. Bobby Knowle, came straight down and hit the beach about 100 feet from the water line. He went down with his airplane. It was a sobering event for all of us. Later in combat, I found firing the eight 50-caliber guns was effective in getting out of compressibility.

Later on we started to use Bradley Field at Windsor Locks, Connecticut where the 62nd Squadron of the 56th was based as a check-out field because the runways were longer and the approaches to the runway were better. Stratford was simply not an adequate or safe field for checking out new pilots in the P-47. We had many accidents due to the approaches and the short runway. Moving the new pilot check-out to Bradley solved most of these problems.

My first squadron commander, Loren McCollom, was strict and serious, a fine man. He always said, "Just stay on my wing. When I start a maneuver, don't try to outguess me. You don't know what I will do or where I will go. Stay with me and I will get you back." In combat flying, I remembered his lesson, and used it often in training the pilots who would fly my wing position in combat.

One morning in October 1942, my squadron commander told us, "I have just learned we are going to England and from there as part of the newly formed Eighth Air Force we will fly and fight the famous German Luftwaffe." He also said that the weather was usually bad, and if we were not confident of our instrument flying ability, we should practice as much as possible during the short time we had remaining before the airplanes would be taken away and prepared for shipment to England.

I didn't know much about flying on instruments. I had had the usual under-the-hood instrument flights as a cadet and had a bit of time in the Link trainer but I certainly did not feel qualified. I usually flew at least one mission each day with a flight of four to the south side of Long Island for gunnery practice over the Atlantic Ocean. As we started back from the next flight, I told my No. 3 man to take the other two pilots back to Stratford because I planned to climb up into the clouds and fly instruments back to the base. I got into the clouds and flew along using needle, ball and air speed. The attitude indicator was still foreign to me. This did not seem too difficult, so I thought I should try rolling the airplane. As I did this roll, all the instruments tumbled. I had no reference to my attitude, and I lost control of the airplane and came spinning out at the bottom of the clouds. I recovered, but I also discovered there must be more to flying in clouds and on instruments than I thought or knew about. In hindsight, this event seems strange, but at that point in my career my instrument experience was, to say the least, limited. After this flight I practiced instrument flying at every opportunity.

We stopped flying in late November so that the airplanes could be prepared for shipment to England; hence we had a lot of time on our hands. Fortunately we had a lot of jeeps, and with snow on the ground we organized jeep races. It is a wonder that we didn't kill ourselves. Near Stratford was an area of rough terrain where tree stumps and other obstacles were covered up with snow. We played follow the leader, and trying to cut off the leader, someone would hit the stumps, often throwing the driver clear of the jeep. We were young and physically fit, and fortunately we bounced well.

Finally the time to move to the Port of Embarkation at Camp Kilmer arrived. Dick Allison and I were good friends in the 61st Squadron. We roomed together at the Port of Embarkation for three or four days. On the first day we had a number of meetings and learned a little about what we should prepare for in England, such as warm and proper clothes for the cold damp weather. We loaded our aviation kit bags full. One day when there wasn't much to do, we talked of how long the ocean trip to England would take, and we knew we would probably get pretty tired of it. We went over to the Class 6 store to buy some bourbon, 12 quarts of it in a case. We planned to put six bottles in each kit bag, which was already fully packed.

We opened the bags and started asking ourselves, "Do I really need this and that?" We said, "Probably not," and we tossed out stuff and put in a bottle until we got all six bottles in each of our bags. That night the trucks came about 11 p.m. to take us to the port for boarding the Queen Elizabeth which was to sail the next morning. The trucks took us only part way. We had to walk the rest of the way. I have no idea now how far we walked. It seemed to me we walked for miles. I know that that aviation kit bag was heavy. It was hard to carry; it was so fat. When I carried it in my hand, it hit me on the leg. When I tried to get it up on my shoulder, I found it didn't fit there either. There was no way to get it under my arm. So Dick and I said to each other, "We have too much damn stuff in these bags. Let's stop and throw something out." We did this three or four times while we walked, but I don't remember that we ever considered throwing out any of the bourbon. We boarded the Queen Elizabeth on 3 January 1943 with a case of whiskey and felt better when we heard, though we did not see, that Major David C. Schilling, commander of the 62nd Squadron, had walked on board openly with a bottle of whiskey under each arm.

Dick and I were assigned to a stateroom designed to have two people, but on this trip it housed 12 guys in three tiers of bunks. That whiskey came in handy as it turned out that we were the only ones who had brought any quantity. We became quite popular. A lot of "new" friends made a trip to our stateroom. But we also had time to review what we had accomplished since becoming aviation cadets about 16 months previously. I accumulated 59 hours, three minutes of flying at Chickasha; Basic at Randolph provided an additional 74 hours, 10 minutes; and in Advanced at Ellington I acquired 74 hours, 5 minutes. My grand total of flying time in cadet training amounted to 207 hours, 18 minutes. With the 56th Fighter Group, flying planes from the P-35 to the P-47, another 171 hours, five minutes was added, 159 hours of that time in the P-47. When I added my fighter time and cadet time, I counted a total flying time of 378 hours, 23 minutes.

Looking back on that experience, I realize that that wasn't very much time as a basis for going into combat. However, I knew we had a great airplane in the Jug and we were eager to test its capabilities against the powerful and experienced Luftwaffe.

I found my primary flying school airplane -PT-19, at the Pima County, AZ Museum in 1991.

CHAPTER 2
COMBAT OVER EUROPE AND GERMANY

The Queen Elizabeth was a luxury British ocean liner, converted to a troop carrier, a pretty fast ship, capable in an emergency of a maximum 37 knots. The winter weather caused a rough voyage in many ways, and we were always aware that enemy submarines maneuvered somewhere out there. At least 12,000 men were on board, including Army troops, some Royal Air Force pilots returning home, a medical evacuation unit from a New York hospital and the 56th Fighter Group. The Army troops had been issued clothing impregnated with a treatment that resisted penetration by gas. This clothing of heavy olive drab wool was scratchy and smelled awful. These soldiers occupied the lower levels of the ship. However, there were twice as many soldiers as there were bunks for them. Half of them had to stay on the upper decks with many outside in the weather while the other half slept below. Then the groups changed places. Several 56th officers were selected to help in this alternating procedure. I was one of them. Although it was cold at topside, at least the smell of the clothing was dissipated in the fresher air.

One night when we were seated in the dining room, we realized why the tables had edges built up to avoid spillage of tableware. All of a sudden, the Captain must have spun the liner's wheel a full 90 degrees. Everyone and everything went crashing across the room. Stuff slammed into the wall. Later we understood that the "Liz," running across the Atlantic without escort, had encountered a submarine pack and the Captain was trying to evade and outrun them. Fortunately he was successful. Many more times during our crossing we felt the ship turn quickly and violently with changes in power as the Captain skillfully and safely maneuvered us across the submarine-infested waters of the North Atlantic. It was reported that one man had gone overboard, but this great ship could not jeopardize the lives of all the men aboard by attempting a night rescue of one man.

In addition to the violent maneuvers of the ship in avoiding submarines, it was a rough crossing weather-wise. I had never before crossed the Atlantic Ocean. I was amazed at the height of the waves and at the huge swells. One moment this mighty ship could be sitting high with great visibility of nothing but water for miles and the next moment be totally surrounded by walls of water much of which came over the decks.

We dropped anchor at Gourock, Scotland at 4 p.m. on 11 January 1943. I got off the ship at 5 o'clock, and with my 61st Squadron mates was marched to a train. It was 9 o'clock that night before the train started the trip to Peterborough, which was the closest town to the 56th's base at Kings Cliffe. We arrived at Peterborough at 3 p.m. the next day. Just as on my first day at Chickasha, and again at Stratford, I arrived at an unfinished airfield. We stayed in several small hotels in Peterborough for a few days until the barracks at Kings Cliffe were completed. Everything around the town and countryside was blacked out.

I didn't understand English hotel customs too well. The hotel staff asked me what time I wanted to be "knocked up" in the morning, giving me no warning that this meant someone would walk into my room and say, "Good morning, Sir, your tea." The next morning a maid knocked, walked into my room, opened the drapes, and put the tea beside my bed. Shades of the female voice that awakened me at the hotel in Chickasha. Even in war-torn England life seemed pretty good to a new young pilot who was involved in the greatest adventure he had ever known.

In a couple of days, we moved to the base. Kings Cliffe in the East Midlands was one of the new wartime airfields with temporary Nissen-type buildings. It had three short hard surface runways and a paved perimeter taxiway that connected the three runways. The mud because of the ongoing construction on the base, the cold damp climate of England which the small iron stoves could not overcome, and the unfamiliar English food made our first January in England somewhat unpleasant. We longed for the arrival of our P-47s that would take our minds off the daily discomforts. In the meantime, ground training, using bicycles to simulate flying formations, courses in geography to familiarize us with the terrain over which we would fly and fight, and instruction by a couple of Royal Air Force officers on the British flying control system helped us to think we were moving toward flying again.

Finally the airplanes arrived on 24 January and were warmly received. The base jumped with excited activity. As the aircraft had only recently been assembled at the Burtonwood Depot, it was necessary for each one to be thoroughly inspected by the ground crews before they could be flown. Fortunately that inspection was accomplished swiftly, and we eagerly took to the air to regain our feel for the P-47 that we had learned to love.

After I had had a couple of flights around the area, late one afternoon, Col. Hub Zemke, Commanding Officer of the 56th Fighter Group, came in the pilots' lounge with a manila envelope in his hand. He announced, "I've got to get this message to 8th Fighter Command this afternoon. Anyone want to take it?" My hand went up immediately. The old man told me that Fighter Command Headquarters was near Bovington just west of London. "I think you land at a base by the same name," he said, "and a car will take you from there to Fighter Command Headquarters." So on the map I drew a straight line from Kings Cliffe to Bovington, determined the distance and how long it would take to fly there. A great opportunity. I always enjoyed flying to a strange base. I put on a flying suit, got a parachute, and walked out to the airplane.

I took off, got out my map and tried to do pilotage, i.e., to stay on course by comparing the ground references with the map. This plan just did not work. Whereas the map would show a railroad track or a town, on the ground I would see several of each. I knew the only way I would find Bovington was by time and distance—hold my course and fly out the time; then if I didn't see the town and the airport, I'd do a 360-degree turn and Bovington should be inside that circle. I held the course, flew out the time, and sure enough, I saw the town and an airfield, but not just one airfield but two others, none of them having identifying signs. All road signs and signs on buildings had been removed early in the war as a precaution against letting the Germans know where they were if they were to invade the area. I landed at what I thought was the most likely airfield and left the engine running. A Royal Air Force (RAF) airman came running to see this huge airplane, and I asked him if this was Bovington. He said, "This is not it. You are almost there, right over there. You can't miss it." That last phrase I was to hear the British say every time they gave directions. I was anxious to taxi out and get on with my mission but he wanted to talk about my airplane.

Finally I taxied out, took off, and pulled up the gear, and I found the other field. Since it was late and I wanted to get to 8th Fighter Command Headquarters as soon as possible I headed straight for the end of a runway. Then I realized just in time that my gear was still up, and it was too late to do anything but push up the throttle and go around. This time I had the gear down and landed. Again not being sure of the field I left the engine running. Another RAF type came up to the plane and climbed onto the wing saying, "That's an interesting landing procedure. Do all of you use that procedure, coming in first with gear up, going around and then landing?" I answered, "Yes, we always do that." I learned there was another airfield in the equation of my mission when he announced, "This is not Bovington." The third time I took off, landed at the right field and I had the gear down. I was learning some interesting navigation lessons.

An attractive young WAF driver with a staff car arrived to take me to 8th Fighter Command Headquarters. Along the way the engine quit and the car rolled to a stop on the side of the road. The driver got out, raised the hood and appeared to be just looking at the engine. I stayed in the back seat. I was still in my flying suit and I always carried a few tools. I said to the driver, "Do you want a screwdriver?" Her reply puzzled me, but then I thought maybe due to her English accent I may have misunderstood her.

The car finally started, and I arrived at 8th Fighter Command Headquarters well after dark but had no trouble in finding General Kepner's office and delivering the envelope. I later had dinner, remained overnight and flew back the next morning above a low overcast. Again I figured time and distance, let down through the clouds, did a 360-degree turn and, sure enough, there was Kings Cliffe. I was beginning to like England.

Our flying now was to prepare us for combat, to learn to navigate over England, to learn and use the radio procedures and homing devices available to help us get back to base after combat over Europe, and to practice serious gunnery techniques. We recognized we had arrived in war-torn Europe. The Luftwaffe regularly flew over England indiscriminantly bombing cities, small towns and airfields. The pilots of these aircraft and the fighters we would soon encounter over Europe were highly trained and had already four years of combat experience. We were brand new, had never experienced combat and still did not know just how the P-47 would perform in deadly engagement with the Luftwaffe's FW 190 and the Me-109. However, we were determined, confident and anxious to get started, to get involved in this war, to taste actual combat. More to the point, we wanted to get a German fighter in our gunsight and as we pressed the trigger switch watch our eight 50-caliber machine guns rip their aircraft apart until it exploded in flames.

We soon learned that we were to go to Llanbedr on the west coast of Wales for final gunnery training before starting combat.

Again my tendency to volunteer gave me an interesting experience. It was necessary to send a road convoy to the gunnery site at Llanbedr under the direction of an officer. I thought it would be a great experience to be the officer leading the convoy consisting of ground crew personnel, ammunition, aircraft parts, and tools. However, that volunteer job turned out to be one of the most difficult missions I have ever had. On the road maps I had collected on which to lay out the journey, the route to Llanbedr looked easy enough to follow. I had some difficulty understanding British English and could not understand the Welsh language. Getting directions along the way proved even more difficult. Every road sign and place designation had been taken down. And everyone I asked directions from ended up saying, "You can't miss it." And I would miss it. After each inquiry, I would start out hopefully. When I got to the turn-off described, I would see a couple more, none of them having any signs posted. I don't know how many times I had to ask directions. Dozens and dozens of times I jumped out of the jeep to inquire before we finally arrived at Llanbedr.

Shooting gunnery at this time was serious business. For one week despite the persistent clouds and rain, flights of four aircraft each were launched steadily from early morning until almost dark. We wanted more than anything to be thoroughly prepared for the combat that would soon come. There was no point in being good fighter pilots and being able to find the enemy only to find we could not shoot the enemy down because we hadn't learned how to shoot aerial gunnery. Tow target flights had been set up, the target towed by a Lysander, a British high-wing monoplane. The target usually was nearly as long as the fuselage of a fighter plane plus a little more length to account for error. Each pilot fired individually color-tipped ammunition in order to identify and determine his own score by examining the target for the holes made by his ammunition color.

The squadron pilots stayed in small two-room cottages in a field where sheep grazed. Invariably when someone went to sleep early and left the cottage door open, someone would round up one or two sheep and guide them through the door of the cottage and then close the door. It was fun to imagine that pilot's surprise when he was awakened by the bleat of real sheep.

At the beginning of April 1943, Colonel Zemke told us that we were about to be put on operational status and would move from Kings Cliffe to a new base, Horsham St. Faith, just outside the city of Norwich, closer to the North Sea. This was a well constructed permanent RAF station, but it had no runways, just a relatively flat and smooth grass field. Many RAF fighter plane bases were built in this manner during those days.

When we landed there on our arrival from Kings Cliffe, the grass hadn't been cut. It must have stood about a foot high and this made for a very smooth landing. However, grass field landings could be a little tricky, especially if the grass was wet, which it was most of the time. Then braking action was limited and it was hard to stop the airplane. One time when the grass was wet, I didn't get stopped. I went right off the edge of the field, and the plane went up on its prop. Not only was I embarrassed, I was mad. How in hell could I have let this happen. The plane stayed in that position, and I wondered how I was to get down from the cockpit. When a P-47 is on its nose the cockpit is quite high. My crew chief Sgt. Baltimore came out to see what I had done to his airplane. I was standing up in the cockpit and considering if I could jump to the ground. But it was too far. Sgt. Baltimore didn't seem to care about getting me down; he was only concerned about the airplane. I didn't want to stay in the cockpit, but I did until the crew got the tail down. I think this was part of my punishment. The other punishment was that I had to put a British pound in a glass jar on the bar each week for a month; it was marked "Lt. Johnson's propeller kitty." Any pilot could use this money to buy a drink by placing a note in the jar with his name on it and the statement, "I will never damage an airplane I fly." To my knowledge at the end of a month there were four British pounds in that jar and no notes.

My first combat mission took place on 15 April 1943—a great day. I was scheduled to fly the No. 2 position in the lead flight. Colonel Zemke led the group of 48 P-47s, 16 from each squadron. I was to fly Colonel Zemke's wing. We flew in flights of four aircraft, each squadron having four flights. The airplanes were lined up wing tip to wing tip and after starting engines, the pilots would taxi across the grass field with each flight getting into the proper position for take-off. Take-off time was set for 2 p.m. I had worked on my airplane almost all morning. Sgt. Baltimore and I had cleaned and polished it, not to make it look nice but to make it fly faster.

The excitement of flying my first combat mission was almost indescribable. I must have visited the latrine at least three times during that last hour before take-off. It was a normal ritual for pilots to go one last time beside the tail of his airplane before climbing into the cockpit. I climbed into the cockpit well ahead of start-engine time. There were not many things to do in the cockpit prior to pushing the start switch. One fairly critical item though was priming the engine.

A hand-operated primer on the instrument panel needed to be turned, pulled out and then pumped several times.

The start-engine signal was given. Propellers started to turn all up and down this long line of P-47s. Engines started with great puffs of smoke on either side of me. My engine smoked but did not start. I could not believe it! I had waited so long for this day, my first combat mission, my first time, I hoped, to see a German airplane, and now my damned engine would not start. The other airplanes began to taxi and had almost reached the take-off position before my engine finally started. Sgt. Baltimore was standing on the wing beside me when the engine started. I was in such a hurry to get into take-off position I immediately pushed the throttle forward, and the plane's sudden movement made my sergeant fall off the wing. I rushed across that grass field with the tail in the air to join my flight. Since all take-offs were planned with a few minutes in take-off position for any last-minute checks and adjustment before releasing the brakes, I arrived just as Colonel Zemke started to roll. I spun around, joined his wing, rammed the throttle forward to stay in position, and I was on my way. That is how close I came to missing my first combat mission.

This mission was the first full scale mission for the 56th Fighter Group. It was a fighter sweep over the western edge of Belgium and France during which we hoped to bring up the Luftwaffe. German fighters flew in the area but initiated no engagements. I saw no enemy airplanes and very little of anything. My first combat mission seemed much like any other formation flight. It was the only combat mission I flew in a wing position. After this one I always led at least a flight. On 14 May I had my first opportunity to put an FW 190 in my gunsight and squeeze the trigger. What a really great thrill that was. I scored hits all over that airplane with concentration in the cockpit area. Unfortunately I had to break off my attack because I saw two FW 190s closing fast on me and one had already opened fire. Because the airplane I was shooting at did not explode and I did not see it hit the ground because of the clouds beneath us, I was only able to claim the aircraft as damaged. However, I believe the pilot was killed or totally disabled since he took no evasive action after my bullets began to strike the cockpit area.

By now I began to have a pretty good feel of combat. I liked it. I liked the thrill of the hunt. But one thing I knew I had to improve was my ability to see enemy airplanes and to judge the distance between them and me before I opened fire. I was determined to improve the quality of my aerial gunnery.

Each airplane had a 16-mm movie camera mounted in the leading edge of the wing. When the trigger was pressed, the guns fired and the camera rolled its film. Hence every time I had an engagement with the enemy and fired the guns, this camera recorded a moving picture of the entire action. We flew training missions every day that we didn't fly combat, and frequently on such a training mission, I would be one of two aircraft that would take off, climb to 15,000 or 20,000 feet and do mock combat. I had these airplanes loaded with ammunition so that the weight of the P-47 would be the same as a combat-loaded plane, but obviously the guns were prepared not to fire. When we pressed the trigger, we activated only the camera. We would attack each other in all kinds of maneuvers. The pilot being attacked would do his very best evasive maneuvers to avoid having his partner's gun camera show that he could have been hit if the guns had fired. After development, this film was closely analyzed and studied to learn whatever we could about how effective the attack had been and how effective the evasive action had been. It was a rewarding way to improve an individual pilot's combat ability. We also would fly away from each other for a considerable distance to practice and train our eyes to focus on the small speck of an airplane rather than just to look to infinity.

This lack of ability to see enemy airplanes at fairly great distances was a problem for all of us during the early days of combat. Some pilots overcame this lack better than others. I seemed to see enemy planes quite often before other pilots saw them. I had a keen eye—so much so I was called the flying Daniel Boone, no doubt an echo of my Kentucky origin. However, I expect a good bit of my ability came from my early life when I tried to see any airplane that I heard passing overhead.

The P-47 had eight 50-caliber machine guns, four mounted in each wing. Those eight guns loaded with a mix of armor-piercing and incendiary bullets could shred and set on fire an enemy aircraft if the pilot was in proper range before opening fire. Most pilots tended to open fire out of range, thereby alerting the enemy that he was under attack and could then get away.

I had my guns bore-sighted so the trajectory of the left wing guns and of the right wing guns would cross at between 200 and 300 yards in front of my airplane. I also had the guns set so that the trajectories were not on the same plane. The effect then was that from about 150 yards to about 350 yards all my bullets were on trajectories through an imaginary square about 8 x 8 feet. I planned then that, if I were closing very fast on the enemy, I would open fire at 200 to 300 yards, and if I were closing more slowly, I would not open fire until 200 yards. That turned out to be a great and effective concentration of fire power. I spent a lot of time at the bore-sight range with my crew chief and the bore-sighting team. They were just as anxious as I was to make those guns just right.

As I was growing up I did a lot of duck hunting. Sitting in a duck blind for hours waiting for the ducks to fly over us, too often I would not hit a duck. I shot out of range, or so my Dad told me. I do not remember what my Dad had done to learn to shoot them in range, but I know what I did and it helped a lot. Using a couple of boards, I put together something that did not look like a duck but it was the same size as a duck in flight. The next fall for a week or so before the duck season opened, I put this wooden duck on top of a pole and measured from it the killing distance of my particular shotgun and load. I then spent a lot of time standing at that distance looking at the wooden duck down the gun barrel of my shotgun until I knew exactly what a duck should look like at my killing range. When hunting season opened that year I downed a lot more ducks.

During the early summer of 1943, I decided to apply my duck hunting experience to combat flying. I had my crew chief position my airplane and put another P-47 200 yards directly in front of my airplane and raise the tails of each airplane so that they would look generally the same as in flight. I spent a lot of time in the cockpit looking through the gunsight of my airplane at the other airplane and getting fixed in my mind just how large an enemy plane was when it was in range. The P-47 was larger than the FW 190, but nevertheless I now had a fairly good picture fixed in my mind of what I was looking for. My crew chief Sgt. Baltimore was very tolerant and helpful in my continuing search for ways to maximize my combat ability. In turn I let him use my bicycle most of the time (Each pilot was issued a British-built bicycle for his ground transportation).

After each mission, all pilots who had made contact with an enemy airplane wrote a mission report. This was a personal combat report according to a formula of detail, i.e., date, kind of mission, the squadron or group section flying the mission, take-off time, location of encounters with enemy aircraft, weather, claims of destroyed, probably destroyed or damaged enemy airplanes. Although the information gleaned from this type of report lacked the excitement of over-the-bar war storytelling, they became the historical record of the individual pilot, of his squadron and group, and of the 8th Fighter Command and 8th Air Force in Europe. I regret that I did not record more fully the details of the missions I flew. I disliked writing down more details than I had to. Nevertheless, the more than 22 personal combat reports I still have today refresh my memory of some of the most exciting moments in my combat life.

On the morning of 26 June 1943, The 8th Fighter Command operations order for this day directed us to escort B-17s fairly deep into the south of France. Since our base Horsham St. Faith was just south of the wash in East Anglia, we were directed to fly to Manston, an RAF base southeast of London, land, refuel, and take off from there to join the B-17s near Forges, France. By taking off from and returning to Manston, we could stay with the bombers much longer.

I led Shaker Yellow flight in the second section of the 61st Squadron. We joined up with the B-17 bombers and took our escort positions. I was to the right and 1,000 feet above the bomber formation. I scanned the sky constantly expecting to see enemy aircraft. We hadn't been there very long when suddenly I spotted them—at least

30, probably more. They approached with the sun behind them and in the opposite direction from our formation about 2,000 yards out and several thousand feet higher. I immediately called my leader, "Large number of bogies 3 o'clock high." I heard, "Roger, " meaning my leader had received my message. By now the German planes were at about five o'clock and they started a descending turn to come in on our tail to the rear of the bomber formation. I immediately called, "Enemy aircraft coming in fast from five o'clock." I received no response. I could not believe this was happening. We were about to come under attack by dozens of enemy aircraft with whom we would have to tangle and fight, and our group made no move to prepare for the attack.

I called again with no response. I could not wait any longer. I called, "Yellow Flight, break hard left, NOW." It was a perfect break. The FW 190s could not stay with us but passed right through our turning flight. I was so close to these aircraft I could easily see the pilots as they shot by. I tangled with several of the enemy but could never get in position to fire. It seemed they wanted to attack the bombers and were not much interested in me and my flight.

Everything happens very fast in an aerial battle. To me, this encounter seemed rather long; however, I doubt that it lasted more than a few minutes. I now tried to reform my flight, but to my surprise I could not find another P-47. I could see the bombers far ahead still on course, but I could see no fighters. It was very quiet, almost as if the enemy fighters had never been there. I started to climb in the direction of the bombers, hoping to find my squadron or some part of the 56th. After all, we had been 48 airplanes in formation just a few minutes before. I reached 26,000 feet, scanning the sky. I knew there just had to be fighters, enemy or friendly, out there somewhere. Suddenly I thought I saw three P-47s, about 3,000 feet below me far to my left and headed in the opposite direction. I immediately rammed the throttle forward and turned in their direction to join them but decided to hold my altitude. As I got closer, I realized that these were not three P-47s but two FW 190s and one P-47, which was being chased and was being badly shot up by one of the FW 190s. The P-

47 just flew straight ahead, trying no evasive action. The other FW flew lower and to the side of the one shooting at the P-47. Still at full throttle, I quickly started a diving turn for the aircraft doing the shooting and I was glad I had kept my altitude. I needed to get that FW 190 quickly or the P-47 would be shot down. Both Fws were concentrating on the P-47 and never saw me coming. I held my fire until about 200 yards, then squeezed the trigger and yanked the throttle back in order to stay behind him a bit longer. What I saw was unbelievable. That FW was just saturated with strikes and almost immediately it started to smoke, then flames and a huge explosion enveloped it. I rammed the throttle forward, pulling up in a tight turn to see what the other FW 190 was doing. I located him down near the ball of flame that was hurtling to the earth. I saw no parachute from that airplane before it crashed. I then pulled up to see if the P-47 was all right. I saw him far off still flying straight and level and heading in the direction of Manston, England. I thought he would make it home o.k. so I turned back to find that other FW 190.

I had shot down my first airplane, I liked the feeling, and I wanted a second one. I could see the first one still burning on the ground, but I never could find the second one. I suddenly realized that I had been at full power now for sometime and that wonderful P-47 had been responding to my every move of the controls as if we were one. I throttled back, checked my fuel, which was getting low, looked at my watch and turned for England. I was far over the time we were scheduled to turn back and head home.

I selected maximum range cruise settings to save fuel and then sat back enjoying the ride out of France and across the English Channel to Manston.

This days activities were not yet finished, however. I had barely gotten settled down for what I hoped would be a pleasant and safe ride back when suddenly as I was scanning the skiers for enemy aircraft there they were–several thousand feet above and slightly to my right rear about a five o'clock high position. I couldn't identify how many but at least 4 to 6. They were in a sorta loose gaggle.

What to do–if I tried to tangle with them and fight and won I didn't think I would have enough fuel to get back to England. I f I tangled with them and didn't win, I certainly wouldn't get back to England. I had just had my first victory and I wanted more but these odds didn't seem to be in my favor.

My only chance to survive, I felt, was to try a maneuver I had practiced several times but never really thought I would ever use in combat. It was one that could only be used when you were alone– it was a last resort–a SYA maneuver and it was dependent primarily on two things. First, the enemy must think they are taking you totally by surprise and, second, the maneuver must be started at exactly the right moment and while the enemy is closing rapidly. So I'll do it. I continued with the same low power setting, straight and level pretending I had no idea there were enemy aircraft anywhere near. And this wasn't easy to do because the adrenaline was really flowing and my heart rate must have topped 200. But I continued and watched them start their decent and turn to a firing position behind me. They were at high speed and closing fast. I didn't make a move but I was prepared and knew exactly every move I must make to be effective. Just as I thought they were within firing range and I almost waited too long because they were closing so fast, I jerked the throttle to idle, rammed the propeller pitch control full forward, slammed the flap control lever down, threw the stick full left, and kicked the right rudder pedal to the fire wall. That P–47 jumped left like a horse shying from a rattlesnake. The bullets first and then those FW–190s went scream-ing past me and slightly high–good–I was in their blind spot. I had no time to lose, I must act and quickly. I hit the flap handle up, rammed the throttle full forward, cut in water injection, rolled the airplane and in an instant was going straight down at fantastic speed. At about 8,000 feet and approaching compressibility speed I began to ease the stick back until the aircraft was level probably about 6,000 feet but still with full power. Carefully then I scanned the sky for any sign of those FW–190s. They were not in sight. I then eased the power back , established maximum range cruise settings and took stock of my fuel situation. It would be close but I thought I could make Manston.

After getting over the English Channel I began the think about what had just happened. There was no doubt in my mind–that maneuver had saved me but I didn't look forward to ever using it again.

On my way back to England, however, I couldn't help wondering why had the P-47 pilot taken no evasive action but had just continued straight on while he was being badly shot up. It seemed as if he had simply frozen on the controls. I later learned that this reaction in combat was not too uncommon.

I was the last to land at Manston. My crew chief had worried that I might not make it back, but when he saw that the tape covering the gun barrels had been shot away and I told him I had destroyed a FW 190, he was excited. He pointed to a P-47 that was badly shot up and that had landed with the wheels up. Before going into operations for debriefing, I went by this airplane. I could easily see from the damage it had received it was the airplane that the FW that I had destroyed had been shooting at. I still did not know who the pilot was. When I went inside for debriefing, I immediately recognized him. The pilot of this badly shot up P-47, standing with his shot of after-mission bourbon in his hand, was telling a wild story about his combat with two FW 190s, about how he had fought them off and finally escaped. I decided I would not spoil his glory by relating what really happened. That was a tough mission for the 56th Fighter Group. We lost three of our senior captains and one fine young lieutenant. Several more aircraft were badly damaged. I had fired 860 rounds of 50-caliber ammunition and had the only kill. That was not a very good trade.

One of my most challenging flights occurred on 17 August when we escorted bombers on their way to hit the industrial targets at Regensberg. I led Keyworth Red flight in the first section of the 61st Squadron. I wrote an unusually long personal combat report on this encounter with ME 109s and an ME 110, which recounts the details of this spectacular mission.

> We made landfall over Walcheren Island at 1555
> hours at 20,000 feet. We proceeded on course at this
> altitude to just north- east of Antwerp where we pulled

up to about 22,000 feet and dropped belly tanks. Shortly after this point, White flight led by Major Gabreski made an attack on two ME 109s coming in from the rear. We followed him in the attack and soon he and his wingman returned [home] because of fuel shortage… When we reached the bombers we crossed over the top to take a position on the left side of the last box [of bombers]. As we came out on the left side north of Liege [Belgium] about 25,000 feet, I saw a twin-engine plane almost solid white, or very light gray, flying across the front B-17s in the last box at about 20 degrees to their course. The pilot was flying at about their speed and about 1,000 feet above them. I immediately rolled over and went down on him from dead astern.

At about 150 yards I opened fire and could see strikes all through the center of the plane. After about a two-second burst he exploded into what seemed like tiny pieces with a flame about 50 feet in diameter and the little pieces seemed to just hang in the air burning. It is my opinion from his position and action that he was preparing to drop bombs on the B-17s and that my bullets exploded his bombs before he could release them because I don't believe anything else could have caused such a tremendous explosion.

We then pulled up toward the sun to about 23,000 feet and upon leveling out I saw a single ME 109 going in head-on to the bombers. I came down on him at a steep angle and opened fire at about 200 yards. I could see hits and flashes on the fuselage and wing roots. At this point he started to turn left and a full burst seemed to hit between the cockpit and engine. There was a large flash of flame and smoke, and he started to go down in a slow spiral. As I pulled back up in a climbing turn, I saw the pilot bail out and the chute opened immediately. We then pulled back up to about 1,000 feet above the bombers and to their left. We were approaching the rear of the front box when I saw another single ME 109 coming in from about 10 o'clock to the bombers. I couldn't get within range until he broke away from the bombers. I then easily closed to 100 yards without being seen by the enemy aircraft. I fired about a three-second burst, observing strikes all over the fuselage and smoke and flame coming out. Without any evasive action he slowly rolled over to the left and went straight down. As I pulled up in a tight climbing turn, I saw the ME 109 hit the ground in a cloud of smoke. I then found that I was by myself (my No. 2 man and second element had chased two ME 109s off my tail during my last attack) and started for the coast at 17,000 feet. As I neared Antwerp, two ME 109s came up behind me and out to the side, but when I turned into them, they broke down toward Antwerp. I then proceeded home without further incident. I attribute the success of this flight on this mission to the splendid cooperation and team-work of my wing man, Lt. Foster, and my second element, Lt. [Paul] Conger and Lt. R. S. Johnson. I claim one ME 110 destroyed and two ME 109s destroyed.

I now had downed four enemy aircraft. The incident that was so spectacular—the explosion of the ME 110—was a German maneuver that allowed the pilot to drop bombs with instantaneous fuses through the bomber formation. If the bomb touched a bomber, it would explode and the bomber would be destroyed. When I got back to England, I found from everyone in the formation, and I heard later from bomber crews, that they had recognized the explosion and understood what the plane was to do. In other words, I had exploded his bombs before he was able to drop them. That was one of my greatest missions. So much happened in so short a time. It is hard to remember how it all felt.

A little more than two weeks later, this 17 August mission was featured on a weekly radio program, A Story from Britain. On 4 September, four pilots and I read a script titled "60 Seconds over France" that dramatized four recent combat missions. Frank McCauley and I read the prepared dialogue that described the story of that exploding white ME 110 and its pillar of flame about 1,000 feet high and 50 feet across. That event lasted maybe 20 seconds in the air, but Frank and I related it in four minutes on the radio program.

On 19 August, I became an ace, the first one in the 56th Fighter Group, the second one in the 8th Air Force in Europe, by downing an ME 109 near Gilze-Rijen in CAVU (ceiling and visibility unlimited) weather. At 25,000 feet, I watched three ME 109s approaching the bombers about 2,000 feet below my flight. We made a tight 360-degree turn and came out on the tail of the three ME 109s flying line abreast. The leader did a very quick roll and then continued flying straight. I fired about a three-second burst from about 250 yards at 15-degree deflection at the number three plane. I saw strikes on the wing near the fuselage. He immediately flipped over and went straight down. I let him go and pulled up in a tight left turn and found the leader of these three right in front of me at about 100 yards. I started firing and he tried all kinds of maneuvers with the exception of breaking down as the Germans usually did. I could see flashes on his fuselage and I knew I was hitting him. Pretty soon there was a large red flash near the center of the fuselage and he started down in a rather steep dive, trailing smoke. I watched him go down for about 10,000 feet and then pulled up to try to get my flight together again. Lt. Biales, who flew in the second flight in our section, saw him hit the ground. I claimed one ME 109 destroyed and one ME 109 damaged. I was proud of becoming the first ace in the 56th Fighter Group and to be second to Jack London in the hierarchy of aces in the 8th Air Force in Europe.

To honor me and in recognition of the first 56th Fighter Group Ace, Colonel Zemke asked someone to pick up my best uniform jacket (it was called a blouse in those days) and take it to a tailor in London, who replaced the lining with a brilliant red lining, a privilege in adjustment to the uniform allowed only for an Ace. That was one of my most cherished pieces of uniform. The blouse with the red lining is now displayed in the United States Air Force Museum at Wright-Patterson Air Force Base, Dayton, Ohio, along with the story of its origin. The only thing I can say about becoming a fighter ace is that it was a very nice feeling of accomplishment. To shoot down five enemy aircraft was just the beginning. It meant that I wanted to keep right on doing what all of us had been trained to do. Of course, when a pilot got that second five, and even the third five, little attention was paid to that achievement.

It had been a busy and very interesting summer for me. In June I had met Group Captain Milan and Wing Commander Deane at the RAF Club in London. We had talked at length about our respective airplanes, the Spitfire and the P-47. They were from Biggin Hill, a RAF station just southeast of London, and they asked me to fly down when I could and we would exchange airplanes for a familiarization flight.

On the 4th of July I flew down to Biggin Hill. I stayed several days during which time I flew two combat missions with my P-47 and also flew the Spitfire 5B for one hour and 15 minutes and the Spitfire 9B for one hour and 15 minutes. In turn Milan and Deane each flew my P-47. The Spitfire 5B was very light and its performance seemed to me to be rather ordinary. The Spitfire 9B was another thing. It also was very light but powerful and could really climb and turn. Both airplanes in a fast dive, if the pilot did not keep them perfectly trimmed, seemed to slip sideways slightly. I did not feel I would really like this airplane in combat. Likewise, the RAF guys liked the big roomy cockpit of the P-47 but felt it was a bit too heavy to be effective in combat. I left Biggin Hill with each of us having enjoyed the experience but happy with our own flying machines.

On 10 August, I was promoted to captain. That rank and title I really liked. It just seemed to sound right. Gen. Henry (Hap) Arnold, Chief of Staff of the Army Air Forces, arrived in England in early September. On 4 September, I flew to Duxford, home of the 78th Fighter Group, to meet with General Arnold and Gen. William E.

Kepner, Commanding General of the 8th Air Force Fighter Command. Capt. Jack London, the first Ace in the European Theater of Operations, and Major Roberts, the third Ace, were also there. We were the only aces in the ETO (European Theater of Operations) at that time. We had a nice meeting over lunch and General Arnold, after congratulating us, presented each of us with an engraved Bulova Navigator watch.

Each American base in England had a C-61 aircraft, which was used for administrative flights. This was a small four-place, single-engine airplane. I had flown this C-61 over to Duxford because after lunch with the generals I planned to fly down to London, taking two news reporters with me. The reporters were to accompany me because I was to broadcast that night from the British Broadcasting Corporation (BBC) studios back to the United States. During lunch, one of the reporters asked me if I would mind another passenger on my flight from Duxford to London. As the C-61 was a four-place airplane, I said, "Not at all."

When I arrived at the airplane that afternoon, my three passengers were waiting. When I saw the third passenger, I was concerned. He must have weighed 300 pounds. In those days we did not compute weight and take-off distances; we just assumed we would take off regardless of these factors. The third guy climbed in the front seat beside me. I felt the little airplane settle to the right and my right arm felt somewhat restricted due to its being tightly pressed against my third passenger. At that time, Duxford had a grass field which caused a lot more friction and resistance on take-off than a hard runway would. I thought of Lindbergh's take-off from Roosevelt Field on his way to Paris. I started the engine, taxied out to as close to the edge of the field as possible to give me maximum take-off distance. Since the airplane had not been refueled at Duxford, I thought that loss of weight might offset the extra passenger weight I had aboard. I pushed up the throttle, checked the instruments and released the brakes. Immediately I noticed the hedge row at the other end of the field. The little airplane struggled across the field, the hedge row got closer and the air speed increased very slowly. I thought of trying to stop; I thought of trying to open my third passenger's door and pushing him out, but I kept going. I pushed hard to get that throttle a bit farther forward. At the last second I carefully eased back on the wheel and my little airplane struggled off the ground and over the hedge row missing it by inches.

When some color had returned to the face of my fourth passenger, he said, "You know, I have noticed on almost every flight I make with you Americans, you take off very low; it's rather unnerving." I didn't say anything.

After the evening broadcast, I was invited along with Bud Mahurin to have tea the next afternoon with Queen Elizabeth at Buckingham Palace. This was an extremely interesting event. Bud and I had agreed that as we met the Queen, he would say, "Hi, Queen," and at my turn I would say, "Hello, Queen." However, we didn't do this. Gen. Omar Bradley was also present and it seemed after our meeting and responding to the Queen's questions, most of her time was spent with General Bradley. This left Bud and me to entertain or be entertained by the two princesses, Elizabeth and Margaret, who were both present. We thought both seemed rather young but they were charming. The tea, small sandwiches and cakes were excellent and we enjoyed a memorable afternoon. After tea, I went to the airport, got my airplane, and flew alone to Halesworth. As I taxied my little C-61 to the parking area, remembering how well it behaved with its heavy load, I patted the instrument panel and said, "You have done very well."

The Fairchild Aviation Corporation had developed a completely new self-computing gunsight for fighter airplanes. A few of these had been shipped to the RAF to be mounted in their Spitfires and tested. Col. Chesley Peterson of the 4th Fighter Group at Debden, England and I had been selected to go down to Exeter, a RAF station somewhat like our Wright Field at that time and fly these Spitfires with the new K-14 gunsight and then report our findings and recommendations to 8th Air Force Fighter Command.

On 17 October, I flew down to Debden, joined Colonel Peterson in his C-61 and we flew down to Exeter, which is right on the English

Channel in the southwest of England. An interesting incident happened as we landed. With any cross wind, the C-61 had a tendency to ground loop as the pilot rolled out from touchdown. Colonel Peterson was flying and sure enough, as we slowed down the airplane started to ground loop. He was unable to stop it so around we went on the runway. It is an embarrassing and humbling experience, but Colonel Peterson handled it in his own way. As he taxied back to park in front of operations where the ground crew signaled us, we noticed a red carpet had been laid out on the tarmac and quite a few people had gathered for our arrival and, of course, had observed the ground loop. He shut off the engine; we climbed from the airplane and walked up the red carpet, returning the salutes of the RAF officers. After some conversation with the people gathered there, suddenly Colonel Peterson said, "Hey, did you see that ground loop? By the way, Jerry, where is my pound (British money)? You see I bet a pound with Jerry that I could ground loop that C-61 on landing." I wondered if they believed him, but at least they accepted his story.

Colonel Peterson and I were at Debden for a week. I flew 16 missions with this new K-14 gunsight mounted in a Spitfire 5B, firing live ammunition at a flag target. It was far superior to the ring and bead sight I had been using. All I had to do was to put the pipper on the target and the amount of lead needed, for the angle I was off was computed for me. I could hardly wait to put this gunsight in my P-47 and fly into combat using it. We spent this week with Group Capt. Ford, Squadron Leader Denton, Flight Leader Sheppard and a civilian, Mr. Jones. It was a fascinating week and I learned a lot, not all from flying since I met a very lovely and charming WAF (Women's Auxiliary Forces).

On 19 November I flew down to London, had dinner with a small group of RAF pilots and a fascinating Mrs. Mitchell from Glasgow, Scotland. The next day I was presented the Distinguished Service Cross by Lt. Gen. Jacob L. Devers at 8th Air Force Headquarters. Lt. Gen. Ira C. Eaker, Commanding General of 8th Air Force, was also present. Afterwards there was a reception and a dinner. On Thanksgiving day, 25 November, I again flew to London to have a holiday dinner given by the RAF at the Wings Club. I am not sure how this happened but somehow the same WAF I had met at Exeter was present at this dinner. I was scheduled to return to Halesworth the next morning, but to my surprise the weather totally socked in and I had to stay in London another night. I can't say I was disappointed.

In the first two weeks of October, I shot down a ME 110, a ME 109 and a FW 190. My personal combat report for 10 October recounted the details.

> As we [Blue Flight, Keyworth Squadron] turned left to take our position on the bombers, I saw 12 to 15 enemy aircraft to the rear of the second box and slightly above them, about 27,000 feet. I saw an ME 110 starting an attack from about 4 o'clock on a bomber that had fallen back somewhat from the main formation. I called my attack and started down. As I neared the ME 110, I could see large bulges under each wing just outside the engines, which probably were rocket guns. I opened fire at about 300 yards and saw strikes on the fuselage and starboard engine, which started smoking. By this time we were within 200 yards of the B-17, and the enemy aircraft went under the B-17 very closely. Since I was attacking from slightly above, I had to pull up hard to miss the Fort and went over the top. I then half-rolled and came out on the tail of the ME 110 again. At about 250 yards, I opened fire and the port engine started burning. There were strikes near the cockpit and along the fuselage. Then pieces started flying off around the tail and the aircraft fell off to the left in a spin. I then pulled up in a tight left turn and the last I saw of it, it was still spinning down with the left engine and wing burning and the right engine pouring out black smoke. I couldn't observe it any longer since an FW 190 dived past my nose so close I had to break down to avoid hitting him. I then turned back toward the bombers and there was

a ME 210 slightly below me headed toward the bombers from about 8 o'clock. I started after it and opened fire at about 250 yards. There were strikes on the fuselage and right engine, but since I was closing fast I had to pull up and come down in another attack. On the second attack there were hits all over the fuselage [and] wings and the right engine started to burn. The rear guns fired at me through the first attack and part way through the second and then stopped firing. The ME 210 started down in a shallow dive to the left and I made another attack. This time the left engine started burning and pieces flew off. When I pulled up from this attack, one person bailed out and the aircraft continued going down and burning. We pulled back up to our position on the left side of the bombers and escorted them to the coast without seeing any more enemy aircraft. I claimed one ME 110 destroyed and one ME 210 destroyed.

On 14 October, the bombers were going after the ball bearing plants at Schweinfurt. This escort mission was a major effort but badly handicapped by severe weather over England. Apparently planners at 8th Bomber Command Headquarters considered scrubbing the mission and waiting for better weather. However, they decided to go on as planned. The 56th Group took off on time. Several fighter units were delayed and a few did not launch at all. Several bomber groups were also delayed in taking off and forming up.

The result of all this delay by weather was that a well-planned mission with fighter protection for the bombers was very poorly executed. Consequently the German fighters had a field day. We had to wait at the rendezvous point with the bombers for some 20 minutes before the bombers arrived. These 20 minutes caused us to have to discontinue escorting the bombers sooner than planned. As we approached the time when we would have to break off escort and start home, we could see what looked like many squadrons or groups of enemy fighters in the distance just waiting for us to leave the bombers.

We stayed much longer than we should have because we hated to leave the bombers all alone to face the certain slaughter that awaited them on the long remaining flight to Schweinfurt and then back out from the target toward home. This limited range was the only problem the P-47 had in escort missions. The longer-range P-51 Mustang would solve this problem, but it would not arrive in England in any great numbers for several more months.

On this mission I led Keyworth Blue One flight. As I made my last turn over the bombers before leaving the area, I spotted two FW 190s flying line abreast about 2,000 feet below me. I called the attack, started down to take the one on the left. I opened fire at about 200 yards and continued to close on him. He rolled over, started to spin down with smoke and flames coming from the airplane. My No. 4 man, Lt. Sam Hamilton, saw the pilot bail out. As I had become separated from the rest of my group and was low on fuel due to staying too long with the bombers, I had to bring my flight back to Halesworth at a maximum range cruise setting. As I approached England we flew above a solid overcast and I could hear the conversation of other aircraft ahead of us that were trying to find their home base. I heard Halesworth control tower report the weather as zero-zero, meaning no ceiling and no visibility. That message ruled out our landing at home base. I knew my flight was low on fuel, and we had no time to waste and certainly could not consider going to Wales or Scotland as some bombers were doing.

I remembered the morning weather briefing and the expected weather conditions that would prevail at the time of our return. I had to find a place to land and soon. I decided to go southwest and hope for an opening in the overcast. During World War II every English or American military base had a very bright light on the left side of the landing end of the runway. I had already called my flight and told them to form in tight echelon formation off my right wing since we might have to land suddenly. The top of the overcast at this time was about 3,000 feet—I was right on top of it. Suddenly through a thin spot in the clouds, I saw that bright light and knew what it meant. I had flown with the three guys with me, knew their qualifications and knew they would not screw up the landing pattern I had in mind. I called, "I'm going down to land, stay close and don't lose me."

Down I went in a tight spiral around that bright light, knowing there would be a runway just to the right of it. As I passed 1,000 feet, I called, "Gear down, flaps down." We weren't very much above landing speed at this time. Sure enough, there was the runway— visibility was no more than one-half mile. I touched down long enough to give the others room to maneuver, rolled out and off the runway onto the grass as soon as I could. I could not have been prouder of these guys. With so little total flying time they had handled those P-47s like true professionals. We had practically landed in formation. Before that little hole above the landing light closed over and visibility dropped to zero, many more airplanes landed with no attempt to properly park them.

Eighth Air Force airplanes had landed all over England, Wales and southern Scotland on that day. It took almost a week to get them back to their proper bases. Sixty bombers had been lost and many more were badly damaged on this Schweinfurt mission. That day became known as Black Thursday and the numbers of lost and damaged bombers and their crews came close to causing the end of daylight bombing over Europe.

In this same month of October, Gen. Jesse Auton, Commanding General of the 65th Fighter Wing, under which the 56th Fighter Group operated, thought that an aggressive fighter ace like me would be helpful to the 356th Fighter Group at Ipswich. This Group had arrived in England rather recently and was new to combat. General Auton believed I could be helpful in getting them started. I really hated to leave the 56th. It was my outfit. I had been with it for almost a year and a half, knew well the older pilots and had helped train all the new ones. Nevertheless, I had no choice, I had to go. The 356th was based not far from the 56th. Their base, Martlesham Heath, was near Ipswich, and the 56th had recently moved to Halesworth from Horsham St. Faith. The reason for the 56th's move was to place us as close to the east coast of England as possible and thereby be able to go deeper into Germany with the bombers.

At this point after I was selected to go to the 356th Fighter Group, I was one of 15 aces in the 56th Fighter Group. Our success was probably due to our aggressive and determined attitude toward combat. Also, we were well trained and proud of our outfit. Like a big family of carefree combatants, when the new pilots came in, we took them up in training missions and dogfights over and around our own base to indoctrinate in them the same aggressive spirit and attitude that we knew we had. Not everyone in the 56th had it as fully as desired. A lot of the success of combat pilots depended on their leaders. A leader's objective should be to put the pilots in a combat position where they would have the advantage over the enemy and thereby be effective. I always encouraged pilots by practicing with them. If I had a pilot who had joined the squadron recently, I always flew with him several times before he actually went into combat. I took him through all the maneuvers that he would be expected to encounter. I gave him an opportunity to find out how difficult it was going to be just to stay on his leader's wing. All of these things, I believe, made him a better pilot. We taught our new pilots the 56th way. I planned to try and implement these same techniques with the pilots of the 356th Group.

I arrived at Martlesham Heath and joined the 356th on 29 November and flew my first mission with them on 1 December. Since the 356th was new to combat they were not given difficult missions and did not penetrate very deeply into enemy territory. Consequently the German fighters did not come up to meet us.

On 12 December I did find a few FW 190s. We engaged them and I was just closing on one when he went into the overcast below us and I never found him again. The weather was really bad all over Europe and England during December and January of 1943-44. On this mission when we returned to the base, we landed in a heavy snowstorm with almost no visibility.

Three days later our group took off with 48 airplanes. The ceiling was about 600 feet so we were unable to form up the Group before entering the overcast. So each of the 12 flights climbed through the overcast alone. We were almost at 20,000 feet before we broke out.

As I looked around in the bright sunshine above the overcast, I would see a flight break out here, another there, and soon all 12 flights were above the overcast and not too badly separated. Then we joined in proper formation for the rest of the mission. Later we learned the bombers we were to escort had aborted and we were directed to return to base.

Before taking off that morning and since the weather was briefed to be very bad on our return, I briefed and implemented a plan for getting the 48 P-47s back on the ground at Martlesham Heath. I had developed this plan while I was with the 56th. Each base had a homing device and the control tower could give incoming aircraft steers (compass headings) to the base. We did not have landing systems such as GCA or ILS. My landing plan required the pilots' close attention to timing and speed. Before reaching the base on our return, I put the 12 flights in trail with space between flights. We descended to 3,000 feet on a heading of 180 degrees off the landing runway heading and held a speed of 180 mph, carefully maintaining this formation as we approached the base. The tower had reported the top of the overcast to be no more than 2,000 feet, but the ceiling was only 200 to 300 feet with no more than one mile of visibility. An airman with a white flag tied on the end of a long pole stood in the center of the field. When he heard P-47 engines directly overhead, he would drop the flag. The controller in the tower would see this flag fall and tell us we were overhead. The lead flight would then turn 45 degrees right in a one needle width turn, start the let down at 500 feet per minute and hold for three minutes, then start a left one needle width turn, continuing descent and start slowing down to 120 mph; continue turn until on the runway heading which would be a left turn of 225 degrees. We had received the altimeter settings as we initially approached the base. If we had not broken out by 100 feet, we were to pull up, take a heading to a large crash area on the coast about 30 miles north. Each pilot was to give his airplane's call sign, e.g., Blue One, on touchdown.

Although I had practiced this procedure in good weather conditions several times while I was still with the 56th, I was now very concerned as to whether it would work under very bad weather conditions and with this many airplanes. Before it was my turn to take my flight down, I had heard a few touchdown calls and thought the system must be working. As my flight went down and I picked up that bright light on the left side of the landing runway, I felt real relief. As it turned out, ten of the 12 flights landed at home base. The leaders of two flights had become separated and confused and could do nothing but attempt to find the crash site, which was paved and could be used for wheels-down landings. Six of these landed safely with gear down. Two crashed, one in an open field which the pilot could not see until just before he touched down, the other just short of the crash site. Neither pilot was seriously injured. Needless to say, the bar that night was a busy place. A week or so later at a meeting of Fighter Group commanders I was asked to present this landing procedure. I don't believe very many were convinced it was a workable procedure.

I was promoted to Major on 16 December, but somehow this did not mean very much. I had been a captain for only four months and had not really become used to the title Captain, which was one I liked. Also, it was about this time that I began having severe ear problems. Because of the weather and flying one ear became badly infected and I was grounded. Then as this cleared up a bit, my tonsils became infected and had to be removed. I sat in an ordinary straight-back chair for this operation with minimum anesthesia. It was painful, but worse was the unsweetened canned grapefuit juice I was forced to drink during recovery. I think I lost at least two weeks of flying. I had become good friends with a pilot slightly older than I, Oscar Cohen. He had had many interesting experiences in his life. He was not very tall, and as we stood at the bar for many hours during my time at Martlesham Heath he usually stood on the bar rail as he related his experiences. He had a great sense of humor. While I was grounded and recovering from the tonsilectomy, he would bring over a bottle of gin and make some delicious martinis. He insisted it was the only drink one should ever have.

It was January 1944 before I finally destroyed a FW 190 and damaged another. This was the only kill I had with the 356th Group. It was not a good winter for me.

When I returned to the 56th Group in February 1944, I was given command of the 63rd Squadron. Many pilots in the 56th had by now passed me in total kills since I had gotten only one while I was away. I started to fly every mission I could. Having pretty good luck, I downed one or two enemy aircraft at a time, and was slowly catching up with the guys who had gotten ahead of me.

Fortunately I returned to the 56th just as the Big Week in February got under way. This famed Big Week was a maximum effort by the 8th Air Force against industrial targets in Germany by the largest concentration of bombers and fighters to date. The Thunderbolts were fitted with long-range 150-gallon belly tanks that would enable them to penetrate with the bombers deep into Germany and when the enemy fighters arrived, to stay with the bombers until the enemy were destroyed. Gen. Jimmy Doolittle had taken command of the 8th Air Force in January 1944. One of his first actions was to authorize fighter escort pilots not only to defend the bombers but to pursue the enemy fighters and destroy them. This was consistent with General Eisenhower's objective to ensure that the Allies had air superiority by D-Day. The Thunderbolt pilots also did a lot of strafing as the Jug's 50-caliber guns did a fantastic job on almost anything on the ground—trucks, trains, enemy aircraft, whatever moved or stood still. As strafing was a different kind of mission from dogfighting and escorting, we had to learn by experience to keep up our airspeed on a strafing run, to do the best shooting we could on the target, and to get away quickly.

Big Week began 20 February. On 21, 22 and 24 February, I downed a FW 190 each day. On 29 February I destroyed a Ju 52. On this mission we were escorting bombers on their way to Berlin. It was a quiet peaceable Sunday morning. The continent was snow-covered. We had been with the bombers at 23,000 feet for some time and it had been totally quiet—no radio transmission, no enemy airplanes anywhere. I happened to look down and spotted a single airplane going due north and at probably about 5,000 feet. We were over Germany, east of the Zuider Zee, and it was obviously an enemy aircraft. I decided to go after it. I was leading the second section of the Group with my squadron of 12 airplanes. I called my leader to tell him I had a bandit low and I was going to go down with only my flight and get it. I relayed this message again to my squadron and started down.

It was a long way down to this aircraft from 20,000 feet. My speed was very high in that dive and the enemy plane was slow compared to my speed. As I approached, he was going under my nose. I realized I would not get a shot at him. So I said to my wingman, "I'm overshooting this guy; you take him." There was no answer. I pulled across on top of the enemy aircraft in a tight turn to watch my wingman shoot him down. By that time I could see the swastikas and two engines on it and I identified it as a Ju 52, a German medium-sized bomber. As I made my turn, to my amazement I saw 11 P-47s behind me. All three flights had come down with me. No one was shooting at this airplane. I thought this reluctance was strange, and I guessed they were just saving it for me. So I came back around and got behind the Ju 52 and shot it down. A big ball of fire rose as it went down; no parachutes blossomed. We all climbed back up, joined the bombers, and finished the mission. I was anxious to know what caused everyone to go down with me. Back at the base I learned that nobody in my squadron had seen that airplane until I set it on fire. They had misunderstood my transmission; they thought I was in some kind of trouble which caused them all instead of just my flight to dive down with me. On that particular day I was the only one in the entire 8th Air Force who had seen an enemy airplane and I destroyed it. That event got quite a bit of news coverage in Stars and Stripes.

My luck continued in March. On 2 March, I destroyed a ME 109, and on 8 and 15 March, I downed two ME 109s on each day. My total of destroyed aircraft now stood at 18 and I had probably destroyed two more and had damaged three others. My long-practiced tactic of diving on an enemy from above, attacking and zoom-climbing back to altitude still served me effectively. My personal combat records repeatedly describe the success of this tactic. However, despite my best efforts to fine-tune my shooting ability, my guns were not always effective. There were six other times that I fired at one or more enemy aircraft but I did not feel my strikes were sufficiently effective to report a claim of damage.

During this February-March period, my combat reports record that I led either the A Group or the B Group of the 56th on all missions. In the beginning due to the aircraft and pilot authorizations at this time, each squadron could fly 16 aircraft plus two spares on each mission for a total for the Group of 48 aircraft plus six spares. The spares would take off after the 48 had taken off and would fly with the formation until we reached altitude or the enemy coast. If a pilot had a problem with his aircraft and had to abort, a spare would immediately fill the vacated slot. It always seemed some pilots had more problems, imagined or real, than others and would abort. In some 90 missions I never had to abort.

In the early part of 1944 as P-51s started to arrive in considerable numbers in England, the P-47 authorization of aircraft and pilots to our Group was increased. By reducing the number from each squadron to fly a mission from 16 to 12, and then by flying two Groups instead of one, we could put up 72 airplanes on each mission versus the 48 previously flown. These extra airplanes visibly seen by the bomber guys were much appreciated.

On 27 March, the day I was shot down, I flew with B Group on a bomber escort mission that attacked the submarine pens at Bordeaux on the southwest coast of France and nine Nazi air-fields southwest of Paris. B Group was about 15 minutes behind A Group and I could hear the radio transmissions of A Group. Bud Mahurin, my long-time friend and classmate in flying school and now my squadron operations officer, was in A Group. I overheard them getting involved in some type of aerial battle. Then I heard Bud say he had been hit and was bailing out. This upset me very much and may have caused me to be over-zealous and over-confident later in this mission, resulting in my going down on the same day as my good friend.

That 27 March had started out as a good day. James Cagney and his group were on our base and had put on a wonderful show the night before. He had with him a beautiful young, blond accordion player.

I thought she was terrific. When she removed the accordion and I saw how perfectly proportioned she was, I could not understand how she could manage that accordion. I was determined to find out. After the show, I got her separated from the group and we had a marvelous evening until quite late and we planned another similar event for the night of 27 March.

The escort mission we were scheduled for on 27 March was to take off about 10 a.m.. I felt great, was properly dressed for combat and ready to go. However, we were put on a standby status due to weather. Two hours passed and nothing happened. Then about 1230 the mission was scrubbed. I had lunch, then went to my room, undressed and prepared to rest a bit before the affairs of the evening. I had barely dozed off when suddenly the combat mission alarm sounded and I was told we had only a very short time before take-off. I was now out of the mood for combat. I felt it would be only a milk run and therefore did not dress properly. I put on only uniform slacks and a pair of English street shoes. We did take off in a hurry.

We left the bombers at the appointed time; we had seen no enemy aircraft and no action. I wanted to find something to shoot at on the way home. Lt. Everett was flying my wing position. He was a new pilot whom I had flown with twice after he arrived in the 63rd in order to teach him the fundamentals of combat flying. It was my desire to have all new pilots in my squadron fly their first couple of combat missions on my wing. This was Everett's second combat mission flying on my wing.

We had let down to 8,000 feet on the way home and soon I saw a long freight train winding through a slight canyon in a rather rugged area. I called it in and started down toward it. I got strikes with some small explosions indicating the train was carrying ammunition and explosives. At that time the Germans were moving a lot of equipment and explosives to the west coast of France in anticipation of an Allied invasion. As I pulled up and came around for another pass, I could see some of my guys getting large explosions and I realized we had lucked into a valuable target. On my second pass I still did not see any small arms fire from the train. It was fairly well shot up by this time, and I should have terminated the attack and taken my outfit home. However, I was still thinking of my friend Bud, who had gone down earlier, so I decided to make one more pass and really finish off this train.

By this time, my air speed was quite low, making me vulnerable to small arms and cannon fire. I had had very little strafing experience up to now, but I did know the cardinal rule for strafing was to come in fast, hit the target, and get out. I was over-confident. It seemed that by the time I started my third pass, the German anti-aircraft defenses on the train were prepared for action. The barrage of fire I ran into sounded something like the sound of large hail hitting a car. Almost immediately the windscreen was bathed in oil, and I heard horrible noises from the engine. It shook the entire airplane as it struggled to keep turning but it could not make it. I was about 200 feet in the air with low air speed and a dead engine. Instinctively I pulled back on the stick and reached for the canopy handle. The airplane was too slow to climb.

Now I was trapped—I was too low to bail out and had only heavily wooded and rugged terrain to crash into. I had no options. This airplane was going to crash in seconds. I could only help it crash as safely as possible. In this situation the aileron was ineffective because of my low speed, I could maintain the wings level only by use of the rudder, known as "walking the rudder pedals." This I did and the airplane came down and just slapped the tops of these big trees when suddenly to my utter amazement I saw a small open and cultivated field right ahead. The airplane mushed through the tops of the trees and dropped to the ground at the edge of the field. It could not have skidded more than 200 feet. My head hit the gun sight and my left arm hit something else, but at the time I felt no pain. There has never been any doubt in my mind that this was one of several times in my life when God was with me.

I opened the canopy, got out of my parachute, and pulled the rip cord. The parachute billowed out in the cockpit. I pushed it down under the fuel primer pump, pulled out the pump, kicked it until fuel leaked onto the parachute, and with my Zippo lighter started a fire. I did this to keep the Germans from getting the airplane.

As I started the fire, I noticed several of my friends flying around above me, and one had his wheels down. I tried to wave them on. I thought what they were doing would pinpoint my position to any Germans in the area. I was too busy to continue watching what my flight was doing. It was many years after the war was over that I learned the tragic truth of what happened that afternoon. Lieutenant Everett, my wingman, had thought he could land, pick me up and get me back to England. His airplane was the one I saw with its wheels down. In his attempted landing he had hit some trees apparently causing severe damage to his P-47. He pulled up and headed west to England, and he was alone. Not long after he was heard calling "May Day, May Day," the international call of distress. He was not heard from again, and nothing of him or his plane was ever found. When I learned of this outcome, I was terribly upset. It bothers me very much to this day that he was willing to risk his life to save me. No greater tribute can be paid to any man. He was the only pilot who flew in my flight with me that I ever lost in all my combat missions.

Quite a few Frenchman from a small house and barn nearby ran toward the plane. Some of them understood and could speak a bit of English; I spoke no French. I asked for their help in concealing me. They said, "No," as it was too dangerous for them; the Germans were everywhere. By this time the airplane was burning very well. I threw my leather helmet which I used all through combat into the fire. I really hated to part with it. I gave a few items to the Frenchmen. Since we were instructed to get as far from the crash site as possible within the first hour, I started to run toward the woods I had just flown over. As I ran, I saw what I thought would be a rather deep ravine on the other side of the field, which I thought would provide better cover. I changed course. The field was not flat and I could no longer see the airplane, only the black smoke and flames shooting up. I must have been just about directly in front of it when suddenly there was the sound of guns and a swish of machine gun bullets right over my head. I thought the Germans were firing at me. I hit the ground and tried to dig myself in. Then I realized that the sound of guns I heard was the sound of 50-caliber machine guns. The Germans had no 50-caliber guns. These had to be my own guns firing from my P-47. I concluded that the fire in the cockpit had burned the insulation off the wires leading to the gun switch. Since I had left all switches on in the cockpit, when the wires touched, the guns were fired using up the remaining ammunition. I thought how ironical it would be had I shot myself with my own guns. I had a better thought. Here is this great airplane, which I had flown for quite awhile. It had my name on it and the swastikas for the 18 enemy planes I had shot down. It was named " Jackson County, Michigan Fighter" for the people in that county who had bought war bonds to purchase the P-47 to fight in the war. This great airplane that had been my friend and had taken me home so many times and safely now was firing its last salute to me as we both departed.

I continued running toward the ravine. That's where I probably made a mistake because it was a deep ravine and fairly heavily wooded. I saw little caves where tree roots had been eroded by water. I took off some superfluous things I was wearing and disposed of them in holes I dug because they were obviously of military origin. I should have stayed in that ravine and dug myself in. However, following instructions, I knew I had to get as far as I could from the plane within the first hour. I proceeded on, following the ravine until I came to a road. It was a kind of dirt road, not much used. Creeping up to the edge of it, I couldn't hear or see anything in either direction. Actually I couldn't see very far for there was a turn in the road. I deliberated with myself on whether I should take the chance of exposing my where-abouts by crossing the road. As I still didn't see or hear anything, I thought I was o.k. Just about the time I started across and was about to reach the other side and enter the woods, shots rang out. I looked around and thought I saw perhaps six German soldiers in uniform and with rifles raised, nearing the curve of the road. I thought that if I had waited just a little longer before crossing the road, I would still be free. As the odds seemed to be in their favor, I decided it better not to try to resist. They reached my spot in the road and searched me. I became a prisoner. A German vehicle with a German major in it arrived. He spoke a little broken English "For you ze war is over."

RECORD OF ENEMY AIRCRAFT ACTIONS IN WORLD WAR II

Date	Aircraft	Location		Result
14 May 43	FW 190	Near Antwerp	A	Damaged
26 June 43	FW 190	Dieppe	A	Destroyed
17 Aug 43	ME 109	Near Eupen	A	Damaged
17 Aug 43	ME 110	Near Eupen	A	Destroyed
	ME 109	Near Eupen	A	Destroyed
	ME 109	Near Eupen	A	Destroyed
19 Aug 43	ME 109	Gilze-Rijen	A	Destroyed
19 Aug 43	ME 109	Gilze-Rijen	A	Damaged
10 Oct 43	ME 110	Near Munster	A	Destroyed
	ME 210	Near Munster	A	Destroyed
14 Oct 43	FW 190	Near Eupen	A	Destroyed
24 Jan 44	FW 190	N.W. of Lille	A	Destroyed
24 Jan 44	FW 190	N.W. of Lille	A	Damaged
21 Feb 44	FW 190	N.W. of Zwolle	A	Destroyed
22 Feb 44	FW 190	S.W. of Guterslob	A	Destroyed
24 Feb 44	FW 190	Near Minden	A	Destroyed
29 Feb 44	JU-52	Near Horderwijk	A	Destroyed
3 Mar 44	ME 109	S.E. of Aachen	A	Destroyed
6 Mar 44	FW 190	Near Wensendorf	A	Damaged
8 Mar 44	ME 109	Dummer Lake to	A	Destroyed
	ME 109	Celle area	A	Destroyed
15 Mar 44	ME 109	N.E. of Hanover	A	Destroyed
	ME 109	N.E. of Hanover	A	Destroyed
14 May 43	1 FW 190	St. Nicholas Vicinity		Damaged
		AECR No. 1		
26 June 43	1 FW 190	10 Miles N. of Dieppe		Destroyed
		AECR No. 5		
17 Aug 43	2 ME 109s	Near Diest and Hasselt		Destroyed
		AECR No. 12		
17 Aug 43	1 ME 110	North of Liege		Destroyed
		AECR No. 12		
17 Aug 43	1 ME 109	Near Hasselt		Damaged
		AECR No. 12		
19 Aug 43	1 ME 109	Gilze-Rijen		Destroyed
		AECR No. 12		

19 Aug 43	1 ME 109	Gilze-Rijen AECR No. 12	Damaged
10 Oct 43	1 ME 210	N. of Munster AECR No. 14	Destroyed
10 Oct 43	1 ME 110	N. of Munster AECR No. 14	Destroyed
14 Oct 43	1 FW 190	Vicinity of Eupen AECR No. 14	Destroyed
24 Jan 44	1 FW 190	4 Miles NE of Ypres	Destroyed
21 Feb 44	1 FW 190	N.W. of Zwelle CVCB Rpt. No. 56	Destroyed
24 Feb 44	1 FW 190	Near Minden CVCB Rpt. No. 56	Destroyed
29 Feb 44	1 JU-52	Horderwijk CVCB Rpt. No. 59	Destroyed
3 Mar 44	1 ME 109	S.E. of Aachen CVCB Rpt. No. 58	Destroyed
6 Mar 44	1 FW 190	Near Wenzendorf A/D CVCB Rpt. No. 60	Destroyed
8 Mar 44	2 ME 109s	Dummer Lake CVCB Rpt. No. 61	Destroyed
15 Mar 44	2 ME 109s	Near Nienburg CVCB Rpt. No. 61	Destroyed

AECR VIII Fighter Command, Assesses Enemy Casualty Report.
CVCB VIII Fighter Command, Confirmation of Victory Credits Board.

This was my last and favorite airplane. It was provided through war bond purchases by the people of Jackson County, MI.

Top Left: *Brig. Gen. Jesse Auton was also from Kentucky and he never lacked for words of advise and encouragement.* **Top Right:** *George Baltimore always told me my airplane was in perfect condition just before I climbed in the cockpit - and it was.* **Just above:** *My first squadron commander presenting mission briefing prior to take-off for combat.*

Just Above: *A typical 12-ship P-47 formation enroute to combat in Europe.*

Center Left: *Gen. Arnold, Commanding General, Army Air Forces (far right) and Gen. Bill Kepner, 8th Fighter Command Commander (far left) congratulate the first three Aces in the ETO. R to L: Capt. Jack London, Capt. Jerry Johnson, and Major Gene Roberts. Duxford, England Sept. 1943.*

Bottom Left: *My P-47 "In the Mood" (for combat) and my ground crew. L to R: Cpl. Lazanjian, asst. crew chief; Cpl. Asplint, armorer; Cpl. Brickner, radio mechanic; and Sgt. George Baltimore, crew chief.*

Right: *Gen. Kepner has just presented me with my second Distinguished Flying Cross. November 1943.* ***Above:*** *This photo was taken shortly after arrivng at the interogation center, Oberursed, Germany. March 28, 1944.* ***Below:*** *P-47 Thunderbolts lined up prior to start-engines at the grassfield Horshan St.-Faith, Norwich, England 1943.*

CHAPTER 3
SURVIVAL IN STALAG LUFT I

When the German major announced that for me the war was over, I had only a vague idea of what French ground my feet stood on. We had flown a mission to support withdrawal of the three Bomb Divisions of B-17s that attacked the submarine pens at Bordeaux and nine Nazi airfields and rail yards. When we finished the escort part of the mission, instead of heading directly toward Halesworth in England, I decided to look for targets of opportunity on the way back. We had sufficient fuel and I was still upset that my squadron operations officer and very good friend had been shot down. I was determined, if possible, to make the Germans pay for my loss and make them pay today. That freight train in the area southeast of Caen was my opportunity but also my fate on 27 March 1944.

The major took me to a little French town not far away. I was not interrogated; he just took my name off the dog tag that hung around my neck and told me that I was seen going down and that my movements had been watched after the crash. He made some notes and then talked on the telephone to someone. After that, he took me to the local town's prison. My cell had a pull-down steel frame for a bed. The door was locked and I was left by myself.

Suddenly I had to go from the life of an active fighter pilot flying out of England to being locked in a cell. This change was quite a shock. I had time to think about that as I sat in my cell. I was 24 years old. I had downed 18 enemy aircraft. I had been awarded the Distinguished Flying Cross with two Oak Leaf Clusters, the Distinguished Service Cross, and the Air Medal with three Oak Leaf Clusters. Before today I had not had a direct hit on my airplane in over 200 hours of combat during some 90 missions. I could have gone home at the end of my first tour a couple of months ago, but I liked what I was doing as a fighter pilot. It was the most interesting and exciting job I ever expected to have. "Hell," I said to myself, "this is no way to end my part in the war."

In about an hour, the major returned with two guards, guns and one dog. He said nothing, only motioning me to follow. The two guards walked on either side of me and the dog sniffed at my feet. Needless to say, I was concerned and wondered what would happen next. We got into a truck that already had a driver and started out. There was a lot of conversation between the driver and the Major. It was very dark with no lights except those the truck made. The driver made many turns, stopped twice to study a map. After about two hours we arrived back at the jail. I thought I would try to find out what we had been looking for. The Major said, "Ze aeroplane." I supposed he meant my airplane, the one I had crashed and burned. After being placed in my cell the second time, a Frenchman brought me some very thick broth, which was good, and a piece of bread. I was given a blanket, and I spent the night on that pull-down steel cot. The guards left the light on all night, and I could hear people walking up to the door quite often. I must have been some kind of novelty in the small town. I did not know who was looking at me, whether they were French people or German guards.

The next day I was taken from that jail by a guard and together we boarded a train to Paris. In Paris we had about a two-hour wait for the train to Frankfurt, Germany. It was the 28th of March, a bright sunny and warm day. We sat outside the train station on a bench and watched the activity of the area. I had never been in Paris before. There were many Germans in uniform and many healthy-looking and well-dressed French people moving about in the station area. This scene seemed so strange. A terrible war raged almost all over Europe. I knew well the conditions in England that I had left only yesterday. Yet here in Paris things seemed so normal. I kept thinking of the song, "April in Paris." I could have enjoyed this time except that I knew I must escape, I must get away from this guard. He seemed relaxed as he held the rifle and the Luger on his belt was holstered. However, everytime I glanced at him I noted that he was intently watching me. The French people passing by paid no attention to me. I wondered what they would do if I somehow managed to get away from the guard. Finally I concluded that it was just not the right place for an attempted escape; it was too open, too many German soldiers all around.

I was very hungry having had only a croissant and coffee for breakfast and I guessed that now it was about 2 p.m. Soon we boarded the train to Frankfurt. It was very crowded with many German soldiers and officers. In all of this crowd I was sure there would be a chance to mingle with the crowd and free myself of the guard and get off at one of the train's stops.

The guard must have read my thoughts because suddenly he produced a length of small but strong rope and rather roughly tied it tightly around my waist, knotting it behind my back and tying it around his waist. This action really upset me because I now began to feel for the first time since I had been shot down that I probably would not be able to escape and would go to prison, not again having the great thrill of lining up a German fighter plane in my gunsight.

The British had bombed Frankfurt the night before and the rail line was torn up. There was quite a lot of damage to the city. The interrogation center, the Dulag Luft that we would be taken to, lay about 12 kilometers north of Frankfurt. The train dispatched us about 12 kilometers west of Frankfurt because that was as far as the train could go because of the condition of the tracks.

As I was put off the train I realized that on the same train were 10 or 12 other American prisoners. They were bomber crews. I was the only fighter pilot among this group of prisoners. I had not seen them until that point in our journey. We were all herded into one little group, and four or five guards walked us up the tracks and into the city of Frankfurt and finally to the Luftwaffe interrogation center called Dulag Luft.

We had a rough time going through Frankfurt. The German civilians were very belligerent. They threw rocks at us and spit on us; they made all sorts of comments, much of it in English; but the guards made no effort at all to protect us from the civilians. They gave the local populace plenty of opportunity to throw their stones at us without hitting a guard, and they let them get close enough to prod us with sticks. The people apparently were trying to punch us in the face; we could have lost an eye. We realized that we had no alternative but to keep going, ignoring the jibes and jabs. Fortunately no one was seriously hurt by these attacks. I was particularly concerned with the bomber crews who had lost their boots. The only clothes they had on were a heated suit which they had when they bailed out, and without boots they wore out the foot part of the suit quickly. They had a lot of trouble walking on the railroad tracks. It was pretty cold and snow covered the ground. By the time we arrived at the Dulag Luft, their feet were in really bad shape. However, we made it through the ordeal, and all we received were small puncture wounds from the pointed sticks, a few hits from rocks, and a good bit of saliva.

I had had nothing to eat since breakfast. I was hungry and exhausted. Early in the evening, the guards stopped at a German farmhouse to get some water for us. The farmwife actually drew water out of the well and brought us a whole loaf of real black bread. A German guard used a huge knife and cut off a little piece of bread for each of us. It tasted delicious. With some water and that piece of bread, I was again fortified and was prepared for whatever lay ahead. The guards assured us we would have a fine dinner of hot food when we got to camp.

Finally we did arrive at Dulag Luft, the interrogation center. It was long after dark. We were herded into a room where we were totally stripped and completely searched; both our person and our clothing were carefully searched for compasses, maps and various other things that we might have secreted as aids to escape. We then had a hot shower with some strong soap that I suppose was meant to take care of lice and so forth. Then they returned our trousers, shirts and socks, but they kept rings, wristwatches, boots and belts. After that, we were put into individual cells, cubicles about eight feet long and perhaps five feet wide; I could touch each wall with my arms outstretched. The door was tightly sealed on the inside, and the cell contained an electric heater which was controlled from outside the cell.

When I was put in this cell, it was dark because there was no window and there was no light inside it that I could control. I was still hungry and expected to get that big hot dinner the guard had promised.

After an hour or so, a guard opened a little slot under the cell door and scooted in a bowl of very thin soup and a piece of black bread. I did not want to eat it because I thought I would ruin my appetite. Talk about being naive.

I had been told that to call a guard, I could pull a string in the cell beside the door that dropped a latch outside which the guard would see and he would come to my cell. I did this. When the guard arrived, I told him I was hungry and wanted food. He just stood there, signaling that he could not understand me. I began to say in a loud voice that I wanted food. Although a prisoner was restricted from talking to any other prisoners, people in the adjoining cells could hear if I spoke loudly, but this type of communication was not permitted. This time the guy in the next cell did hear me, and he took a chance and answered me, "You'd better eat what you've got for that's all you're going to get." I now realized that I was in solitary confinement; there would be no hot dinner. I ate the thin soup and piece of bread.

Still exhausted, I lay down on the cot that had a very thin mattress of wood shavings and one blanket. It was hot in this cell, but with my pants on I dropped off to sleep. When I woke up freezing cold, I put my shirt on and curled up under the blanket. As this was the end of March and the temperature was pretty cold outside, I did not warm up. I pulled the latch again to summon the guard. Although guards really did speak English, they gave the impression they did not know what anyone asked for. Unfortunately, my complaint about the cold did get a response. After I had bundled up to escape the cold, the heat came on. The temperature went from extreme cold to extreme heat. This alternating temperature went on every night; there was no in-between. Of course, I understood this was part of the treatment along with my never seeing any daylight. When I had to use the latrine, a guard escorted me to it, stood over me while I took care of myself, and swiftly took me back to my cell. I never saw another POW. This solitary confinement lasted for 23 days.

What I assumed to be the next morning, the second day in my cell, I was given a breakfast consisting of a small piece of bread and a bowl of thin, watery soup. There was no lunch; two meals a day was my diet. The objective now was to stay alive, try to keep up my strength and cause the Germans as much trouble as possible.

On this second day, the guard came and took me to the office of the interrogator Hans Scharff, who after the war lived in the United States and operated a book store in New York in 1966. He also wrote a book about interrogating American prisoners of war and later moved to Los Angeles where our paths crossed again. Scharff jumped up from his desk, invited me in and said, "Jerry Johnson, we have been waiting for you. We thought for awhile we wouldn't get you, but then we get all of you American Ace pilots eventually. You know we've welcomed Loren McCollom, (my squadron commander at Bridge-port in 1942); he's in one of our prisons." Scharff named several other guys who I knew and who had been shot down. He went on talking, "Great guys. How's old Hub Zemke getting along? We haven't got him yet, but we will, and Gabreski too." He named some other guys and then began a personal approach to my situation.

"You don't look very good. Are you sure you're getting enough to eat? Are they treating you all right? Here's a cigarette. You do have plenty of cigarettes, don't you?"

I recognized these comments as the friendly softening-up technique.

"Here we are going to take care of you. You're a Major in the Army Air Forces. With your record—you've got 18 confirmed, haven't you?—I'm not going to let anything happen to you."

He kept spouting this disarming stuff while I sat enjoying the conversation and a cigarette, knowing full well what he was doing. He told me he was a Canadian, educated in Canada and fluent in English. I was a pretty heavy smoker in those days and I had smoked several of his cigarettes by the time he had gone through this preliminary nonsense.

Briskly he became very business-like and picked up some papers, informing me that there were a few formalities that we had to complete before he would put me on my way to a regular POW camp where my friends were. He apologized for the place I had stayed the preceding night, and he wanted to take me quickly to the good living conditions in the prison camp where I would get plenty of food, Red Cross packages, and the like.

"Now," he began, "you are Gerald W. Johnson, Major, right? And your serial number is?"

I gave it to him.

"And the name of the airplane you were flying was?"

My answer was my name, rank and serial number.

"Come on," he urged. "Now you know we know what airplane you flew. You burned it, but hell, we got its tail number. We just want to confirm that that was the one you were in."

Again I gave him my name, rank and serial number.

"You're from the 56th Fighter Group, right?"

"Sorry," I replied, "my name, rank and serial number is all I'm permitted to tell you."

We played this charade for awhile. Suddenly he jumped up, pounded the desk, and the guards came running in. He said something to them in German. It was obvious he was showing his anger, but indirectly I understood that he was telling me he would control himself.

"I am not sure under these conditons whether I will be able to protect you or not," he declared. "After all, you know you've been accused on several occasions of killing civilians on some of your raids over here. We know how many times you've flown over here. If you're not going to cooperate with me, I don't know what I can do for you, but I will try to do my very best."

After he finished that tirade, the guards grabbed me roughly, took me out of the room and back to the cell. He was acting, I knew, but I was still on my own, not seeing another American.

About three or four days went by back in that cell, never seeing anyone, never seeing daylight, eating a piece of bread and watery soup in the morning and evening. Hours can really drag on for someone my age used to a lot of physical activity and ambition to fly combat. Sometimes the light bulb would be turned on, but I did not know if it was daylight or night. I tried to keep track of time but that was difficult. Solitary confinement was a very severe punishment for me.

As time dragged by, I began to develop ways of coping with it. I found things to do to exercise my mind, reliving in great detail every moment of my life that I could remember. Having nothing to read, I tried to reconstruct books that I had enjoyed reading in the past. I tried to visualize the actual print and I wrote the book in my mind just as I had read it earlier. I was good at math. I attempted to do mathematical problems in my mind, constructing every little detail because it was the detail that took up time. In my situation, I had to use up time, and I made the greatest thing of eating that piece of bread, inventing different ways of eating it, mostly to be as slow as I could because I wanted that breakfast bread and that dinner bread to take up as much time as possible. I wished I had had something to tinker with. I was terribly hungry all the time. My shoes were kept by the Germans. But I would imagine what it would be like to have those leather shoes in my cell, to be able to chew the leather, and I would actually get a simulated taste of a wonderful piece of leather.

I was escorted to Scharff's office a few more times to go through the same rigamarole. I never told him anything but name, rank and serial number. About the 18th or 19th day of my confinement, the guard took me out of my cell and let me shower and shave for the first time since I had been there. I could hardly believe how thin and pale I was. Then I was escorted to the German Officers' Club where I met three German fighter aces. There were cookies and snacks on the table and lots of tea. For the visit to the Club, I was allowed to wear my B-15 jacket. It had an inside pocket. I ate all I could eat of the food as there did not seem to be any restriction on the quantity, and I sneaked these little cookies and sandwiches into my inside pocket. I am sure the pilots observed my doing that, but they did not seem to mind my action. I thought to myself, if the Germans intend to keep me in that cell forever, I intend to take nourishment when I can get it. Needless to say, all that food and drink ingested so quickly made me sick. What I ate did not do me any good for I lost it all before they got me back to solitary confinement. However, it was a nice break in my dull routine. Somehow or other, I managed to get the food in my inside pocket back to the cell with me. I hid it in the shavings of the mattress I slept on. During the following days, I ate it very sparingly not knowing how long it had to last me, and I did not know if I would ever have a chance to sneak any more.

About the 22nd day, Scharff brought me to his office again. Although he had told me a lot about the 56th, which I would not confirm, he still maintained that he did not know anything about me. Letting me smoke some of his cigarettes, he asked, "Do you think there is anything that I don't know about you?"

After a bit I replied, "Yes, my mother's maiden name."

Scharff picked up the phone and spoke into it, and in a very short time a little fraulein arrived with a rather thick folder. He thumbed through it for some time before looking up and saying, "Reeves." And he was right. I do not remember what I said, but in Scharff's book he wrote after the war, he recorded that I said, "That breaks my heart." Scharff also remarked in his book that I and one other pilot were the only ones among all American pilots who never told him anything but name, rank and serial number. I never held a grudge against him. He did his job. In 1975 he lived in Los Angeles and came to my hotel on one of my visits to Los Angeles. It was the first time I had seen him since April 1944. There were three of us in the hotel room plus Scharff. For the next two-and-a-half hours we had such a great conversation that we almost missed dinner. His memory was unbelievable; he had many stories to tell about the individuals he interrogated, many of whom I knew.

The next morning after this last meeting with Scharff, a guard came and told me very pleasantly that I was being sent on to prison camp, Stalag Luft I at Barth on the Baltic Sea. Barth is at the southern end of a small peninsula jutting out into the Baltic Sea not far from Stettin which is north of Berlin. He brought me my B-15 jacket, shoes and belt. My watch, the engraved one that General Arnold had presented to me in England when I became the second Ace in the ETO and my ring were not returned. I was taken to the railroad station and put into a box car with about 30 other POWs. Many had serious burns, some were on crutches because of broken legs and other injuries. I felt very fortunate to have escaped serious injury. The box car sat in the marshaling yard for a long time before it was slammed by another car, and then after several more violent jerks we were hooked to another car and became part of a freight train. These movements were very painful for those who were injured. There was a bit of straw on the floor of the box car, nothing more that we might have used to make the injured more comfortable. A fairly large pail sat in one corner which would serve as our latrine.

We reached the marshaling yard at Berlin that first day. After many more jerks and violent smashings of one car to another, we apparently were disconnected from this train and were left as a single car. Through the many cracks in the sides of the car, we could see guards outside the car, but there were none inside.

It had been dark for some time and it was getting rather cold. We had had no water or food since morning. Shortly thereafter lights appeared outside. The door was unlocked and a basket of bread and a large container of water was set inside the car. One guard came inside, took the latrine bucket outside, emptied it, and brought it back. I took charge of the bread and water, and with the help of several other POWs managed to dispense this food and water equally without any serious incidents but with considerable grumbling.

Several of the injured we began to realize were in more serious condition than we had at first thought. I was greatly concerned about their ability to survive the night in that car that seemed to get colder all the time. I started banging on the door to get the attention of the guard. After awhile he opened the door just enough to talk. Fortunately one of our group spoke a little German. I had him relay to the guard that we had some very sick men that should be removed to a hospital. His reply, "Nein, nein." I then had our interpreter beg for blankets, get the guard's name and give him assurance that the Americans would take care of him after the war. This promise must have been effective because the guard spoke to some other German soldiers and before long a few blankets arrived and were thrown into the car. We then managed to get the ones who were suffering most to lie close together and be covered with blankets.

Then came the sound of air raid sirens indicating an air attack was imminent. By then it must have been midnight. I knew it would be the RAF bombers, and I thought the marshaling yards and rail station would be one of their targets. The sirens got louder and louder and I forgot the cold. Through the cracks in the box car we could see the search lights criss-crossing the night sky, and then we heard the sounds of the first explosions. The explosions came closer and closer and the car began to move from shock waves and concussion. It was terrifying to be locked inside this box car with no way to try to protect ourselves. Just as we thought the raid was over, another wave would come in. There were three. I do not know how long this bombardment lasted, but it seemed like hours. Finally the bombers were gone. It was quiet. We had escaped being hit.

I sat down on a bit of straw, leaned against the side of the car and thought about how close I had come to being shot by my own guns after the crash landing and how close now I had come to being wounded or killed by British bombers. I thought, "I guess I just don't understand war."

The next morning, again with much smashing and banging, our little box car became part of another freight train which eventually got us to Barth. By the time we arrived it was almost dark. We had been confined in this car for two days and one night. Throughout this second day the stench from the burn victims and the open latrine bucket got pretty bad.

At Stalag Luft I, I was placed in a room with seven other POWs. One was Maj. John Fischer, a lawyer from the Bronx, New York and a P-47 pilot. We immediately became friends. Before lights out he toasted a piece of black German bread over a stove made from a Klem can. Klem was the name of the powdered milk we received in Red Cross parcels. It was about the size of a one-pound can of coffee. This empty can became our No. 1 source for the making of many things. That piece of toast he made for me I believe was the best food I have ever tasted. The eight of us talked until very late that first night, and for the first time since 27 March, I was with Americans who had been through essentially the same experience as I had; they had been shot down too. I began to know and realize that being a prisoner of the Germans was my fate, and although I didn't, and would never be able to accept it I must learn to live with it.

Stalag Luft I began as one compound, occupied mostly by British airmen who were captured during the evacuation of Dunkerque on the north coast of France in August 1942. Following this crisis, the Germans had their greatest opportunity to invade England. However, they failed in their assessment of British strength at that time and let this opportunity pass. When this first compound occupied by the British was filled, another one was constructed. Because American airmen were being shot down in great numbers during 1943 and 1944, new compounds were continually under construction until there was a total of five. Each compound contained many long rectangular buildings, constructed from rough hewn lumber and with rooms on either side of a hall. The rooms, usually 12 feet by 20 feet, housed a large number of prisoners in double- and triple-deck bunks. Each time a new compound opened, I moved to the new one in order to carry out my responsibility to interview all new POWs primarily for two reasons first, to make sure the new POW was not, in fact, a German plant, and second, to determine what information they may have been given at their home base to deliver if they happened to be shot down and became a POW. The purpose of my efforts in each new compound was to find out what the incoming Kriegies (from the German word <u>Kriegesgefangenen</u>, meaning prisoner of war) could tell me about what was going on in England, North Africa, or wherever they had come from. They could inform us on situations in those areas that we didn't know about. My interrogation of them helped me to authenticate their identity as Americans. In turn I briefed them on their responsibilities in prison camp, the behavior we expected of them, and the manner in which they should conduct themselves among their fellow Kriegies and with the Germans. We discussed the question of escape and evasion in general terms at that point, because with the new people arriving, we were never quite sure who would be interested in that activity or who wanted just to sit it out in prison camp. I set up an escape committee. It met regularly and secretly, but there was no established pattern on how to meet. A good deal of discussion concerning this type of activity occurred while we walked around the compound. This outdoor informal meeting avoided any possible recording by microphones planted by the Germans somewhere in the barracks.

The barracks, the individual buildings within a compound, stood along the sides of the compound. There was an open area in the center, and twice a day everyone had to attend an <u>appell</u>, or head count. This permitted the Germans twice a day to ascertain there had been no escapes. It was a loathsome experience but an excellent opportunity for us to frustrate and infuriate the Germans. One way we frequently used in cold weather was to have two small prisoners, maybe turret gunners, to stand under one great coat (issued to those who had no jacket). This camouflage made the guards think one of the prisoners was missing. Another trick was to have a prisoner fake a fainting spell just as the counting guard passed and to fall into him. This upset the guard's count and he would have to start counting again. Another maneuver was faking insanity with much screaming and yelling. As a result of these tactics the count sometimes would take two or more hours. But we had nothing to do anyway.

We had a lot of opportunity to walk around the area within the fence, talking with other prisoners, playing games, and even sunbathing when the weather permitted. Within the compounds we were relatively free, but the guard towers where German soldiers with rifles watched us constantly, the electrified barbed wire fences and the constant hunger that was always with us reminded us of our real condition.

We were hungry all the time. What food we received was prepared in a central kitchen by Prisoner of War (POW) volunteers. It usually consisted of a few small pieces of potato or turnip. We were most fortunate when a small piece of horsemeat from a horse killed by shrapnel was included in a thin barley soup. In the beginning when I first arrived, each prisoner received one Red Cross food parcel per week, each parcel containing a few different foods in small cans or packs plus soap and cigarettes. Some of the men adapted the heating stove in the barracks to a cooking surface, and others used the contents of the Red Cross packages to make meals more palatable. There was so much talent and imagination among the prisoners that almost any kitchen utensil or tool or implement was made by using materials saved from Red Cross packages and parcels from home. Tooth powder was used in place of baking powder; whipped cream was made out of powdered milk and margarine, and ice cream was created from snow, powdered milk and jam. However, it wasn't long before Red Cross parcels arrived about every two to three weeks and in the winter 1944-45, they stopped arriving all together.

I was fortunate to serve as executive officer to my compound commander, Col. Ross Greening. He not only survived several harrowing wartime experiences himself, including being a pilot of one of the Doolittle raiders in April 1942 and crashing in China. He organized a Kriegie Kraft Karnival in July 1944 to showcase the creative work of the Kriegies. Some examples on display were a full model violin made from bed slats and a leg of a chair with no other tools than a small penknife, a razor blade, a broken piece of glass and sand. Ovens, little stoves, egg beaters, food graters, saws, coffee pots, lamps and toys came from Red Cross tin cans that were opened up and flattened out and heated so as to obtain the solder. Baseball bats were shaped from bed posts, balls from the uppers of old shoes. Chess sets were whittled from broom handles; model homes and ship models were carved from bed and floor boards. Several men knitted dresses and pocketbooks from blanket threads to wear in plays performed by the actors group; German uniforms were made for possible use in escapes.

Colonel Greening painted many portraits of Kriegies and their activities that record this story of prisoners creating a community behind barbed wire. Greening could have painted his own adventures. Instead he painted portraits, camp scenes, aerial battles and the like. He painted portraits of me, Gabby Gabreski, Hub Zemke, and Loren McCollom, among many others. He made caricatures of The Flying Boxcar (the B-24 Liberator), The Fortress (the B-17), The Time Bomb (the P-38 Lightning), and The Flying Milkbottle (the P-47

Thunderbolt). He portrayed scenes of new arrivals entering the Main Gate of Stalag Luft I, the Guard Tower, the Field Kitchen building, chow call, the twice-daily roll calls, and the men sunbathing and counting the hours by Block Nine. Colonel Greening left a visual legacy of survival to the next generations.

Long before I arrived at Stalag Luft I in April 1944, the camp was organized in accordance with military order and tradition. The Allied camp commander was the Senior Officer. Although Royal Air Force officers made up part of the population, after the middle of 1943 the flood of American prisoners increased rapidly. When I arrived, Col. Jean Byerly was the commandant. By December 1944, Col. Hub Zemke, whose date of rank was May 1943, appeared and he became the Senior Allied Officer (SAO) of the camp until the war ended and we were liberated. Under the Allied commander was a commander for each of the compounds. When I arrived I was placed in North 1, which Colonel Zemke took over as the "head shed." The shape of the whole Stalag Luft I looked like a reverse "L", a shape that more or less followed the curve of the bay estuary of the Baltic Sea to the west. Under the compound commander was a group commander, squadron commanders, and a commander for each barracks. This familiar chain of command provided a sense of security and discipline in the uncomfortable circumstances of being caged within barbed wire and guard towers.

We not only dreamed of escaping from our cage but also planned it. The primary method of escape from a prison camp was to dig a tunnel under one of the barracks out to and under the fence. That was a major event that has been described many times in books and movies. We faced many problems before getting started on a tunnel. What to do with the excavated dirt, how to shore up the tunnel, how to supply air down to the diggers, what kind of digging tools were needed—these questions kept many Kriegies interested and involved so that their boredom was reduced. There was always the danger of the digging being discovered and of punishment by the Germans. The Tom, Dick and Harry tunnels created by the British at Stalag Luft III's old North Compound in September 1943 provided temporary freedom for 72 prisoners, 52 of whom were shot when they were captured by the Germans. The tunnels at Stalag Luft I did result in a number of people escaping. They were usually caught right away or within a few days, however, and they came back to serve a long period in solitary confinement.

Since our objective was to keep the Germans occupied as much as possible and to use up German manpower, we became good observers of their capabilities and attitudes. Toward the end of the war the quality of the German guards deteriorated. At first, they seemed constantly worried about being sent to the eastern front to face the Russians. They worked hard at not making mistakes in dealing with the Kriegies. They were very careful that a prisoner would have no reason to squeal on them to the guard's superior, who had the power to send them to the eastern front. Whether they liked it or not, all of them eventually went to the eastern front or somewhere else. On their departure, elderly men who should not have been in uniform at all replaced them. As the Germans also did not get much to eat in those days, we could not help but feel sorry for the older guards. We traded with them for little pieces of equipment that helped us to build things. Through one guard we obtained a crystal radio receiver which was never discovered by another guard. That radio receiver enabled us to monitor British Broadcasting Company programs from which we we were able to stay fairly current as to how the war progressed. Sometime in March 1945, a rumor began in Boston that the war was over, that the Germans had surrendered. Listening late at night, I picked up that information on our set. I could hardly believe what I heard. However, as everything continued to go on as usual the next day, I assumed it was not accurate, which it wasn't.

By April 1945, bits of news of the oncoming Russians and the disintegration of the German war effort reached us. On the morning of 30 April, the German commandant von Warnstedt asked Colonel Zemke to walk outside the camp area with him. He announced, "Der Krieg ist jetsk uber fur uns" (The war is over for us). Warnstedt asked if Provisional Wing X, the overall POW organization of Stalag Luft I, would take over the camp and permit all German personnel to leave without bloodshed. A handshake between the two commanders sealed the agreement. Colonel Zemke had already organized several teams of his staff to plan for such an outcome. I was among those who met with him to devise the plan of how we were going to carry on without German guards. The Germans had given Zemke the keys to the gates, to the food supply, and to the munition storage. Our planning group thought it was unwise to have the camp just turned loose because we thought the soon-to-be-free Kriegies would scatter all over Germany. In trying to make it back to the West, many of them would probably be killed. We thought it best to maintain control of them, an order similar to this already having been received from U.S. military leaders over the secret radio. We decided to maintain the kind of military organization that we already had in place.

At roll call the next morning, all 10,000 Kriegies were told what had happened the German staff and guards were gone; we expected to be evacuated by air very soon; and we wanted to maintain order and control over our lives until liberation. That order was what we tried to attain and maintain. The first thing we did was to select a small cadre of people to go to the village of Barth to try to get food. Because the village had very little food, we commandeered a few head of cattle that happened to be near by and drove them to the camp, slaughtered them, and built a few barbecue fires. We ate better than we had for a long time. We maintained the usual routine of the camp for several days, but we still had all the fences up and the gates locked.

Some days later, as we looked down the road that came into the camp from Barth, we noticed that over a rise in the road came a horse with two riders. As they neared, we identified the horseman as a Russian soldier with a German woman astride behind him. He was drunk, swaying back and forth so that he was about to fall off the horse. Holding a bottle of cognac in his hand, he demanded to see the senior American. In broken English, he said to Colonel Zemke, "The war is over. Why are you locked up? Tear down the fences." Some of our Kriegies, tired of being locked up, heard his words. Those words were enough to sound like an excuse for mutiny. Very quickly, down came some of the fences and gates. We lost control of many of our people, who did move into the countryside, trying to make their way to the West. Most of the people, however, remained in the camp, and many who left came back. Among those who left on their own, some sustained injuries from accidents and from angry Germans, and a few died because of careless behavior in a dangerous environment. The countryside at this time was not safe for the recently liberated men.

Colonel Zemke had organized scouting parties to make contact with the real Russian army. The main army of Russians appeared to bypass Barth, but an advance guard of the Russian army did enter the village. We could hear machine gun fire on and off in that direction, and we learned that these uncouth Russians lived off the plunder of German civilians, raping and looting at will. Eventually the real Russian army arrived and began to put some administration and organization in place. In ledgers, they recorded our names laboriously in big letters in Russian before any of us left camp. After a myriad of negotiations among Russian, British and American generals, on 12 May a B-17 Fortress landed at the airfield at Barth as the first of many B-17s and C-46s that would evacuate the more than 8,000 ex-Kriegies remaining. By 14 May all of them had boarded American airplanes and left Stalag Luft I as a place no one wanted to see again.

The liberated men of Stalag Luft I were flown to various places where the Army processed them back into American military care, and then they boarded ships for transport to the United States. In my case, because of my involvement in intelligence at Stalag Luft I, I was flown to Supreme Headquarters Allied European Forces (SHAEF) in Paris. There I was interviewed for several days and acquired new uniforms. After the war I was awarded a Bronze Star for my work in intelligence as a POW. From Paris I flew to England to meet my flying buddies of the 56th Fighter Group. Although most of my friends had returned to the States, we nonetheless celebrated far into the night. I had not had that much to drink in 14 months. Despite my rocky condition the next morning, my friends were convinced I could not wait to climb into the cockpit of a P-47. They insisted that I fly it. After a few minutes to get the cockpit familiar to me again, I took off, flew around the area for about an hour, and then made a less than precise landing. But it was a thrill to be free to fly again. I knew that I had not yet got my fill of being a fighter pilot.

The next day I got in touch with Mark Hubbard, who had been the commander of the 20th Fighter Group when he was shot down and became a POW. We had become friends in Stalag Luft I and he was visiting his old Group as I was doing with the 56th. I told him I thought we should do some aerial reconnaissance of Germany. After all, it had been more than a year since we had flown over Germany and I wanted to see just how thoroughly the the major target areas had been destroyed by air bombardment. Mark thought it was a great idea and said he would work on it.

Later that day he called to tell me that he had found a B-26 complete with a crew chief, tool kit and spare parts and that we could leave the next day. In those days after the war there were so many airplanes of all types throughout England it wasn't a problem to borrow one and it didn't matter if it was never returned.

We had a great four days, flying very low over almost all of Germany. We landed wherever we could get fuel and visited with the people who had been there during the final period before the Germans surrendered. It was a very educational and informative four days. There was almost no control of the air at that time, and we flew without flight plans and rarely with radio contact with anyone. We had a few close calls but our crew chief was a real jewel who knew that airplane and kept it flying. He was delighted to have this opportunity to see Europe and Germany. The destruction we viewed was unbelievable and everywhere. We wondered how the Germans had been able to carry on for so long. I always valued the experience of this trip and the fact that I was able to see just how totally Germany had been destroyed.

Once again I faced a great transition time in my life—from the horrible and inactive life of a POW to what I hoped would be a challenging assignment that would help me catch up with my fellow flying officers, especially if I decided to make the Army Air Forces my career. First I had to go through the military reintegrating process.

I had several weeks to spend with my family in Kentucky before traveling to the Miami Beach Redistribution Center where in June 1945 I received my first post-European war assignment. I became the Coordination and Compliance Officer with the Air Training Command at Minter Field, California. Like many other pilots coming from prison camps or from the European Theater, I hoped to get to the Pacific theater before that part of the war ended. Being assigned to the West Coast gave me a jumping off place toward that goal.

My father had died, and my mother knew I wanted to continue flying and to get to the Pacific War before it ended . During that short time in California, a bizarre incident occurred. Since my liberation as well as during my POW days, I had not written to my mother as often as I should have. She knew I had left for California duty, she did not know if I was still there. One morning she picked up the newspaper and saw my picture with a story beneath it that reported that I, a leading ace, had been killed in an airplane crash in Japan. She was frantic. That same morning I also saw the same newspaper story in a California paper telling of my death in a crash in Japan. I telephoned my mother immediately to assure her that I was still in California and that the dead pilot was not her son. Coincidentally another pilot by the name of Gerald R. Johnson flew in the Pacific. His mother had read the news report when I was shot down in Europe and wrote to my mother. They became friends by correspondence and remained friends from there on by writing to each other. Somehow when the other Gerald R. Johnson was killed in a B-25 crash in Japan shortly after the war ended, my picture was retrieved from a wire service or newspaper morgue and was used with his story. I was glad to agree with Mark Twain that the news of my death was greatly exaggerated.

Mark Hubbard was also assigned to Minter Field. We both wanted to get to the war in the Pacific as quickly as possible. Therefore, we started writing letters and making phone calls soon after arriving at Minter Field. To us, it seemed that the Pacific War ended too quickly. When VJ day arrived, somehow we didn't feel like celebrating. Bakersfield, the nearest town to Minter Field, celebrated wildly the end of World War II, while Mark and I sat in a bar quietly drinking and discussing what the hell were we going to do now.

During the following months in California I had time to think about whether or not I should continue flying or take one of the several jobs I had been offered. I am sure that I could have had a very good career in some other endeavor. I finally decided to stay in the Army Air Forces for a while and monitor what happened in the postwar period of my military life. I promised myself that if at any time I did not have a military assignment that challenged me or if I became tired of flying, then I would leave the service and try something else. The first step toward that big decision to stay or not to stay arrived with the chance to attend the Army Command and Staff College at Fort Leavenworth, Kansas. Although I did not recognize its significance at the time, that experience helped to set me on the course that resulted in a 33-year total military career.

CHAPTER 4
A POSTWAR BEGINNING IN THE USAF

In the Army Command and Staff School at Ft. Leavenworth from February through May 1946, I not only caught up with what had happened during the last 13 months of the war when I was a prisoner at Stalag Luft I, but I also discovered more about the Army, as it was then, and more about World War II than I knew or suspected because I had looked at both only from a fighter pilot's point of view. When I flew combat many other people did all the planning and handled the operations and the administrative detail.

Because the Army Air Forces had contributed significantly to the victorious ending of the war in Europe and the Far East, I could imagine that the role of air power in the future would be significantly increased and its responsibilities greatly expanded. Undoubtedly the leading Generals of the Army Air Forces in World War II, such as Henry (Hap) Arnold, Ira C. Eaker, James A. Doolittle, Carl (Tooey) Spaatz and others, would be the prime movers in organizing the United States Air Force which would have a role in the defense of the nation such as the Army had on land and the Navy had on the sea. Working through the military and political channels to envision and then to organize an independent service would be a major challenge requiring the efforts of the best World War II Army Air Forces officers. With these thoughts in mind I began to get some feel of what the military world of the near future could evolve into. And I liked it.

Sitting in the classrooms of this last class of Command and Staff School at Ft. Leavenworth, I had the chance to study how the Army worked, how it was organized and administered, and how it recruited and trained its personnel. But perhaps more importantly, I was exposed to and studied the strategic and tactical planning efforts that had been used in World War II. I began to understand better that the orders and directives we had received at the fighting level, both air and ground, did not just happen. Many long and grueling hours of "what if" questions had been carefully evaluated before a recommendation was made and a command decision resulted in an order received at the fighting level. I was also impressed with the quality of the School's curriculum and of its faculty. I learned a lot from the varied experiences of the other students, who were members of the Army and the Army Air Forces as well as of foreign military units. I enjoyed getting to know many of my military contemporaries whom I had not met before. This experience helped me to explore more deeply the question of whether I would make the military my career.

I learned that the Army was planning to select from the many Reserve Officers of World War II those that would qualify for a regular commission. Since a regular commission is an important step to a military career, I decided to try for one. This effort required taking several written exams, and ultimately appearing before a board of senior Army officers, led by a major general. The two brigadier generals and a couple of colonels making up the board appeared to me to be formidable types. I remember that I was pretty scared when I was ushered in to sit before this group and to be asked all kinds of questions covering a multitude of subjects. I answered them to the best of my ability, but I walked out of that session with the feeling that I hadn't impressed them very much, but then I felt they hadn't impressed me either. I guess that I had been intimidated by all of that brass. Therefore I was greatly surprised about a month later to receive a letter advising me that I had been selected for a regular commission. I was very pleased but also mindful that this was only the first step and that I must now continue to work and study in order to be prepared for whatever might await me. Since I had a fairly good record made in 15 months of combat, and I had lived through 13 months of prison camp without any scars, I decided that I would stay as long as the military assignments were challenging and interesting to me and also offered the opportunity for further advancement.

Overwhelmed as I was by the senior Army officers before whom I appeared, I was alerted to the fact that the Army Air Forces was something the Army did not yet quite accept. I noted that officers who wore wings did not hold responsible positions in the Army school;

only one colonel on the board wore wings. It is true that the Army Air Forces had only a few senior officers who had had combat experience and command experience with flying units of World War II. Even after the Air Force became an autonomous service in July 1947, it was recognized and often said that its officers did not pay much attention to organization and administration, that all they wanted to do was to fly airplanes and to do what was exciting. Nevertheless, the organization of the Air Force was solid from the beginning, and I had become for the second time a commander of a fighter squadron in the field at the time of the Air Force's birth. As I look back on 1946 and 1947, the early years of my career, I realize that I already had served with units that were to continue to make outstanding contributions to the new Air Force. I joined the 56th Fighter Group in April 1942. It became a leading Group in the 8th Air Force which, formed in January 1942 at Savannah, Georgia, became primarily responsible for conducting the air war against Germany and carried out the destruction of the Luftwaffe in preparation for the invasion of Europe. In July 1946, I became a part of Strategic Air Command, organized the previous March, that was designed to implement the nation's strategic bombing policy.

An experience while I attended the Command and Staff School in Ft. Leavenworth resulted in a major change in my life a few months later. I met my first wife Lou Ann Schaefers of Omaha, Nebraska, and we were married in August of 1946. Our meeting happened in a hospital, after a wild drive of a ball on the golf course hit me in the head and momentarily knocked me out. We usually finished classes about 4 o'clock in the afternoon so when spring came, even though none of us played very good golf, after class we headed for the golf course. On this particular day, the tall grass nurtured by recent rains obscured the lie of the balls on the fairway. We drove off the No. 1 tee. None of us had a very good drive. Because of the tall grass, each of us went looking for our balls. I found mine and hit my second shot, not realizing that another member of our foursome was farther back off the tee than I was. When he found his ball, without looking up to clear the area ahead of him, he hit the ball with his three wood. His ball went off to the side, still lifting, and it caught me in the back of the head. That blow knocked me down, and I was unconscious for a little bit. My friends rushed over to me, and as I was bleeding, as a precautionary measure they put me in the golf cart and took me to the hospital. Shortly after my admission to the hospital, the cutest blond nurse arrived on the scene. That white uniform fitted her so perfectly. Several months later she became Mrs. Johnson and joined me in my career with the soon-to-be independent Air Force, the Strategic Air Command, the 8th Air Force and the 56th Fighter Group.

Although as a commander of squadrons in the field I played no part in the development and evolution of the system of American air power, I look back with admiration at the tremendous planning and design of an Air Force within two years after the end of World War II. In March 1946, while I was still at Command and Staff School, the United States Army Air Forces created the Strategic Air Command (SAC), the Tactical Air Command (TAC), and the Air Defense Command (ADC). Tactical Air Command was to provide air support to ground troops and forces; Air Defense Command would provide air defense of the United States. Under its first commander, Gen. George C. Kenney, Strategic Air Command would provide the nation with a striking force of long-range bombers so powerful as to provide deterrence against another major war. Although charged indirectly to maintain peace, SAC's real mission was to prevent a nuclear war. To carry out this primary mission that required powerful weapons, mobility and flexibility, SAC developed the concept of forward deployment, on a rotational basis, of bomber and fighter units to air bases in countries close to our potential enemy, the Soviet Union.

In those days SAC's bombers were B-29s and B-50s. The fighters were P-51s. Airborne refueling was still some years away. These airplanes simply did not have sufficient range to reach global targets from the United States and return. Consequently, base rights were negotiated with England, Spain and Morocco. NATO was still in its infancy.

By the time these bases were usable SAC was making a transition to an all-jet force. The primary jet bomber was the Boeing-built B-47; the fighter was the Republic-built F-84. Both the bomber and fighter units would rotate to a forward base for six months TDY. This period was later reduced to 120 days. Some form of control of these TDY deployments had to be established, and Provisional Air Divisions near the site of the deployed units were created to fulfill this need. An early test of deployment under division control came in December 1946 when I was directed to deploy my 62nd Fighter Squadron from Selfridge Field, Michigan to Ladd Field, Alaska. More details about that later.

Col. Dave Schilling, who was with the 56th Fighter Group during World War II and commanded it for a time, served in the Branch of the Flying Training Division of SAC Headquarters which at that time was at Andrews Air Force Base near Washington, D.C. He was selected as the first commander of the 56th reactivated at Selfridge Field in April 1946. He started to get in touch with many of the old 56th types, including me, and I requested to be assigned to the 56th when I left Ft. Leavenworth. Immediately I was given command of the 62nd Squadron, then flying P-47Ns.

Being newly married, I was also involved in getting settled into a big set of quarters on Selfridge, buying furniture and getting reacquainted with flying fighters. I enjoyed flying the P-47N for a short time because it was quite different from the P-47D that I was shot down in. The wings were somewhat longer, and it was designed to have a longer range primarily for use in the Pacific theater. It was an interesting airplane to fly, but I don't think I would have enjoyed fighting in it as much as I did the P-47D. It seemed to be less responsive to the aileron and somewhat more difficult to maneuver than the smaller P-47D.

Soon my squadron received the P-51H, the last series of the Mustangs that were built. It was designed to cost less because it was not expected to last a long time. It was determined that the average P-51 in World War II lasted through only 35 hours of combat flying. Some of the lighter materials used in the P-51H resulted in malfunctions of some systems. In the case of the tail wheel cable control, the mounting bracket would bend and the tail wheel would not extend for landing. We fixed this problem by disconnecting the cable and putting the tail wheel in a permanent down position. Overall, it was a nice airplane to fly, very light, maneuverable, having plenty of power. We flew a lot at Selfridge. It was a pleasure to get back into real flying after spending more than a year in prison camp and then during the past year, having only a few support-type airplanes available to fly.

In September 1946, I was advised I was to take my squadron of P-51s to Ladd Field, Fairbanks, Alaska, for cold weather tests, departing Selfridge Field in December. A squadron of B-29s from Rapid City, South Dakota, would also be deployed to Elmendorf Field at Anchorage, Alaska. This was SAC's first attempt at forward base deployment of units. Both units would be scheduled to rotate back to their bases at the end of three months. This time was extended by one month. The 57th Provisional Air Division reporting directly to SAC Headquarters in Omaha was formed at Ladd Field, Fairbanks to complete the chain of command between the two SAC units in Alaska and SAC Headquarters.

My squadron consisting of airplanes, pilots, crew chiefs and some maintenance personnel was augmented by personnel from the Supply Group, the Maintenance Group, Administration and Finance of Selfridge until I had a provisional squadron of some 340 people. Leading and managing this augmented squadron was a new experience and involved me in details of the military structure I had not known before.

All personnel except pilots and crew chiefs left Selfridge by train in early November for Seattle, Washington. From there they went by boat to Anchorage, Alaska and then by train to Fairbanks, Alaska, arriving in early December. Such was the system of movement and deployment in those early days in the development of air power. This advance group would prepare the base for the arrival of the pilots and planes.

I left Selfridge in a light snow storm on 18 December with 27 P-51Hs. Crew chiefs with some spare airplane parts and tools followed in three B-29s, led by Col. Bill Bacon who commanded a B-29 Group at Rapid City, South Dakota. When we stopped at a base enroute to Alaska, Colonel Bacon enjoyed pulling his B-29 right up to within two feet of the door of a hangar. He knew that we dumb fighter pilots would wonder how from that position he would ever get his B-29 back into a position to taxi. Of course, he was right because we did not know that the B-29 had reversible propellers and that he could simply back away from the hangar door.

Shortly after take-off from Selfridge during climb-out, one of my pilots lost his engine and crash-landed in a cornfield. The P-51 came to rest about 100 yards from a farm house. It was early morning; the farmer and his wife were having breakfast and did not hear the P-51's arrival. My pilot climbed out of the cockpit and carrying his parachute walked to the farm house and knocked on the door. The wife opened the door and needless to say, was somewhat startled to see this young man standing there dressed totally different from other people who sometimes arrived at her door this early in the morning. He asked to use the telephone and called back to Selfridge. I had already told Selfridge operations control that he had gone down in a cornfield only about 50 miles from Selfridge and told them to prepare the spare P-51H which was standing by just in case of such an emergency; I also told operations to tell him to take off immediately in the spare plane and to meet us at Great Falls. When my pilot reached operations at Selfridge by phone, the controller told him, "Your boss has called in your misfortune and wants us to tell you to get your ass back as soon as possible, get the spare airplane and meet him in Great Falls." He followed these instructions immediately by asking the farmer to drive him back to Selfridge but only after having a second delightful breakfast.

We were delayed in Great Falls, Montana for several days while some minor airplane parts needed for severe cold weather arrived and were installed in the P-51s. We finally got off on Christmas Eve but ran into severe weather as we approached Edmonton, Alberta, Canada. I decided to land and wait out the storm. However, before landing we did manage to fly across the city a couple of times, at a very low altitude and in beautiful tight formation. We just wanted Canadian citizens to know they would have guests for Christmas. That worked, too. We were housed in the best hotel and during our Christmas stay of two days we met many interesting and hospitable Canadians.

The weather finally cleared and we took off for Ladd Field. One of my pilots, a very fine young man, a bit younger than most of us, developed problems with his engine. We were then about 45 minutes from Whitehorse over rugged terrain. Whitehorse had a narrow landing strip that would accept the P-51. I relayed this to my pilot and asked him to try to nurse the plane to Whitehorse. He thought he could. I kept him in our formation and started a slow let-down. When I had the landing strip in sight, I asked him to leave the formation and land at Whitehorse. This would later provide a very sad outcome. I then set up a slow circle of the strip, and after seeing him land safely I advised him I would send maintenance personnel and a new engine from Ladd Field. We then climbed back up to cruise altitude and proceeded on to Ladd Field, landing about 3 p.m. Our ground support people whom we had not seen since early November were happy to see us and the airplanes.

With this happy landing we had completed this first SAC deployment. I had lost one airplane and had another one with a pilot down at Whitehorse. Not bad, I thought, considering all the unusual and challenging experiences we had encountered.

Although we arrived in bright sunshine, the temperature stood at 18 degrees F. This relative mildness would not last. The temperature started to drop that night down to minus 50 degrees F, and by morning ice fog, which forms at about minus 35 degrees, restricted visibility to no more than a few yards. For the next 23 days the temperature never rose above minus 50 degrees F and ranged down to minus 70 degrees F. It was the longest cold spell this area had had in 12 years. This cold allowed us to identify the problems in human and plane performance. I kept some oil used in the plane's engine outside in order to see how thick it would get. It froze to such a thickness that I could not even dent it with a screwdriver.

Because of the severe cold I was delayed in getting the pilot and plane back from Whitehorse. Just as soon as there was a break in the weather, I sent a new engine and maintenance personnel to recover the P-51. It took several days to accomplish the necessary maintenance. During this period a few of the maintenance personnel had been returned to Ladd by an airplane passing through. Finally the P-51 was ready to fly and the pilot was prepared to fly it to Ladd Field.

I was in my office at Ladd when my 1st Sergeant came in to tell me one of my maintenance sergeants, whom I knew very well, was outside and insisted he see me immediately. I said, "Send him in." He related to me in a very excited manner how he had been told the night before while he was at Whitehorse working on the P-51 that an airplane was available to return him to Ladd and that he must leave immediately. The reason he wanted to see me was to tell me he had been reinstalling a major fuel line to the engine when he had been interrupted and had to leave his job. On the airplane coming back to Ladd he had thought about this interruption and was not sure that he had replaced and tightened the main clamp on this fuel line or had only replaced it and not tightened it. He had tried to reach me from the airplane he was riding in but had been unable to get through to me. Communication in those days was not very good. Immediately I started to get a call through to Whitehorse to tell them not to let that airplane take off until this fuel line was checked. This fuel line was about one inch in diameter and the fuel in it would be under some pressure. If it were to come loose in flight, the engine would immediately stop and the fuel would undoubtedly be ignited and a serious fire would result.

Before I could get the call through my operations officer burst into my office, (the sergeant was still there), and told me the pilot at Whitehorse had taken off but shortly after take-off the engine had burst into flame. The pilot bailed out but his parachute failed to open and the pilot was dead. The airplane had crashed and was burning. The maintenance sergeant in my office looked as if he were in shock and about to collapse. I said to my operations officer, "Get my P-51 ready for immediate take-off. I'm going to Whitehorse." I had to determine if this accident had been caused by a fuel clamp not being properly installed.

As I flew to Whitehorse that cold afternoon over terrain deep in snow and ice I thought through the events leading to that fatal accident and wondered if I would ever be able to determine just how and why a critical maintenance operation had been interrupted before the job was completely and satisfactorily done. This kind of interruption was absolutely forbidden. I also wondered about the maintenance sergeant I had left in my office, a person I knew well and whose total reliability and responsibility I acknowledged. Would he be able to survive without knowing whether or not he was responsible for the accident? I must find that clamp.

There were no landing lights at Whitehorse at this time, and by the time I arrived, there was barely enough light for me to find the landing strip, but somehow I made it. I wanted to go to the crash site immediately, but decided to wait until morning when there would be sufficient light to make sure nothing was overlooked as we sifted through the debris. I formed a make-shift accident review board and briefed them on what we would be doing the next morning.

I then proceeded to the room where the pilot and his gear had been placed. I wanted to know why the parachute did not open. To my utter disgust I found the answer. The ripcord cable and handle had been attached to the left main parachute support strap by ordinary thread. As the pilot climbed from the cockpit and the flames from the engine hit the parachute, the threads had burned away. As a result the parachute cable then flew back over the pilot's left shoulder, totally out of his reach. On his right hand, the hand used to pull the ripcord handle, his nails were broken and the tips of his fingers were bloody as he had clawed at the parachute trying to find the ripcord handle. I did not sleep that night but found some comfort in a bottle of bourbon someone was considerate enough to bring to my room.

Early the next day I took my accident review team to the crash site and we carefully searched through the wreckage. Since the airplane had crashed with a full load of fuel it had been almost totally consumed by fire. I could never find anything that remotely resembled a fuel hose or clamp. Late that day I discontinued the search with the knowledge that positive proof of the cause of that accident could never be determined from the wreckage. As I flew back to Ladd Field that night there was about a quarter moon shining, and strong displays of aurora borealis lights raced across the sky. This natural phenomenon coupled with the snow on the ground made a bright and beautiful night to fly. I thought long and hard about the information I had been given the day before in my office by my maintenance sergeant. It seemed like a long time ago. What should I do with this information? These thoughts almost totally occupied my mind that night and still by the time I reached Ladd, I had not arrived at a conclusion as to what my next move should be. Even though it was after midnight when I landed, the maintenance sergeant was waiting to meet me at my airplane. I briefly explained what had happened that day and asked him to meet me in my office the next morning.

Again, I slept very little that night, but I did not want any help from bourbon. I felt this decision was mine alone. I did not want to go to my superiors for counseling or guidance. Above all, it seemed to me there was nothing to be gained by sacrificing the career of another fine young man. At this point, nothing could bring back the life of the pilot who had tried so desperately to save himself and would probably still be alive if the parachute had been properly designed. I prayed hard that night.

When I arrived at my office the next morning, my mind was clear. The maintenance sergeant was waiting and over a cup of coffee I told him I admired and respected him for coming to me two days before with his story and expression of concern. I also told him that his apprehension as to whether that fuel line clamp had been tightened after it was installed could never be determined. I described for him the condition of the parachute ripcord that was released when the attaching threads had burned away and how the pilot was unable to pull the ripcord handle because it was not within his reach. In fact, this was the cause of the pilot's death regardless of why the engine had burst into flames and stopped running.

I do not know what effect this incident had on the future life of this sergeant. I am sure it was never forgotten. We stayed in touch for many years and he rose to the highest sergeant grade and carried out the responsibilities of that grade with distinction. I have never forgotten the incident nor have I ever been sorry about my decision.

The problems of arctic operations were many, both for the airplanes and the crews. There is a lot of difference in flying, maintaining airplanes and surviving if a crew goes down in moderate temperatures with lows down to zero or maybe to 10-degrees below and with temperatures down to minus 50 degrees and more. From the pilot's point of view the very bulky and heavy flying suits that were the best available at that time along with the cumbersome fur-lined cloth mukluks just didn't fit very well in the relatively small P-51 cockpit. Also, the cloth mukluk tended to become wet if it was exposed to any melted ice or snow. We became convinced the uniform engineers at Wright Field who designed these things had never tried them for comfort or practical use in airplanes.

The two major problems with the airplane were freezing oil and hydraulic leaks. At these low temperatures the oil in the engine crankcase simply froze. Emersion heaters were available and successful in thawing the ice so that the crankshaft was free to turn and the engine would start. What we didn't know in the beginning was that except for the oil around the crankshaft the rest of the oil was still frozen and could not be pumped to the critical parts of the engine for lubrication. Consequently after a short time the engine would seize and stop running because of lack of oil. This, of course, could have been overcome by keeping the airplanes in heated hangars until time to fly and then rolling them out, starting engines and taking off. This procedure, however, would lead to the second problem—hydraulic leaks from the neoprene seal which at that time was the best seal material available. It was the rather sudden change from the temperature of the warm hangar to the outside which caused the leak. If the airplane stayed outside in the cold, the seals leaked very little or not at all.

Another problem was a phenomenon of weather. If there is any moisture introduced into the air at about minus 35-degree F, ice fog forms and can become so thick as to reduce visibility to a very few yards. And the white ice fog together with the snow on the ground causes a white-out. One simply couldn't see. A similar situation existed in flight; if you were flying under an overcast with the ground totally covered in snow, you had to fly on instruments. You had no horizon. As the temperature hovered between minus 35 degrees and minus 40 degrees the visibility would improve and we would get suited up and prepare to launch a few flights. As the airplanes started engines and began to taxi, the exhaust from 12 to 16 airplanes produced enough moisture to make the visibility drop to almost zero. This caused an accident one day when while taxiing one pilot failed to see the airplane in front of him. As a result his propeller chewed up the aft section of the plane in front.

We tried to solve this problem by towing the airplanes to the end of the runway and then starting engines and immediately taking off. This worked for one flight of four airplanes, but after they got off the runway visibility would be socked in. We finally decided that flight operations below minus 35 degrees F were not feasible.

We were fortunate that winter in having available in Fairbanks Sir Hubert Wilkins, the famous Arctic explorer. He very graciously agreed to present a few lectures to our pilots concerning his explorations and experiences. What was most interesting to my pilots was how to survive under conditions of extreme cold if they had to bail out or crash-land.

An Army Battalion was conducting Arctic exercises that winter on the tundra near the Tanana River just south of Fairbanks. Some of their officers came to Ladd Air Force Base almost every weekend. I met one of their majors who was a very nice guy and we became friends. After a few weeks he invited me to spend a night with him where they were operating. I gathered up my Arctic gear and accompanied him to his unit. We stayed in an igloo that night which had a pot-bellied stove red hot and two areas covered with pine boughs on either side of the stove for sleeping. When chow time was called we crawled out with mess kits, food was dumped in and we crawled back inside to the hot stove. The food was almost frozen before we got back to the fire. We consumed a bottle of bourbon that night before going to sleep, and I slept rather well. Early the next morning I was ready to return to the Army Air Forces at Ladd Field.

After this experience I got my pilots together and described this night I had spent with the Army and told them I would like to do a bit of recruiting. Through the local Air Force recruiting office and a Fairbanks travel office we managed to get quite a few Army Air Forces recruiting posters and posters depicting the beaches and weather of Florida. At that time a relatively small metal cannister filled with sand and fitted with a spotting charge on the end was used for practice dive-bombing. For our recruiting plan we put enough sand in the canisters to make them ballistic and then filled them with the posters we had gathered. I called my Army friend and told him I was planning to drop some posters in his area and asked if he thought it would unnecessarily upset his commander. He said he didn't think so and gave me a spot to make the drop. In a few days the weather was perfect for such a mission. I had two of these cannister bombs attached under the wings of each of four airplanes. I then led this flight for a dive-bombing mission against the Army. In addition to the posters each cannister had several large papers inscribed with "Don't walk. Ride. Join the Army Air Forces."

I found the target spot my friend had suggested, and we made near-perfect dive-bombing runs and all the bombs were released. When they hit the ground, they opened and we could see the posters being scattered about.

The next day I was called to the office of my Division Commander. I was very seriously received and escorted into his office. Without any preliminaries he proceeded to tell me of a complaint he had received by phone from the Army Commander, a colonel. According to the Army colonel, he had been dive-bombed by four P-51s. This had resulted in a disruption to his command and a drop in the morale of his troops. The Army colonel wanted to know what my Division Commander intended to about it. I then proceeded to tell him the full story and to explain the contents of the bombs. By the time I was finished he was laughing and he picked up the phone and called the Army Commander. Apparently they were soon laughing together. When he hung up he told me the Army Commander had told him to remind that damned Johnson that his Air Forces is not a separate service yet—he's still a part of the Army.

In the early spring the ice in the rivers starts to break up. Due to the thickness and the great amounts of this ice, it is not uncommon for the ice to jam the flow of water in the rivers, causing the water to back up and cause flooding in the town of Fairbanks. The early spring of 1947 was one of those years. I was asked by the mayor of Fairbanks if I would be willing to assist in relieving their potential flood problem by bombing the ice flows and thereby permit the water to flow. I told him I could handle that mission and we did. It was a perfect opportunity for dive-bombing practice and at the same time help our neighboring civilian community.

Capt. Billy Edens, my ground training officer, and several other pilots during this period conducted cold weather survival tests which provided valuable information. They took with them into the wilds of Alaska only the survival items carried by each pilot in his airplane. In addition, they were dressed in the flying suits worn by pilots. The first objective was to see if a downed pilot could survive with only the equipment he was carrying with him when he went down and the second was to test with only this equipment and in the snow-covered terrain whether he could mark his location sufficiently to be found by search planes. The pilots flying the search planes were given only a general area in which to search. Many things were learned during these exercises. The basic one was that in most areas the snow was so deep that without snowshoes the pilots could not travel and in most cases could barely maneuver enough to gather fire wood or pine boughs. Therefore, to find their location on the ground was extremely difficult. We found the colored smoke flares and the small reflecting mirror, both carried in the pilot's survival kit, to be the most helpful items in attracting the attention of search planes.

Despite the loss of flying time in early January we had followed a strenuous flying schedule and by the end of March had completed the training planned for this temporary duty (TDY). Our activities in the frozen North had attracted the news media who visited us and reported, quite accurately I believe, what it was really like to operate

P-51s under these conditions. In addition we were visited by many SAC Headquarter's people who were more interested in our deployment from an operational and administrative point of view than in our cold weather activities. During this time at Ladd Field we had represented the fledgling Strategic Air Command in an oustanding manner. The permanent echelon of people at Ladd had developed great respect for us and our determination to carry on despite the weather. It turned out that during this same time period my P-51 squadron under far worse conditions had flown more hours than the B-29 bomb squadron at Anchorage.

The manner in which my first TDY to Alaska was terminated is interesting in the sense that it explains the way things were done in those days. By this time in the development of air power subsequent to World War II most of us had friends from those war days in commands and in many different positions of responsibility. Through these people we could get things done. Also, it turned out, my present unit, the 56th Fighter Group at Selfridge, was receiving its first jet fighters, the F-80 Shooting Star, and Dave Schilling, its commander, was far more interested in those new airplanes than he was in what the 62nd Squadron in Alaska was doing. Time passed, we flew expertly and accomplished all assigned missions plus others we dreamed up. However, I did not hear anything about our returning to Selfridge.

I had become pretty well acquainted with the Commanding General of the 57th Air Division. I was determined that my support personnel would not have to spend another month getting back to Selfridge by land and sea transportation as they had done on the way to Alaska. My Division Commander had shown no interest or concern in the termination of my TDY so I asked him if it was permissible for me to work with Alaskan Air Command to arrange for the return of my unit. He said it was o.k. I then had my people work up a list of equipment to be returned, an estimate of the weight and (cube) volume and a list of personnel. With this information I flew to Elmendorf and met with my friend as I presented my proposal, which was to have my squadron and equipment flown back to Selfridge by Alaskan Air

Command aircraft. I had been accompanied on the way up to Alaska by SAC B-29s. I didn't need them on the way back. I knew Alaskan Air Command had a small number of C-54s and I guessed that the pilots that flew them probably would enjoy a trip or two to Michigan. At first the answer to my proposal was "Absolutely, No." However, after my friend had brought in a few of his workers and enthusiastic young pilots, his opinion began to change. As it grew late on that day, I suggested we retire to the Club for a drink, dinner and continuation of the development of my plan. The drinks may have been several more than one, and the dinner may have been a bit late, but by the time I went to my airplane late the next day to fly back to Ladd Field, I had in my pocket not only an approved plan but signed orders directing that my squadron be returned from Ladd Field, Alaska to Selfridge Field, Michigan by airlift to be provided by Alaskan Air Command. I had learned a lot about how to get things done, and it had only cost me two days and a rather expensive evening at the Officers Club.

As I led my squadron back to Michigan, now consisting of only 25 airplanes since I had not received a replacement for the one lost at Whitehorse and another one that had crashed later at Ladd, I had much to think about. These four months had been filled with events that had taught me a lot. I was now a much better pilot. I was, I felt, an experienced and capable commander, and I had learned more about people and how to get the best performance from them. This higher performance I knew resulted from giving them a lot of my time and attention and being responsive to them as individuals. After all, I could be no better than the people who worked for me. These views never changed as my later commands grew in responsibility.

On my return to Selfridge, Col. William Hudnell, the wing commander, had a surprise for me. When he met me on the flight line and congratulated me on the fine job we had done and on the excellent experience the squadron had gained, he added that he had good news or bad news for me, depending on how I looked at it. He announced, "You are going to Grenier Field, Manchester, New Hampshire to take your entire augmented squadron as a nucleus to form the new 82nd Fighter Group." I do not remember what my initial reaction was, but

I recognized that I was being given a new and challenging job. I spent the weekend at Selfridge. Monday morning I took off with the pilots and the 25 airplanes that we had just brought back from Alaska and flew to Grenier to begin the activation of the 82nd Fighter Group under the command of SAC. This was a career path that I desired.

After we landed at Grenier in a strong cross wind, most of the pilots flew right back to Selfridge Field in a C-47. They were to meet their families there and start their leave time, their first since leaving Michigan for Alaskan temporary duty (TDY). I remained at Grenier and prepared for the challenges that lay ahead in the development of a new fighter wing.

Two incidents stand out in my memory of my 14 months with the 82nd Group—my selection of the best personnel director for the Group and my second TDY to Alaska from March to June 1948. Since I was starting a new Group, I had to interview every officer that arrived in order to find out his qualifications and where to assign him within the Group. In those days, we did not have Military Occupational Speciality numbers (MOS), and only later did we acquire the Air Force Speciality Code (AFSC). I assigned several people, mostly senior NCOs, to interview the airmen and place them most effectively.

At Grenier, my office was an unairconditoned room in a one-story World War II tar paper shack down by the flight line. About 4 o'clock one hot July afternoon, my adjutant came in to say, "Major Dixon is here to see you." Uniform protocol then required a long-sleeved shirt and a tie, and the khaki material was heavy. Into my office came a perspiring major in a somewhat wet and wrinkled shirt.

"Major Dixon reporting, Sir," he said.

I asked him to sit down, and we started talking. I thought him a bit belligerent and not easy to talk with. After a few minutes I realized I was learning nothing about him. Finally I asked, "What kind of assignment are you looking for?"

He replied, "I want to fly airplanes."

"Where did you come from?" I asked him. He said he had been shot down in World War II flying a Spitfire, a subject we had already discussed. He emphasized he just wanted to get back to flying as he had been away from it for some time. He wanted very badly to fly a P-51.

To point our conversation in another direction, I asked, "What was your last assignment?" Again he changed the subject. "Tell me," I insisted, "what was your assignment just before you were sent to Grenier?"

Almost reluctantly he said, "Teaching English at West Point."

As one who loved to fly, I understood his desire to work in a cockpit more than before a classroom. Nevertheless, I told him that what I needed more than anything else in this organization right then was a personnel officer. I thought that he as a major (I was a lieutenant colonel) was going to come right over my desk and hit me. He left no doubt in my mind that personnel was a career in which he had no interest. Nevertheless, I had already decided that I liked this officer's attitude and I had the feeling he would do well in any assignment.

"Major Dixon," I told him, "as of right now, you are Director of Personnel of the 82nd Fighter Group."

"All right, Sir," he said. He stood up, saluted, and left my office.

Major Dixon had to find a place for his family to live, and two days passed before I saw him again. I had the habit of going to my office after dinner almost every night to do some work. My office was at one end of the building; down at the other end was another office, and the rest of the building was open with desks. As I drove into my office area that evening, I noticed that there were several cars parked at the opposite end of the building from my office. The lights were on inside. That was unusual. I looked through the window to see what was happening. There was Bob Dixon at a desk, his sleeves rolled up, his shirt open. Stacks of regulations and whatnot were spread all over the desk. Three sergeants and one of my captains who had some personnel experience were with him. Dixon was starting to learn the personnel business. My hunch about him was correct. He was the same kind of worker I was, and we became good friends. From that summer of 1947, Dixon became one of the finest personnel officers of the Air Force, rising rapidly to four-star general. I did not get to keep Dixon very long in the Group, for his ability was soon recognized by the Wing Commander, Brigadier General Tucker. But General Tucker did not get to keep Dixon for long either. Maj. Gen. Horace Wade, then the Deputy for Personnel at the new Strategic Air Command Headquarters at Andrews Air Force Base, immediately recognized in Dixon just the person he was looking for to help him in the formation and development of the Strategic Air Command under Gen. Curtis E. LeMay. He therefore moved him from Grenier down to Andrews, the temporary home of SAC and later to Offutt Air Force Base, Omaha, Nebraska when SAC moved its headquarters. General Wade recognized that he needed Dixon to identify responsible individuals, train them well and put them where they should be in SAC. In building SAC to carry out its deterrent mission, there was hardly anybody or any group in SAC Headquarters that was more important in developing SAC for General LeMay than the personnel people.

As a group commander at Grenier with the purpose of developing pilots and airmen for their role in SAC's mission, I called on my experience as a squadron commander in combat and on TDY in Alaska. About that time, Col. Henry Viccellio had taken command of the Group, and I was his deputy. We worked well together. On a Saturday in March 1948, Col. Viccellio came to my quarters saying, "I've got something to tell you. I have just received a message from SAC telling us we are going to take the 82nd Group to Alaska, leaving early next week. Since you have already been in Alaska once, you have a lot of experience. I'd like you to take the advanced echelon and get things set up for the air echelon's arrival."

Instead of one squadron of P-51s going to Ladd Field, I had to prepare for the entire Group to move and train there. That meant preparation for some 75 P-51 pilots and planes and for 1,800 men who would be flown to Alaska instead of going by ground and water. The P-51s went to Ladd Field, and a bomber group went to Elmendorf Field. This deployment had an added significance in light of contemporary world politics. Italian elections were to take place about this time. SAC leaders were somewhat concerned that if these elections resulted in any significant communist gains, the outcome might cause the Soviet Union to think that things were moving well for them and that they might plan some activities against the peripheries of the free world. That perception caused SAC to move these fighter and bomber units to Alaska, a periphery of the United States, as a kind of message to the Soviet Union that the United States really did have some degree of deterrence alive and well in our policy.

Besides training on the ground and in the air from March to May, the 82nd responded to calls for help in alleviating some problems in the Alaskan environment caused by the cold weather. One of these could be dovetailed with the group's practice of dive bombing. Ice jammed the Yukon River at Tanana, more than 50 miles northwest of Fairbanks. Since I had done this the previous year, it was old hat. Our P-51 pilots dropped 500-pound demolition bombs at three separate spots on the river where the ice had thickened and threatened the area. The success of this three-month TDY by an entire group proved that SAC's concept of deployment on a rotational basis and with increasing speed from base to forward base was feasible as a vital part of its deterrent mission. It is fair to assume that the move of an entire group from the east coast of the United States to the extreme northwest of the North American continent was noticed by leaders of any potential enemy.

Returning from this second Alaskan assignment in May 1948, I was still much concerned that I had only two years of college, which was all that was necessary to enter the Army Aviation Cadet Training program in 1941. I thought that if I were to make a career out of the military, it would be best to earn at least a baccalaureate degree. Such a degree would also provide me with a solid background for attending special military education programs beyond the Command and Staff School I had already completed. Since I had been occupied for two years with strenuous leadership duty, I thought this was a good time for a break. I applied, and Boston University was the institution selected for me, probably because of its proximity to my base at Grenier. I enrolled in September 1948 and through a concentrated schedule finished in January 1950.

My next assignment as plans officer with the Air Force Engineering and Development Division at Wright-Patterson Air Force Base,
near Dayton, Ohio, seemed logical for career development and
broadening. My boss was Col. Melvin McNickle, who was a twin
brother to Col. Marvin McNickle, a P-47 pilot in World War II and
now was also stationed at Wright-Patterson. Lt. Col. Bill Clough, a
non-rated administrative assistant to Mel, taught me a lot about staff
work and administration. These were areas in which, he believed at
that time, not very many Air Force officers had much interest or knew
very much about. Clough stressed many times that unless the officers
wearing wings learned how to administer and control the Air Force,
non-rated people like himself would take over and run the recently
formed and authorized United States Air Force. We both got to work
about seven in the morning, and the time from then to 8 or 830 was
almost always a period of learning for me.

During the war Muroc Dry Lake, northeast of Los Angeles, had
been a test center for newly developed aircraft. In 1950 the decision
had been made to build Edwards Air Force Base adjacent to the dry
lake with a hard-surface runway 15,000 feet long that terminated in
the dry lake. Test aircraft would have almost unlimited distance for
take-off and landings. Necessary hangars and support buildings
would also be constructed. The new base would cost approximately
$100 million, a very large amount of money for that time. I was made
project officer for this development. It was a demanding job with
almost weekly quick trips to Washington and California. I had little
time to do my work at Wright-Patterson and to keep the people I
worked for and coordinated with abreast of the developments. Consequently almost every weekend I could be found in my office and
very often with several others who were assisting me. This I believe
was the time when I noticed a difference between Air Force personnel
and civilian employees of the Air Force. And there were many at
Wright-Patterson. An Air Force officer or enlisted person worked
whenever he was needed or he was asked. The number of hours or
week-day or weekend hours worked didn't matter. A civilian em-
ployee worked the authorized number of hours and regardless of his

grade was reluctant to come in for extra and necessary work unless he was paid overtime. This used to really bother me. I became so fed up with one of my civilian employees that I fired him or thought I had. He not only would not work extra hours but did hardly any thing during the hours he worked. And that was the time when I learned it's not possible to fire a civil servant. The process one must go through and the records to be kept and the paper work involved required so much effort that most Air Force people just gave up or else they were transferred before the elimination of a worthless worker was ever effected.

The Korean War started in June 1950. As it progressed I began to realize this conflict was not something that was going to be quickly finished. With this thought I also knew that I should be involved. If one's chosen career is military, then one should fight every war in which his country is engaged. Also about this time the Air Force Research and Development Command was organized with Headquarters at Baltimore, Maryland and was commanded by former CINCSAC General Thomas Power. I was being advised that this was an excellent opportunity for career progression and was urged to move to Baltimore.

I liked what I was doing and the level at which I was working wasn't too different from command. I was pretty much my own boss. However, I didn't like the fact that I was meeting my monthly flying requirement by flying a B-25.

It wasn't too long before this problem was solved for me. Col. Dave Schilling, whom I had joined in the postwar 56th Fighter Group at Selfridge Air Force Base, Michigan after finishing Command and Staff School had become the commander of the 31st Fighter Wing at Turner Field, Albany, Georgia. The Group was flying the Republic-built F-84E. He called me to say he had a position open in his Wing and very much wanted me to come to Turner and join him. This I did in July 1951 and I became Director of Operations of the 31st Fighter Wing. This position was the beginning of a long stretch of assignments at Turner Air Force Base under SAC that included two TDY tours of peripheral fighter operations during the Korean War, a nonstop air-refueled flight of 20 fighters to England, command of a Strategic Fighter Wing and command of a Strategic Reconnaissance Wing.

Upon return from Alaska to Selfridge Field, MI in April 1947 I am met by Col. Bill Hudnell, 56th Wing Commander and Lt. Col. Dinghy Dunham.

CHAPTER 5
MY CAREER IN SAC: A FIGHTER PILOT

A t Turner Air Force Base, I began my first real experience in flying jet fighters. At that time the 31st Fighter Wing flew the F-84E. It was the forerunner of the F-84G Thunderjet, the latter a much improved fighter because of its aerial refueling capability, and the F-84F which had swept wings.

The need for increased range in fighter aircraft had been recognized early in the development of airplanes. Many attempts had been made and some very simple systems had been devised to transfer fuel from one airplane to another while in flight. However, between the two wars, World War I and World War II, no concerted developmental effort toward solving the problems of aerial refueling took place. This omission is understandable since during these years great progress was made in improving the flying machine; better engines, stronger fuselages, increased ceiling and speed, and of course, increased reliability and safety. This progress seemed sufficient at that time. There simply was no interest in keeping the plane airborne beyond the extent of its inherent fuel supply.

As Strategic Air Command developed in the early years following World War II, it became apparent that the oceans on either side of the United States needed to be crossed and that these oceans must not detract from SAC's deterrent mission. Thus the stage was set for the development of aerial refueling. Historically an individual able to solve great problems has always arisen to meet the need. To a very large degree this man was Dave Schilling, Colonel USAF, who made the first nonstop east-to-west crossing of the North Atlantic in September 1950 by use of inflight refueling.

The probe and drogue system was the initial method to effect aerial refueling, but we needed a more effective system. In the boom system developed by Boeing Aircraft Company and initially installed in KC-97s and later in the jet KC-135 tanker plane, a boom operator lying on his stomach in the tanker extended the boom into the fuel receptacle of the receiving plane. Republic Aviation designed the F-84G with a receptacle for air refueling. The F-84G allowed the 31st Wing and the 508th Wing to pioneer flights for great distances over the oceans nonstop.

I did not participate in the first mass deployment of the F-84Es of the 31st Fighter Escort Wing to Misawa, Japan, in July 1952. Gen. Jesse Auton, who was the 65th Wing Commander under which the 56th Fighter Group had served in Europe, had sent me on a highly classified assignment to Oslo, Norway in January 1952 shortly after I had been promoted to colonel.

The classified mission to Norway extended my experience in SAC in a new direction. SAC had forward air bases in England, Spain and North Africa. By this time the North Atlantic Treaty Organization (NATO) was developing rapidly and many bases were being built that could accommodate SAC fighters that were much closer to the Soviet Union. Norway was the obvious choice for development of these bases with the added capability to take care of SAC fighters either as forward launch sites or recovery bases. However, a problem arose because Norway's constitution did not permit foreign troops on its soil in either peace or war. Hence the secrecy of our mission. We always wore civilian clothes, and we always presented ourselves as a part of NATO. I was one of three Air Force officers selected to go to Norway to work with the Norwegian Air Force and with NATO to assure that the requirements of a forward base, adequate for use by SAC fighters included extra fuel storage, munitions, and many other things peculiar to the SAC mission that were designed into these particular bases. I made many trips to NATO Headquarters and became well acquainted with people from most NATO countries and became knowledgeable of the NATO organization and mission. There was only one drawback. Since I had been promoted to full colonel just before leaving Turner to go to Norway, I would have enjoyed wearing the uniform with a colonel's insignia and the hat with braided visor. This preference, however, was denied.

When I returned to Turner Air Force Base in the summer of 1952, I was to become deputy commander of the 508th Strategic Fighter

Wing, which was scheduled to be activated at Turner and to be commanded by Col. Cy Wilson. The designation of this fighter wing as "Strategic" revealed a change in the mission or purpose of fighters in SAC. If SAC bombers were to carry out the strategic bombing policy as a deterrent of aggression against the United States, then the fighters that worked with the bombers on that policy would also have a strategic purpose. By September I officially joined the 508th as deputy to Colonel Wilson. We trained pilots to fly the F-84Gs, to master the aerial refueling procedure that included rendezvous with the tankers and cross-country navigation that involved some instruction in celestial navigation.

In the winter of 1953, the 508th Wing was sent to Misawa, Japan in support of SAC's rotational policies and to provide supplemental support and mission augmentation to the Allied forces of South Korea. The 508th Wing's flight activity while at Misawa provided support, deterrence and augmentation to the United States forces operating from South Korea and the South of Japan.

One day a young lieutenant and I took off in two F-84Es from Misawa. We planned to cross the water to Korea and run some peripheral activity along the eastern side of Korea. It was a very cold day; ice was on the ramp and on the runway. As was our habit, we went to the parachute shop to have one fitted to each of us. The parachutes would then be delivered to and placed in the airplanes that we had been scheduled to fly and that were identified by tail number. It was easier not to have to carry the parachute across the icy ramp and to climb into the airplane when the chute was already in place.

The lieutenant and I completed our mission planning and walked out to our airplanes. We discovered that the parachutes had been placed in the wrong airplanes. My chute had been placed in the aircraft that the lieutenant was scheduled to fly and his chute was in the airplane I was scheduled to fly. Instead of going to all the trouble of changing parachutes, we decided just to change airplanes. I would fly the one my chute was in, and he would fly the one his chute was in. I advised base operations by radio the changes in the tail numbers.

We both fired up, taxied out and took off. We climbed out to the west, and were through about 20,000 feet when I noticed my wingman, the lieutenant, had dropped back a few hundred yards. I immediately called him and asked if he was o.k. He said that he was losing a little power, but the instruments did not indicate any problem. I throttled back but continued the climb.

I could not help thinking of a fairly recent flight from Turner when I had encountered a similar problem of some loss of power as I got to higher altitude. On that occasion I had reported the power loss to mission control. They advised me that my crew chief had reported that his visored cap was missing. It was standard practice that crew chiefs removed their caps and placed them in their pocket as they moved around the airplane after engine start and while they removed power cables and wheel chocks. When I landed we found his cap against the debris screen in the intake of the engine. It apparently had been sucked from his pocket as he went under the nose of the airplane to remove the chocks.

I had been watching my wing man very closely and it appeared that several times he seemed to start to close on me but would then drop back again. I decided to level off and reduce power. I had asked several times if he was o.k. He had responded, "Yes, I think so." It became clear that he had a real problem. I decided I had to take him back to the base. I started a slow turn back to the base and called mission control to advise them my No. 2 had a problem with his airplane and we were returning to base.

Just a few seconds later he called, "I'm flamed out." We had plenty of altitude. I told him to do an air start. He "rogered." I had slowed down and stayed close by him. He said he was unable to get an air start. Because we were losing altitude rapidly, I told him to eject. He said he would do another air start. I said, "No, eject now while you have altitude." He did not. I then called him by his first name and said, "Eject, eject, eject NOW." By now we were really low. I saw the canopy come off, but it seemed long seconds before the seat shot out. He separated from the seat, the chute opened but only streamed before he hit the ground. The airplane crashed and burned near by. When his body was found, it was discovered he had crashed against a fence post and had died instantly.

Needless to say, I have thought about that flight many times. I worried about it at that time and for a long time afterward as to why and how his airplane malfunctioned. How did the ground crew put the parachutes into the wrong airplanes? Why did we unknowingly change the airplanes we were to fly without a second thought? What would I have done, if we had not switched airplanes, and I had flown the one that had the problem? I will never know the answers to these questions. We finished this 90-day rotation sometime in April 1953 and returned the 508th to Turner.

Shortly after our return, Colonel Wilson and I began to think about a mass flight of F-84Gs across the North Atlantic nonstop, utilizing aerial refueling. Fortunately the wing receptacles of the F-84Gs were equipped to work with the boom of the KB-29 or KC-97 tankers. These were propeller-driven converted airplanes. The KB-29 was a converted B-29 bomber. The KC-97 was a converted transport. The difference in speed of the jet fighter in comparison with the propeller-driven tankers did not make refueling any easier. With the tanker at maximum power setting and in a slight dive, the speed differential was still barely tolerable, in particular as the fighter approached a full fuel load. The other problem was altitude difference. The fighters would be cruising at high altitude and would usually have to descend 15 to 20 thousand feet to rendevous with the tankers.

We selected the 14th of August 1953 as the date for this flight, which we had named Longstride. This mission would consist of 20 F-84Gs in five flights and two sections. Cy Wilson would lead the first section of 12 aircraft. I would lead the second section of eight aircraft. Our destination was Lakenheath, England.

I was responsible to Cy for developing the overall plan, selecting the pilots and coordinating with the tanker units for the required number of tankers needed and the three refueling rendezvous points. The Navy also had to be included for positioning certain ships at predetermined ocean positions to assist in navigation and sea rescue if that should become necessary. There was a tremendous amount of work to be done and the 14 August date selected did not provide much time.

The Wing was most fortunate to have an extremely bright and capable young captain by the name of Hank Meierdierck. He was given the task of working out the many details of routing, timing, tanker rendezvous points, missed refueling options, navy ship navigation positions and many other necessary details. Because there were no computers in those days, all of these computations had to be done by hand.

Since none of us had ever flown for 11 hours without landing, which it was calculated would be the flying time of Longstride including finding and getting on the boom of a tanker three different times, I decided I must plan a simulated practice mission. What if the whole idea was not feasible or at least not practical. In order to use fewer tankers I decided to do the practice mission with only one flight of four planes. I picked from those pilots I had already selected for the mission a strong pilot, an average pilot and one of the youngest. I would lead the practice flight. Captain Meierdierck laid out a route around the United States that would take between 10 and 11 hours to fly, including three refuelings. We were to wear the anti-exposure suits that we had to wear in crossing the North Atlantic. Before take-off we ate the same type of food we would be served before the actual mission. I knew this would be a very tiring flight. I wanted to know just how tiring.

We flew the practice mission, and we encountered no serious problems. After landing at Turner some 10 hours and 22 minutes later, I believe I must have poured a half gallon of perspiration from this heavy all-rubber anti-exposure suit. The discomfort of this suit was the biggest problem we faced but there was no fix. I never really knew if this simulated mission produced any tangible benefits for the four of us involved. I do know that we learned we were going to be very, very tired when we made that landing at Lakenheath, England. The four of us debriefed this practice flight to the remaining 16 pilots and I am sure the information was helpful to them.

The 31st Wing was also involved in Longstride. Colonel Schilling, commander of the 31st, took eight F-84s over the warmer Atlantic route to Nouasseur Air Base, Morocco, North Africa. His take-off from Turner was a bit later on the same morning, and since he was flying over the warmer waters of the mid-Atlantic, anti-exposure suits were not required.

Turner Air Force Base had only one air-conditioned facility—the briefing room in the center of the Headquarters Building. Needless to say, during the hot summer of 1953 that air-conditioned room was used for many activities other than as a briefing room. A lot of people temporarily moved their desks into the briefing room. We knew we would have to take off about 230 a.m. from Turner in order to arrive at Lakenheath before it got dark there. We thought it would be a lot smarter if all the pilots slept at the base that night away from their families. We set up 20 cots in the briefing room, and the room was darkened at 6 p.m. The pilots were required to go to bed early because they would be awakened at midnight and fed a steak and egg breakfast. Then we would get suited up in the anti-exposure suit which is a mess to get into and which needs the help of another person both getting into it and getting out. I have never been a very good sleeper, and that night was no exception.

I remember some of the thoughts that went through my mind that evening. Why am I in this damned briefing room lying on an uncomfortable cot? I'd rather be home in my bed. I'd like to see my wife and children before take-off. In six hours I'll take off in an F-84G to fly nonstop to Lakenheath, England. It will take 11 to 12 hours. I'm tired. This had been a busy day—many things to do. Have I done them all? This may be my last flight. Why am I feeling this way and why can't I sleep? I need the rest.

I dozed off. I awakened to a change in the sound of the air-conditioner. I dozed off again and was awakened by bright lights and the announcement that breakfast would be served in 30 minutes. I could care less. I did not even remember dinner at 5 p.m. and without a cocktail or glass of wine. Suddenly I reminded myself that I was a leader. There were at least seven other pilots in this room who were younger and looking to me to guide them safely across the huge Atlantic Ocean in this first mass nonstop crossing by single-engine, single-pilot aircraft.

With that thought, I jumped from that cot feeling new strength and new determination that regardless of how little I had slept, I had the mental and physical reserve to make this crossing and to provide strength to those who would look to me for leadership.

Up at midnight, we ate our breakfast, got into the suit, and got our flight plans and whatever else we had to carry to our planes, including a small bottle of water. One thing I learned on the practice mission, whenever a pilot wears the anti-exposure suit, whatever he needs for navigation had to be tied on a string around his neck. If for some reason he dropped anything on the floor of the aircraft, the rubber suit would never allow him to bend over and pick it up. Navigation equipment for fighter pilots was limited in those days but I did have pencils, flight logs, emergency procedures check list, radio frequencies, tanker call signs, Air-Sea Rescue information and other items. I tied them all in such a way that I could not lose them.

About 2 a.m., with the aid of two airmen, one on each wing, we climbed in the cockpits. It was very dark everywhere, and it was difficult to get everything hooked up and adjusted. It was now about start-engine time, and I suddenly realized I needed to relieve my bladder. There was no way to do that and would not be for the next 12 hours. "What the hell," I thought, "I'll just sweat it out." To make the story of this historic flight complete and accurate, I have to add another element and another participant to it at this point.

Col. Thayer Olds, commander of the 40th Air Division at Turner under which both the 508th and the 31st operated, wanted to earn his first star and become a brigadier general. Although he was in his late 40s (to the rest of us in our early 30s, he seemed a bit old), it was surmised that he had received word to the effect that he needed to do something spectacular to make that star forthcoming. In any case, Thayer approached Cy, and between them they agreed that Thayer would be designated as leader of the 508th on the North Atlantic crossing. He chose not to wear the anti-exposure suit because he said he would never make it if he had to wear that suit.

"I would rather take my chances on not going down than not being able to survive in that damn anti-exposure suit," he declared. He was the only one of our 20 pilots who did not wear one.

Anyhow we all fired up, taxied out to the runway, and took off without any problems. It was still pitch dark at 2:30 a.m. We flew up along the east coast a little west of New York, past Boston, east of Canada. The first refueling was to take place somewhere beyond Boston. Needless to say, the person doing all the navigating and leading of the flight was Cy. We scarcely heard Thayer's voice. It was getting light as we made that rendezvous with the KC-97s; everyone filled their tanks, and we started across the Atlantic. The second refueling took place near Greenland, and the third over Iceland. From there we flew into Lakenheath. The second refueling also went well. The sun was bright as we flew east in a kind of loose formation. It was a beautiful morning to fly an F-84 to England. Everyone was a bit tired when we arrived over Iceland. However, the rendezvous went well but not quite as smoothly as the first two. We had a small problem in locating the tankers and had to do some maneuvering to make the rendezvous.

I had a little difficulty on that third refueling. I just could not seem to get fuel. The process took far longer than it should. I talked to the boom operator in the tanker. He said he thought we had a problem with the pump that pumped the fuel from the tanker to the fighter. I managed to find the spare tanker plane in the area, got on its boom and finished my refueling. It happened that Capt. Hank Meierdierck was the only one that could not get any fuel. He had to drop down to Iceland and land at Keflavik to get refueled and join up with us as soon as he could. Due to heavy haze, we could hardly see Lakenheath or find the runway. We were skilled pilots, however, and we landed without difficulty. As I taxied in I began to feel the fatigue which I had either not felt or ignored in flight. A lot of people met us, including the British news media, and a great deal of interest was shown in our nonstop mass flight of F-84s across the Atlantic utilizing aerial refueling.

After interviews, pictures and debriefing during which time we got out of those horrible survival suits, we made our way to the RAF

Club for a much awaited rendezvous at the bar. We had not been there for more than an hour when Hank, still in his flying suit, rushed in and told his story. He said that when he landed at Iceland, it took some persuasion to get his plane refueled without shutting down the engine. He was concerned that at Keflavik he might not get a restart. His flight from Iceland to Lakenheath although at night had been uneventful. This was probably the only time a jet fighter plane was refueled on the ground with the engine running.

There was real reason for rejoicing because all 20 pilots, including Thayer, had made the crossing safely. The next day I went to a small town nearby and bought a Morris Minor convertible. It was a great little car and Cy and I drove to London for two days of R & R (Rest and Relaxation). I think we had more of the second "R" than the first.

The day after we returned from London, we fired up our 20 birds and flew a low-level mission over most of southern England doing a great buzz job on several bases and small towns that still held memories for us from World War II.

Two days later we were scheduled to fly the 20 airplanes to Goerdermoen Air Base in Norway. Goerdermoen was a large military base about 20 miles north of Oslo. In order to have communiction with Goerdermoen for landing information and updates of weather information, we arranged with 7th Air Division to have a C-97 fly to Goerdermoen with a radio operator aboard the airplane who would stay on the air during the time of our flight and arrival at the air base. The weather over England that August day was beautiful, bright and sunny. The weather enroute to Norway was forecast to be relatively good, including our arrival time at Goerdermoen. Thayer Olds decided to take the lead for this flight. I led the second section, two flights of four aircraft each.

We took off and climbed to cruise altitude which for this flight was about 25,000 feet. Everything went well. Our flight was planned to take us across the North Sea, over water between Denmark and Norway and then at a point just about due south of Oslo we would turn left and take a heading directly to Goerdermoen. I had flown over these areas a lot just two years before and knew them well. I also knew the weather was unpredictable and prone to sudden changes.

After about two thirds of the way across the North Sea, I could see heavy clouds ahead. As we got nearer, it was obvious we were going to enter a solid cloud bank. Thayer was still leading and had said nothing. We flew in a relatively loose and relaxed formation. I called, "Cy, let's get these flights in tight trail formation before we enter the clouds." Typically Cy, he responded, "I'm not leading." Then I heard Thayer say, "Cy, you've got it." Then we went into tight trail formation which put me in the slot position of the fourth flight and I had another flight behind me. Cy tried to contact our C-97 on the ground at Goerdermoen but could never get an answer. We held our altitude until after we made the left turn and were on a heading to Goerdermoen. Cy then started a slow let down. We were still in tight formation, but the air became pretty turbulent and the flights bounced around more and more.

Oslo sits at the north end of a long and slightly winding fjord leading in from the North Sea. It always has heavy shipping traffic. I thought our situation might give us some problems. We were passing 15,000 feet, letting down at about 1,000 feet per minute, and we were still some 20 minutes from Oslo. Flying in heavy overcast, we had no idea what the weather was like at Oslo or Goerdermoen and we had no radio contact with anyone. While Cy and I had stayed in close radio contact, I certainly did not want to say anything that might alarm our pilots. Cy knew that I knew the physical terrain of that area better than he did, and I knew that Cy was the best pilot that I had ever flown with. We would make it but how we did not yet know. I knew that Cy's hope was that we would break out under the clouds over the fjord and then follow it to Oslo. Suddenly at about 7,000 feet the air became so rough it was impossible to keep five flights in tight trail position. I called to tell Cy I would fall back with my eight airplanes and would no longer stay in formation with his 12 aircraft. I told my second flight to move from the slot position below me to a tight formation position in trail above my flight. I did not want to take the chance of losing one or more of my second flight by flying them into the water. In this new formation we continued the let down.

I was also apprehensive about the accuracy of my altimeter. I had not received a new setting since leaving England and had no idea what the barometric pressure in our area might be. At 1,000 feet I was really concerned and feared my actual altitude was lower than the altimeter indicated. My descent rate was now very slow. I was feeling for the bottom of the clouds. Cy and I were in contact; he had not descended as fast as I had and was still at about 4,000 feet. Suddenly I saw a slight break in the clouds and there right under me was water. Then before I could do anything I saw the tip of a sailing ship mast pass my wing (I was very glad I had put my second flight above me). Without saying anything, I very slowly advanced power, started a slow climbing turn to the left until I was on a heading I felt sure would take me over Denmark where I also was quite certain the weather would be good. I called Cy, told him what I was doing and gave him my compass heading and altitude. He agreed and said he was also turning to this heading. Then I got out my maps to find just where in Denmark I could land. To my surprise I had no map of Denmark. We had plenty of fuel; I leveled off at 10,000 feet. I relayed to Cy that I knew there were at least two airfields adequate for the F-84G, one on the east coast of Denmark and one on the Danish west coast about half way down the peninsula.

Soon I broke out of the clouds to bright sunshine and good visibility. I could see the east coast of Denmark, turned in that direction and then followed it south. Cy advised me he was on the west coast proceeding south. By now I was feeling pretty good. I had my section intact and Cy had his section all together including Thayer. I did not need to worry about Cy nor did he need to worry about me. In addition to our command relationship we were good friends, having known each other since we were POWs together, and each of us respected the other's ability.

I was now at 2,000 feet approaching the airfield and runway that I wanted to find when suddenly I had another problem. I could see a barrier right across the runway. It appeared to be about halfway down the runway. Because I could not contact the control tower, I flew by, rocking my wings to indicate I intended to land. I then told my flights I was going to fly down the runway very slowly and at low altitude to determine its condition. This I did and the runway appeared to be fairly clean with some grass and weeds growing through the joints indicating it had not been recently used. I also determined the barrier was at the end of the old runway which I estimated to be 6,000 feet long and at the beginning of the new extension, which was under construction. I estimated it to be 4,000 feet. This observation made sense since the NATO runway standard was 10,000 feet. The old runway seemed safe enough to land on. I told my flights we would go in to land but I did not want my No. 2 man to land until I had turned off at the end and knew for sure the runway was safe. If something I could not foresee were to happen during my landing, I certainly did not want to lose more than my one airplane. We all landed safely. I called Cy, who was still airborne but was approaching the west coast base, and told him we were all down safely and that as soon as I could get to a telephone and find out where we were I would call him. It turned out that was hardly necessary as we later learned the Danish Air Defense Command knew all about this F-84 invasion of both their east and west coasts and about airplanes landing at closed fields, demanding fuel which had to be trucked in and in general creating havoc. Soon after Cy and his 12 airplanes had landed, we talked on the telephone. We agreed that we would spend the night at these airfields, get refueled and if the weather in the Oslo area was satisfactory the next day we would take off, get our two sections together again and fly to Goerdermoen.

The next morning, Cy called to report that the weather in the Oslo area as reported was acceptable, and we agreed that I would take off so as to rendezvous with Cy's flights at noon over the base that Cy had landed on and then proceed to Goerdermoen. This I did, and the flight to Goerdermoen occurred without incident. We were again not able to make contact with the C-97 that should have been our ground control. Since we had plenty of fuel, Cy decided that we would fly around Norway to show the pilots what this northern country looked like. We went down the southern coast, keeping the mountains on our right. Then we turned north, cruised the center part of Norway, and headed back toward Goerdermoen. At the altitude we had been flying, we used a lot of fuel. I was getting low.

I now noticed that the sky was getting pretty black up ahead, indicating that afternoon rain showers had moved in. By the time we reached the Goerdermoen area, a heavy rain storm had arrived and we were low on fuel. We did not have time to fool around any more nor to wait for the rainstorm to pass. We had to land in heavy rain with a slippery runway. I could barely keep the runway in sight until it was my turn to land. Although we had trouble stopping, turning off the runway and taxiing on the wet surface, all 20 aircraft landed safely. Our tour of Norway was an exciting experience, but in retrospect, it was totally unnecessary. We should have landed when we first arrived at Goerdermoen. On the other hand, Cy's decision to fly around Norway in perfect weather was well taken since he was an excellent pilot and I knew he often exposed the younger and less experienced pilots with him to flight conditions very nearly beyond their capabilities. Yet they learned a lot, and a flight with Cy was never dull. He was the only active duty pilot in the Air Force who wore a hearing aid while flying and to some extent that aid was helpful to him on the ground. It wasn't uncommon to see Cy, when being exposed to some discussion he did not care to hear, turn down his hearing aid. However, he never did this in an airplane. During these past two days we had all picked up some new experiences.

We spent just a couple of days at Goerdermoen during which I renewed some friendships which were established two years before. Then we flew uneventfully back to England. After a couple more days there, during which I returned my Morris to the dealer who would have it shiped to Tampa, Florida, we started home. We planned to land at Iceland on the first leg, at Bluie West One (the southwest end of Greenland) on the second leg, at Goose Bay on the third leg, and then on to Turner. We meant to do this all in one day because we gained five hours flying west across the Atlantic Ocean.

The flight to Iceland, landing, refueling and take-off were uneventful. Bluie West One was something else. It was established during the early days of Atlantic crossings by air and was used by ferry pilots during World War II. It was not designed or intended for use by modern jet aircraft. There was only one way in and one way out. Once committed to land, one had to land because there was no space to turn back. In our case with 20 airplanes, we let down from altitude over the Atlantic, put the airplanes in a single line with landing space between each airplane. Then the leader started up the fjord. Everyone had to maintain airspeed and position. The runway started right at the end of this rather long and narrow fjord and went somewhat up hill to its end that was very close to the box canyon wall. At this point there was no way to go around; each one had to land. This really presented no problem. Although we had not seen it before we knew what to expect and how to handle it at jet fighter landing speeds. All aircraft landed safely. We were on the ground just long enough to refuel and check the weather enroute and at the next stop at Goose Bay. Pilots stayed with their airplanes to make sure the refueling was properly done, the tanks were completely full (we would need it all to get to Goose Bay with the head winds predicted), and the fuel tank caps were tightly sealed.

Cy Wilson was a showman and he seldom missed a chance to do something differently. Today was no different. This runway was narrow and not too long. It did slope slightly down hill for take-off, but we would have a tail wind on take-off and would need every bit of runway. Cy called us all together for a five-minute briefing just before we climbed in the cockpit. He told us that we would line up all 20 airplanes on the end of the runway, four abreast and in five flights, and take off by flights. I did not like this flight plan worth a damn. I knew by the way Cy looked at me that he knew I did not like it. However, I said nothing, only grinned. After all, he was the boss.

When I got in my position for take-off, there were 12 jet engines just in front of me and all were about to go to 100 percent power. The first flight off would do great because those engines sucked in cold air. By the time I and the flight behind me released the brakes, the air over that runway would be very hot, this heat would make a big difference in the performance of a jet engine. As I went down the runway, I got no airspeed indication. I thought, "My God, I've left the cover on the pitot tube" (the tube that provides air speed indication). I knew, however, it could not be true that the cover was in the pocket of my flying suit. Due to the tail wind I was far down that runway before I ever got air speed indication.

From some of the pilots ahead of me I heard quick comments of profound terror, some shock and much disbelief. One pilot said he had hit one of the icebergs in the water at the end of the runway. Sure enough, when we arrived at Goose Bay we found his external fuel tank had hit the iceberg, but the tank did not rupture. Despite my air speed indication or lack thereof, 12 airplanes ahead of me had taken off. I would, too, I thought, but it would be a last-second thing. With the end of the runway going under my airplane, I became airborne. All 20 airplanes were airborne on the next-to-last leg of this great adventure. When we landed at Goose all throttle quadrants were carefully checked since many pilots were sure thay had bent the throttle in their frantic effort to get just a little more power on that take-off run from Bluie West One. It was typical of Cy that he never mentioned that take-off.

This leg had taken considerably longer than we had expected due to strong head winds, and we were running quite a bit behind our planned schedule. The final leg to Turner because of the distance required inflight refueling. The weather in the refueling area was deteriorating rapidly. Since we had spent minimum time on the ground at the two previous stops with no check of the airplanes, we all knew that now they really needed a thorough and careful inspection. The decision was then made to remain overnight at Goose Bay and proceed to Turner the next morning. This decision was happily received by all since we were tired. A short visit to the bar with many individual stories from pilots as to what really happened this day followed by a delicious steak dinner and a good night's sleep was welcomed.

The flight to Turner the next day was relatively uneventful. We had to go around a few thunderstorms but nothing serious occurred.

The air refuelings went well and we landed at Turner safely. It had been a great experience that we would never forget. All the pilots had demonstrated exceptional skill and flying ability. We had crossed the Atlantic twice—one nonstop, had flown over most of England, Norway and Denmark and had returned with the same pilots and airplanes we left with. And Thayer Olds got his star. The oceans are now regularly crossed with hardly ever an incident. In the summer of 1953, such a trip was very spectacular to say the least.

In the winter of 1953-54, we returned to Misawa, Japan for another 90-day TDY. The Korean War had ended by this time; however, the situation in Korea was still rather touchy. Our relationship with the Soviet Union had become more difficult. Our presence in Korea was known and was a continuing reminder of the growing capability of SAC, but more importantly, it displayed a determination and will to use the force. The term Cold War had been coined and came into focus and meaning; hence SAC continued its deployment of its military units. The 508th Strategic Fighter Wing was one of several units in the area of Japan and Korea. SAC's position then as it was from its beginning was to be a deterrent force against attack on the United States and the free world. General LeMay thought that a strategically directed military power—air, land and sea—would deter a third world war. He used to say quite often that if he could only send his emergency war plan to the individual in the Soviet Union who had the authority to launch a war against the western world, he thought his plan would deter the enemy leader from deciding to attack. LeMay's concern was that the Soviet leader might underestimate how strong SAC really was and how capable it was to destroy the Soviet Union if it were to start a war.

By constant flying within the United States, on rotational duty in England and Japan, the leaders and pilots of the 508th and 31st Strategic Fighter Wings learned how to achieve the highest performance from the F-84G and the F-84F Thunderjets. Every new aircraft had some unresolved problems or bugs as they were called. The F-84F, which we started to pick up from the Republic factory on Long Island in late summer and fall of 1954, was no exception. This aircraft had swept wings and could go through Mach I. A new hydraulic control system was used for aileron and elevator control. In the beginning this hydraulic system was unreliable and often failed. When this was lost, the only remaining control the pilot had was the use of the electrically operated trim tab switch on the stick. With this method many successful landings were made, but it was tricky and many airplanes were lost. We also lost some pilots, including one of our best, Colonel Cy Wilson, when in December 1954 his swept-wing F-84F lost power and crashed. The F-84F, the Thunderstreak swept-wing version in the Thunderjet series, came after the "G" because Republic Aviation had some difficulty in developing the swept-wing aircraft. Its hydraulic control system caused more accidents in the F-84F than any other single cause. There was also a design flaw in the engine that caused many problems. The metal of the stater blades of the turbine wheel and the shroud around the turbine wheels were made of different materials. At high altitude where it is very cold, the shroud would shrink because of the cold, and the stater blades in the turbine, which were very hot, would then hit the shroud, resulting in a partial loss of power or a complete engine failure. It was not uncommon for the power loss to reach almost an idle speed. However, the engine would most of the time continue to operate.

This circumstance happened to Cy Wilson as he flew from Austin, Texas, his home, back to Albany at Christmas time in 1954. During World War II, Cy had bailed out of his crippled airplane and landed in the North Sea. He had some difficulty with his bailout, and he swore he would never bail out of another airplane. He decided then he would ride an airplane in and crash. On this trip from Texas, because of the engine problem he had let down from high altitude through a heavy overcast to break out under the overcast with a ceiling of only a few hundred feet. The only place that he found that he could land with the little bit of engine power available was a highway. He was not far from Jackson, Mississippi. In that part of the country many of the highways are raised because of the potential rise of water from the Mississippi River and resulting flood of the area. He saw that highway and attempted to make a 270-degree turn to come back around and land.

However, in making that maneuver with the little power he had, his wing tip caught one of the embankments and the airplane crashed. A tree came through the side of the canopy and Cy's head was crushed. I was saddened by the loss of a close friend and flying colleague who had taught me many things about flying and command. I wanted to replace Cy as commander of the 508th and did not waste any time in letting higher headquarters know my desire, and without delay I was given command of the Wing. Not long afterwards at a commanders' meeting at SAC Headquarters, I met General LeMay's personnel expert, Warrant Officer Chrysler. Computers were not yet available but Chrysler was able to keep in his memory detailed knowledge of all colonels in SAC. This was quite an accomplishment. He proceeded to tell me many details about my previous career with dates and facts, including the fact that I was the youngest wing commander in SAC. This was my first major command, and although Cy was not an easy act to follow, I was prepared and ready for this challenge.

I thoroughly enjoyed every part of guiding the outfit through aerial refueling training, celestial navigation practice, gunnery training, and training for delivery of nuclear weapons by a fighter. The Wing competed very capably against all of the other fighter wings in SAC, and we excelled in many areas. I spent a lot of time with both the pilots and maintenance personnel. I never failed to let them know that I knew when they had performed particularly well. One thing I started at this time and continued in all my commands was the use of recognition cards. I had cards about the size of a calling card made up to say "To (the name of a person) in appreciation for your excellent performance" and to have space for my signature. Often and regularly I visited around the base and in the maintenance and supply shops and work areas at night when very few, if any, men were working. Wherever I found a shop or a work area that looked particularly good, I would fill in the card with the sergeant's or airman's name, sign it and leave it for him to find the next morning. This attention was very effective. For many years, and even after my retirement, I would be some place where an airman would recognize me and from his wallet he would extract one of these cards and tell me how much it had meant to him.

One of my strong feelings about command and leadership was that the commander should be known and easily recognized. We were still receiving the new F-84Fs from the Republic factory when I took command of the 508th Wing. I got in touch with one of my Republic Aviation friends and asked him if among the remaining F-84Fs that would come to the 508th Wing, would there be one with a tail number 508? He knew immediately what I wanted and said, "Jerry, that's interesting. I just happen to have one almost ready to come off the assembly line with that tail number." I knew this was not true, but I also knew he could make it true. I said, "That's great, thanks, and let me know when it's ready and I'll come up to get it." The next week I picked up this airplane with 508 on its tail and brought it back to Turner. No. 508 was my airplane and when any one saw it taxiing, taking off or landing, they knew I was in it.

During those days in the early 1950s when SAC had No. 1 priority within the USAF for money, people and materials, the SAC fighters developed many new procedures and concepts for aerial warfare. We also developed "people programs"—ways for improving the status and living conditions of the airmen. These types of things were always first in the mind of General LeMay. Most of these concepts developed in SAC were later accepted throughout the Air Force.

General LeMay was naturally most concerned with perfecting his responsibility for providing deterrence to enemy attack by developing the capability of his bombers to deliver nuclear weapons. However, he was not unaware of his fighters. He told us, his fighter wing commanders, to use our initiative and innovation in ideas to develop and improve the capability of fighter aircraft to deliver nuclear weapons. When we were able to contribute to his overall Emergency War Plan, he urged us to come to Omaha and brief him. We followed his instruction.

A nuclear weapon small enough to be carried under the wing of a jet fighter had been developed. The F-84F could carry the small nuclear weapon. The problem then was to devise a method of delivery that would permit the fighter to escape the blast of the weapon. A number of methods were tried before we found what we believed to be the best one for fighters. This method, called LABS or a low-altitude bombing system, would feature a very low-level delivery at approximately a 300-foot altitude. To prove the concept we practiced at the low-level ranges near Eglin Air Force Base, Florida. We would fly toward the target at a 300-foot altitude, 400 knots of air speed. When we flew over the predetermined IP (initial point) we pushed the throttle full forward and pulled back on the stick to obtain and maintain a 4-G pull-up (four times the force of gravity). At a point approximating 10:00 o'clock, we released the weapon and continued to hold four Gs until we went over the top of the loop, then completed the immelman, rolling to a wings-level position at full power and descended at 2,000 feet per minute until we were again on the deck. At that point we were really a screaming eagle and would have traveled far enough away from the blast. In the meantime the bomb after release would be tossed far ahead of the plane's pull-up point. This maneuver might sound easy, and it was in VFR (Visual Flight Rules) conditions. We had to practice it on instruments. The problem with pulling and holding four Gs is that there is a tendency to pull slightly to the right in pulling the stick. It was easier to fly straight up when on VFR because the pilot could see the horizon and the attitude of the airplane; he knew he had pulled straight up. I cut two strips one-inch wide from a heavy inner tube, attached them to either side of the cockpit and then placed each over the stick. Using both hands on the stick for the pull back and with the rubber bands on the stick worked pretty well for me. After we had practiced this method for awhile, we could do it with ceilings down to 500 feet. With the instruments we had in those days that tumbled as the plane went over the top, this maneuver was a bit tricky. General LeMay liked this method of delivery. Since he was considering having his bombers go in low to avoid enemy radar, he directed that this method be explored for possible use by his B-47 bombers.

I was sent down to MacDill Field, Tampa, to present the concept to the B-47 training wing. Needless to say, there was not a single bomber pilot there that had the slightest interest in doing an immelman from the deck on instruments in a six-engine jet bomber. However, the concept was tried by a Boeing test pilot, who determined that the air speed margin above stall at the top of the loop was too little for this maneuver to provide a safe mission. The idea was abandoned.

I was fortunate to have a KB-29 air refueling squadron, commanded by Major Cobb, attached to my Wing. Cobb and I became good friends. When I could spare the time, I flew with him in the KB-29, the Superfortress converted to a tanker. I always enjoyed flying new and different airplanes and I made many take-offs and landings in this airplane. I also had the opportunity to take the tanker refueler's position and find out first hand what air refueling was like from the refueler's point of view.

In the early summer of 1955, SAC selected the 508th and its F-84Fs to represent SAC in the annual fighter gunnery meet held at Nellis Air Force Base, Las Vegas, Nevada, in September. This was the major gunnery and bombing event of the year for tactical aircraft. It was designed to provide realistic testing of weapons, aircraft and the pilots. Each of the five major commands—USAFE, FEAF, ATC, SAC, and TAC plus the Air National Guard—sent a team of six pilots and six airplanes to this competition. From the six, four would fly each mission. The winner would be the finest in the worldwide United States Air Force. It attracted military and civilian interest around the world. This year 20 generals and 20 Air Attaches representing 18 nations were in attendance and observed the events. All the teams except mine came from fighter commands. Needless to say, all fighter commands did not expect much competition from a command that consisted primarily of bombers. I was determined to show them a thing or two.

I did have a problem to resolve, however. In the 1955 competition, the high altitude gunnery portion, firing at a flag target pulled by another aircraft would be flown at 30,000 feet. In prior years it had been flown at 20,000 feet. The air is much thinner at 30,000 feet and flight tactics, patterns and several other factors would need some adjustment. However, this was not my major problem. My problem was that the only airplanes I had that were modified to tow airborne targets were T-33s. These airplanes did not have the power to tow a target much above 20,000 feet. Most other commands had the new F-86H, and some used a modified B-57 for towing. Hence they had no problem with towing a target at 30,000 feet that would allow their pilots to practice at the higher altitude. I thought at first that this lack of a towing aircraft would be no problem because I had friends in TAC, ADC and other units from whom I would just borrow an airplane that could tow at 30,000 feet. To my dismay no one would let me borrow an airplane. I guess I did not blame them. Why should they increase the competition with their own outfit?

That summer we trained at a satellite base of the Eglin Air Force Base, Florida, complex. Dive bombing and strafing ranges were nearby, and we flew aerial gunnery over the Gulf of Mexico. I had selected a great team consisting of five pilots plus myself. All our gunnery practice went well except we had no training in firing at 30,000 feet. I had to find a way. Up every morning at 4 a.m. we flew missions until noon, and then we let the maintenance team check over the airplanes in the hot afternoons. Most of the pilots went to their quarters or the beach in the afternoons, but I usually stayed at the base and worked with my maintenance officer, Capt. Dick Adkins.

One afternoon I sat at my desk trying to discover a way to solve my altitude problem. Suddenly I had an idea. If one T-33 cannot pull the target to 30,000 feet, why not tie two T-33s together. Of course, that's the answer, I said to myself, but how to attach them? Jet engines were not totally reliable in those days and aborted take-offs were not uncommon. I had to consider that possibility. If two airplanes tied together took off in formation and if one had to abort, what happened to the other one? I got a scratch pad and a pencil and started working this out. Before long I felt I had my solution. I called Dick and asked him to come to my office.

When he arrived, I said, "Dick, sit down, I've got a plan I want to show you. Don't interrupt until I finish." I then explained that we had to start firing aerial gunnery at 30,000 feet and my plan would show how we would do it. We would place two T-33s in formation at the beginning of the runway. The tow cable would be attached to the lead airplane. Another cable 100 feet long would be attached to the second airplane. This cable would be clamped to the lead cable approximately 100 feet behind the lead airplane.

Both airplanes would start engines and take off in formation. If either had to abort the pilot would call, "Abort, abort," and both pilots would abort. "Suppose," I continued, "they are too far in the take-off roll and the aborting airplane may not be able to stop safely?" To help solve this eventuality, I told Dick, each pilot would take off with his hand on the cable release lever in the cockpit, and if at that critical time an abort was called or if at any time one airplane might experience a flame out, both pilots would pull the release cable handle. I believed that if both pilots were ready to release the cable, at least one would succeed and there would be no problem. To me the plan seemed fairly reasaonable.

"What do you think?" I asked Dick.

Up to this point Dick had been quiet, but now he was excited and said, "Hell, I think it is the most ingenious idea I've ever heard. Let's do it."

"O.K.," I said, "get with it and you and I will fly a practice mission before dark today."

After Dick left I began to think about my plan on another level. What am I doing? Here I'm about to launch a mission that could result in a major accident. Dick or I could be killed. I had not even thought about telling my boss, Thayer Olds, now a brigadier general, what I'm planning to do. Then, I thought, if I tell him he will be very nice but will say, "Jerry, you can't do that." If I don't tell him and anything serious happens, it will be the end of my career. If I don't tell him and something happens and I'm killed, it won't matter. If I don't tell him and nothing serious happens, I just might show up those other fighter gunnery guys and win the Nellis meet.

"What the hell," I decided, "I'm not going to tell him."

I was still in my flying suit. I got my helmet and went out to the runway where Dick and his men were just finishing the cables and attaching them to the T-33s. Although the men were pretty apprehensive, I thought they had carried out my plan very well and I was ready to try it. I flew the lead plane, Dick flying the second one in formation.

We had no problem in taking off. The two aircraft climbed up perfectly. Dick stayed in formation. At about 23,000 feet, I asked Dick how he was doing.

"I'm not doing anything," he replied. "I've just got the throttle all the way forward, and there is nothing to do."

We could feel the two aircraft pulling, one being ahead, the other slightly behind. By the time we reached 30,000 feet, the planes were pulling together so well that we could not feel anything different in the pull. We went up and down the range, we made turns, and everything in our plan worked perfectly. We descended to 20,000 feet. I told Dick to disconnect his cable. I flew on back to the base, went across the field, dropped the flag, and landed. The next day we started flying the target flag according to this plan. We always selected two competent pilots to fly the T-33s. The team trained like that the rest of the summer before it left for the Nellis competition. I never told General Olds what I was doing. No one at Eglin knew my team practiced gunnery at 30,000 feet with two T-33s towing the target.

When the 508th team arrived at Nellis, I saw friends from Tactical Air Command and other bases.

"Hey, Jerry," some of them challenged. "What are you going to do when you have to shoot gunnery at 30,000 feet? You haven't had any practice up there?"

"Well," I shouted back, "we'll soon find out."

The 508th had a great surprise for the other teams. We missed winning the air-to-air competition by five points. I could have won that if I had not become over-anxious. On the very last mission our team had a small foul, a foul being a too long mark by the bullet striking the target. That kind of mark indicated a pilot had fired at too small an angle off the line of flight of the tow aircraft. If the angle is too small, it would be possible to shoot down the plane that pulled the flag target. If before we took off for that final mission we had known how close we were to winning the air-to-air competition, we would have flown a more careful mission. But I did not have a coach on the ground; I did not have anyone watching the scores of the other teams. Hence we missed the incentive of being near to victory on that last shoot. We did win the air-to-ground part of the competition and came in second in the air-to-air portion.

When I returned to Turner Air Force Base after the competition was finished, I found the following message from General LeMay, CINCSAC, waiting for me:

> Your victory in the air-to-ground phase and second place in the air-to-air phase of the USAF Fighter Weapons and Gunnery meet is another in a series of superior accomplishments by the 508th Strategic Fighter Wing. The fine airmanship and superior maintenance support necessary to victory reflects the topnotch performance of the pilots and the flightline personnel. Please accept my congratulations and convey my appreciation to those who participated. This was a job well done.

It was a long time after that meet that I told General Olds about tying the two T-33s together in order to obtain practice in firing at 30,000 feet. And it was much later that I finally told General LeMay. The General and I were having lunch together during one of our visits to Maxwell Air Force Base after we were both retired. I casually remarked, "You know, General, I know that during your many years commanding SAC, you knew everything that was going on, but I think there was something that happened that you did not hear about." Then I told him this story of the two T-33s towing a target, and he listened intently.

"You really did that?" he said.

"Yes, Sir," I replied.

"I never knew it." But he remembered how well the 508th had done in the meet at Nellis.

Because for nearly ten years I had flown fighters in a command that was known as a bomber command with the national and global policy of strategic bombing as the instrument of deterrence, I was often asked whether fighter people assigned to SAC believed that they were treated as true SAC personnel. I think it is fair to say that we were tolerated rather than treated truly as SAC people. Most SAC bomber types at that time thought we were a kind of nuisance, using up some of SAC's resources and money. They thought we really did not have any capability of helping the SAC mission much if the nation actually went to war. They were accurate in that assessment. The chance of our delivering a nuclear weapon in an F-84 from Albany, Georgia, to a target in Russia was pretty slim. And SAC's all jet bomber force was just about as fast as our fighters. However, fighter outfits were sufficiently aggressive and innovative to develop some fine missions which Tactical Air Command adopted later and continued to use for a long time. We pioneered inflight refueling to provide a longer range to fighters. As jet fighter pilots we found it extremely beneficial to be assigned to SAC. General LeMay used to say to fighter wing commanders, "O.K. You guys try to work out your own mission and don't bother me. When you think you are capable of my writing you and your fighters into my war plan, then let me know." And go ahead we did, In my opinion, General LeMay has to be commended for permitting fighter wing commanders the leeway, the free rein, to forge ahead with new tactics and new ideas as they did.

Some people in TAC felt that tactical personnel got the short end of the stick not only from the Department of Defense but from SAC. As usual there was not enough money to satisfy every command's need or wish fulfillment. Concern over the Soviet Union's growing capability for surprise attack affected military and political decisions as to where and how defense moneys would be spent. John Foster Dulles, Secretary of State, and the State Department's strategy relied on the theory of deterrence. SAC had a very strong leader with great vision in General LeMay. He believed people were the strongest asset in a command. In SAC he had better dormitories built for airmen; supported automotive and craft workshops on bases for airmen's hobbies; promoted auto racing on runways to raise money to improve the airmen's quality of life. Someone once remarked that all of the major commands were headed by former SAC people. That may have been true in one phase of SAC's strongest period. Yet like me, other fighter pilots had gone to bombers; Gen. Bruce Holloway and Gen. John C. Meyer, for instance, commanded SAC at high points of their careers.

Turner Air Force Base was to be my home base for another year or more with a new experience in reconnaissance. In the early part of 1956, I was asked to go to Omaha, SAC Headquarters, to receive a briefing on high altitude reconnaissance efforts that SAC was developing. I had heard about the U-2, a high altitude airplane designed and built by Kelly Johnson about 1952, a Lockheed engineer who did his engineering and development work in an area he referred to as the Skunk Works in California. After the U-2, Johnson designed and engineered the SR-71, a twin-engine aircraft that flew above 80,000 feet at Mach 3. Under proper environmental conditions, the U-2 had an altitude capability of 70,000-plus feet and flew under Mach 1. It was obvious that air power was expanding, the Soviet threat was increasing, and intercontinental ballistic missiles were in various stages of development. In terms of deployment of air power units, we had to know more about what our potential enemies were doing. Hence the development of airplanes and systems to fill this need progressed. At Omaha, I learned about the Black Knight Squadron, which was being formed to fly the RB-57, a high-altitude reconnaissance airplane built by Martin Marietta, and was commanded by Col. Dan Mulloney. It was a very secret, very classified unit for which Dan would select the pilots most carefully. The most significant part of the briefing at Omaha for me was that my 508th Strategic Fighter Wing would be deactivated but its resources, pilots and support personnel would be used to man and equip the U-2 squadron. The U-2 Squadron and the RB-57 Black Knight Squadron would be under the newly activated 4080th Strategic Reconnaissance Wing. Needless to say, if this change was to happen, I wanted to be the first commander of the 4080th.

I suspected that there might be some competition as to who would command the 4080th. I knew that I had no reconnaissance experience, but I did know that the 508th personnel that were going into the new organization were my people and that I was qualified to command the new unit. Since they knew me as their commander, I believed I would be able to stimulate the best performance from them. I also had complete confidence in Dan Mulloney whom I had met on several occasions. He was an absolutely first-class officer who knew his business, learning the RB-57 from the inside out and spending time with the Martin-Marietta Company, the designer and builder of the RB-57. I had the highest respect for him and we were developing a very close friendship.

I flew to Omaha to meet with Gen. Francis Griswold, the Vice Commander in Chief of SAC at that time. I explained my position on being the best qualified person to command the 4080th, and I let him know that I really wanted that command. General Griswold listened graciously but made no commitment. It was some time before I was notified that in fact I would become the commander of the 4080th. This new assignment became one of those challenging and exciting jobs, totally new and different, that I hoped my military career would offer me.

The Black Knight Squadron arrived at Turner Air Force Base. The U-2s remained at the training base, where the flying strip was a dry lake bed in the desert northwest of Las Vegas. An annual flight physical was nothing compared to the kind of physical tests and examinations my 508th pilots went through while trying to qualify for the U-2 program. Many did not make it. Gary Powers, who had been a member of my gunnery team at Nellis the year before, had no difficulty in meeting the qualifications for this program.

The requirements for this airplane, basically a very high altitude photo reconnaissance aircraft, had been set forth by the Air Force. Kelly Johnson had been left alone in his Skunk Works to design and build it. The SR-71, which Johnson later designed
and built, and the U-2 were magnificent in design and performance. Each was the state of the art of high altitude reconnaissance airplanes for their time.

The U-2 was a very high flying airplane; therefore the pilot must wear a fully pressurized suit. This first suit was very uncomfortable. The U-2 was not difficult to fly but it did have some unusual design features and flight characteristics. The U-2 had a single engine and a very long wing span and utilized tandem landing gear under the fuselage. The wings which drooped a bit when the plane was loaded with fuel were supported by pogo sticks with small wheels; the sticks were mounted under the tip of each wing. On take-off as the air speed increased and the wings lifted, the pogo sticks would drop from the wings. When the pilot landed after his mission, the pogo sticks would be inserted again by the ground crew.

In the mid-1950s, the U-2 had not yet attracted attention in the news media. It didn't seem as if the news media were as inquisitive about aviation developments as they became later. It seemed as if earlier they had much greater respect for security or appreciation for the fact that security in relation to the safety of the nation might quite often be necessary. It was curious that the media had missed seeing a small picture of the U-2 that had appeared in <u>Aviation Week</u> in 1952 with a small caption about a new aircraft under development. No one in the news media made guesses about the photo until finally the Air Force announced the U-2's existence. Thus at Turner knowledge of the U-2 was scarce. This secrecy caused difficulty in the move of pilots from Turner to Nevada for a week or more at a time. When they returned to Turner, they were not free to discuss with their families what they were doing. This necessary reticence caused some personal problems until the security was lifted a bit.

Our transition program to the U-2 went well. My pilots rotated back and forth between Turner and Nevada as their training requirement demanded. Eventually I was told that certain visitors would appear at Turner and that they would report to me and that I was to give them all the assistance they asked for or needed. However, I was also told not to question them on what they were doing or why they were at Turner. This secrecy caused me considerable concern. Soon a couple of young men arrived at my office. They said little other than would I mind if they had access to my base for a week or so and that they would live off base in one of the local motels. Of course, I responded affirmatively to their comments and requests, but I had no idea what they were doing.

One day one of my squadron commanders came to me and said that one of his pilots had been called away from his duty and he could not tell him where he was going. This pilot was gone several hours, and when he returned to his squadron, he could not tell his commander where he had been. Then another squadron commander reported a similar incident had occurred. I still did not know what was happening. Later I learned these visitors interviewed and selected from my pilots certain ones that had passed all their examinations for the U-2 without difficulty and had checked out in the U-2 without any problem. In other words they picked out my very best pilots, those who were willing to voluntarily leave the Air Force for an unspecified period. A few quietly and without ceremony left the base. The pilots would fly as civilians and would receive what at that time was a very substantial compensation, a good deal more than they earned as a lieutenant or a captain in the Air Force. Gary Powers was one of these pilots who accepted this program.

Most people remember what happened to Gary Powers in 1960. That was long after I had left Turner and the 4080th Wing and had served a tour in England. When Gary was shot down in his U-2 and was captured, imprisoned and tried in Russia, I was greatly concerned for his safety. In 1962 after he had been released by the Soviets and returned to the United States, I was again greatly apprehensive but this time because of the way he was being treated by the news media, much of that having to do with whether or not he should have taken his life with the cyanide capsule rather than be captured. It is very easy for some people to form opinions and pass judgement from the safety of their secure offices without any idea of all the facts or the situations the individual they are judging was facing. Knowing Gary Powers very well and having spent time with him on several occasions after he returned, I can find no fault with any of his actions or statements while a prisoner.

In August 1956, two events occurred that affected me personally and professionally. Col. Dave Schilling had died on 16 August while driving his specially fitted sports car in England where he was Inspector General of 7th Air Division. I had flown to Washington, D.C. to serve as a pallbearer at his funeral and burial at Arlington National Cemetery. Many who knew Dave had gathered from all over the world at the Carlton Hotel. The wake we had would be the envy of the best of Irish wakes.

Just before the funeral, Maj. Gen. Bob Terrell, Deputy Chief of Staff for Operations, SAC Headquarters, called me to ask if I could be in Tokyo the following Monday. I said I could and after the funeral I went to Andrews Air Force Base nearby to fly my T-33 back to Turner. On Sunday, Dan Mulloney flew me to San Francisco in a two-place B-57 and I continued on to Tokyo by Northwest Airlines arriving Monday morning.

Colonel Mulloney's RB-57 Black Knight Squadron would soon deploy from Turner to Yokota, Japan. I went to Japan early to brief and to establish proper relationships between General LeMay's Strategic Air Command, which I represented through the RB-57 operation, and the local commanders, i.e., General Lemnitzer, overall commander of Far East Military Forces, and Gen. Lawrence Kuter, Commanding General of Pacific Air Forces. In addition, I had to find space and make necessary arrangements with Yokota base officials to receive and bed down the Black Knight Squadron. General LeMay had made it very clear to me in a letter that I was working for and reporting directly to SAC Headquarters in Omaha and that he, General LeMay, directed through me my Black Knight operational missions. The top local commanders were to be briefed on what I was doing, but they would have no control of my operations. Needless to say, this arrangement was not well received by the powers of the Far East Command and particularly by Brigadier General Small, the Commanding General of the SAC Division at Guam. He insisted that he must be involved and that all SAC operations in the Far East were his responsibility. Up to this time, this assignment was my greatest test in diplomacy. I had to comply with the wishes of General LeMay; on the other hand, I must not ignore the local commanders. After all, they were responsible for that part of the world and some of the things I would be doing just might result in a serious international incident for the Black Knights' purpose was to fly missions over southern Russia in the area west and northwest of Vladivostok. They had every right to feel that they must be involved.

At that time Lt. Gen. Hunter Harris was Deputy for Operations of the Pacific Air Forces. I did not know him when I arrived at Yokota, but I soon did. From the very beginning he seemed to recognize the untenable position I was in and sympathized with me in my efforts to keep everyone happy in the part they played. We became good friends and he smoothed over some very rough spots and on occasion even interceded for me with General LeMay. I was greatly in his debt.

General Terrell had advised me that I would be in Japan only a few weeks and that I could ride with him back to Omaha after he visited the Far East in early September. Therefore, I took with me only a few summer uniforms. It was soon obvious to me that I would not leave Yokota any time soon.

When the RB-57s arrived at Yokota, they were bedded down, and after a few local flights in the area we were operational. I had a perfect team. Dan Mulloney was a superior officer in every way with an outstanding personality. The Black Knight Squadron was his and he ran it. Col. Hawk Austin, a first-class officer, came from SAC Headquarters to provide intelligence coverage for the operation.

We ran a lot of missions that fall and encountered many problems. The airplanes performed perfectly. Although many Soviet MIG fighters were launched against our aircraft, none of ours were lost. We had accomplished our mission and had collected much valuable data. The operation was running smoothly, and the local commanders were satisfied with our relationship and with the information I had continually given them. We had had no serious problems. I had accomplished all that I had come to Japan to do. Although the Black Knight Squadron would continue its operations, I had no further purpose to stay in Japan. I hated to leave Dan; we had worked together very closely. However, he was capable of carrying on by himself, and I suspect was looking forward to having full responsibility. It had been one of the most interesting and challenging assignments I had had, but it was time to get back to my wing at Turner, which I had left in the hands of my very capable deputy, Col. Nate Adams. I flew Northwestern from Tokyo to Seattle where a two-place B-57 from Turner picked me up and we proceeded to SAC Headquarters at Omaha where I was required to brief General LeMay and his staff. This briefing accomplished, I flew to Turner, arriving about 10 p.m. on Christmas Eve 1956.

Nate Adams greeted me when I landed and almost immediately told me that my Division Commander, Col. Hub Zemke, then commander of the 40th Air Division at Turner, was to take command of the 4080th Strategic Reconnaissance Wing, when in the near future it would move from Turner Air Force Base, Georgia to Laughlin Air Force Base, Texas. I had previously selected Laughlin as the permanent home for the 4080th and had looked forward to making this move. I could not believe that Nate's information was correct, but I could not put it out of my mind as I proceeded home to spend Christmas day with my wife and two children.

Nate's information was still in my mind the day after Christmas. Why would Hub Zemke, who was much senior to me, had been my Group Commander during World War II and now was my Division Commander, want to step down to take command of a wing? I could not stand the suspense any longer, and I went in search of Hub to confront him with this information. I found him in his office and after a few minutes of casual conversation, he very nonchalantly confirmed that taking the wing was precisely what he wanted to do. Despite my best efforts Hub became the new commander of the 4080th and took the wing to Laughlin. I was offered command of another F-84 wing, but I turned it down. After all I had already commanded an F-84 wing. But the question remained, What would I do?

I knew that my record was good and that I was highly respected in SAC Headquarters. I decided to fly to Omaha and find another job. After landing my T-33 at Offutt Air Force Base, I went to the office of Maj. Gen. Horace Wade, Deputy for Personnel, SAC Headquarters. He was most gracious and, of course, knew all the circumstances of my losing the 4080th. He told me he thought fighters would not

be in SAC much longer and he was right. He thought I should switch
to bombers where I could continue my career growth.

Maj. Gen. William G. (Butch) Blanchard was to leave SAC Headquarters in early summer to go to England and take command of the 7th
Air Division located on the west side of London. General Wade told me
there was a position, Director of Plans, still open on General Blanchard's
7th Air Division staff. I went to talk with General Blanchard, and he
accepted me for that position. Arrangements were then made for me to
go through the B-47 transition training school at McConnell Air Force
Base, Wichita, Kansas, before proceeding to England. It was time, I felt,
for me to leave Turner. After all, I had been there six years, although
during that time I had been away on TDY for 32 months. My first
assignment had been 31st Wing Director of Operations and I commanded
both the 508th Strategic Fighter Wing and the 4080th Strategic Reconnaissance Wing. I had spent three tours in Japan, five months in Norway
and had flown the Atlantic nonstop. Yes, it was time for me to leave Turner.

The THOR Intermediate Range Ballistic Missile Squadron was
just being readied for deployment to launch sites in England. I became
directly involved in all the complicated and controversial problems
associated with this United States effort to place missiles on British
soil. I worked closely with the Royal Air Force Bomber Command
and Whitehall, equivalent to our Department of Defense. General
Blanchard, commander of 7th Air Division, turned out to be a prince
of a guy to work with and this assignment was a major turning point
in my career. In retrospect Hub Zemke had done me a great favor.

In early April I moved my wife Ann and children Jerry and Debbie
to Omaha, which was Ann's home, and left them with her mother while
I spent three months at Wichita. My family was happy at the prospect of
living in England, and after all these years in single-engine aircraft, I
looked forward to the challenge of flying multi-engine bombers.

In late June my family and I boarded an Army transport ship in
New York harbor and sailed for Southhampton, England. When we
arrived at Southhampton, we were met by our good friends, Hank and
Millie Meierdierck. Hank had flown with me on our Longstride flight
to England in 1953. It was a joyous reunion.

I have finally gotten to Jet Fighters.
The F-84. What a change!

Top Left: *I am being helped out of my anti-exposure suit at Lakenheath, England, after crossing the Atlantic non-stop in an F-84G in August 1953.* ***Top Right:*** *Some of the Gunnery trophies we were presented at the awards ceremony at Nellis.* ***Just Above:*** *My 1955 508th Fighter Wing Gunnery Team representing SAC in the annual competition at Nellis AFB. L to R: Gary Powers, Chuck Stratton, Don Maggert, Col. Johnson, Bob Schneler, and Carl Overstreet.*

CHAPTER 6
MY CAREER IN SAC: BOMBERS AND MISSILES

The B-47 training school at McConnell Air Force Base was a great experience. I was now flying a six-engine jet airplane which had a crew of three. I not only had to learn the airplane, I had to learn how to deal with a crew and share the responsibilities of flight. As a fighter pilot I had done it all including navigation. Now I had a navigator who not only navigated but dropped the bombs. I realized, however, that even though I now had a navigator, I was still responsible for getting safely to where we were supposed to go and also for the accuracy of the bombs' drop. I knew a bomber crew was a team effort and I hoped my confidence would grow as I gained more experience with the crew.

The B-47, designed and built by Boeing Aircraft, made its maiden flight 17 December 1947. After long and sometimes painful development, it became an important military jet aircraft of the time because of its influence on world events and aircraft design. Beginning in 1951, SAC bought more than 2,000 B-47s. It has been called "the one airplane to fly." It was also a marvelous airplane to look at; 35-degree swept wings with six jet engines in four underwing pods, a clear canopy over the cockpit allowing the pilot to have superb visibility, a receptacle in the nose for air-to-air refueling, and tandem gear with outriggers. The cop-pilot was seated under the bubble canopy behiund the pilot and the navigator's seat was in the nose of the aircraft. Learning to fly this airplane was another challenge and one I looked forward to.

The ground school took place during the latter weeks of March, and the training flights occurred for six weeks in April and May. The Wichita, Kansas area at that time of year had many thunderstorms, and we flew mostly at night. Lightning and thunderstorms added an exciting dimension to flying, and static electric buildups caused many occurrences of St. Elmo's fire as it played across the windscreen.

The take-off in the B-47 provided a thrilling, sometimes anxious experience. After taxiing to the take-off position on the runway, the pilot took all six engines up to 100 percent power. After checking the gauges for correct readings, he then applied water-injection to the six engines by throwing the switches on the floor beside the seat. With the added thrust provided by the water-injection, the engine gauges and the airplane would jump and the brakes would be released. That moment held the great thrill. In the cockpit, despite the great roar from the engines, it seemed that speed increased slowly. The pilot now had little to do. The success of the take-off rested with those six great engines. Runway distance markers were conspicuously displayed along the right side of the runway. Before take-off and in consideration of the gross weight of the airplane, a go-no-go position was calculated. This was a critical calculation because if the correct speed at the go-no-go point had not been attained and the take-off was continued anyway, the airplane would simply not become airborne before reaching the end of the runway. On the other hand, if the correct airspeed at that point had been attained the pilot was committed to fly. It did not matter what happened to the airplane after that point, the pilot had to keep going. Landing the B-47 was relatively easy. Despite its size and weight, the pilot's major concern was holding the airplane off the runway to assure that the rear tandem gear touched first. The B-47 spanning the oceans and continents at near supersonic speed made a major contribution to SAC's mandate to maintain peace through deterrence. Between the end of my B-47 school and reporting for duty with 7th Air Division in England, my family and I had time to relax a bit as we traveled from Omaha to New York. I wanted to take back to England my Morris-Minor convertible that I had bought while there during the Longstride mission (somewhat like taking coals to Newcastle). Before leaving Turner Air Force Base I delivered it to the port of Tampa for shipment to England. We kept our other car a Buick until I had finished B-47 school and then sold it and went by train to New York. We visited my wife's brother and family in Dayton, Ohio, and then on to Washington for a few days with Jean Schilling before arriving in New York and boarding an Army transport going to England. My children Jerry and Debbie enjoyed this experience. Capt. Hank Meierdierck and his wife, close friends from Turner, met us at Southhampton. Then began the interesting search for a place to live.

That search was not an easy one. The military housing office gave us leads on places they knew about, but we wanted a place to make our English tour as realistically English as possible. We selected a house in Gerard's Cross, a nice little village on Highway 40 going west out of London. The two-story house was a nice but old house with an absolutely beautiful fenced-in formal garden in front and a great working garden in the rear (actually a vegetable garden with a large hot house). Mr. Bunts the gardener for many years came with the house. It was a pleasure having him with us. The elderly woman who owned the house had to go into a nursing home and rented the house completely furnished. That suited us perfectly. I was delighted to see hot-water radiators, which I was told provided heat. This sounded very nice to us since the weather can be damp and temperatures cool in England.

In our household goods, we had brought a refrigerator and a horizontal freezer. We purchased transformers for them from a family who was leaving for the States. Soon all of the equipment was working. On a chilly evening I decided to test the furnace. A huge stove sat on the stone floor of the kitchen. At one end of the stove was an area with a grate where a coal fire could be started and this heated the water for the radiators. As the coal fire got going, the water in the system of pipes was heated and circulated through the radiators. When the coal fire was burning well, I touched the radiator with a wet finger (I did not want to be burned) to test for warmth but I felt nothing. I touched it again, this time with my whole hand, and I still could not feel any heat. I went back to the kitchen to see if there were any valves that I had failed to open. Despite my best efforts with the coal fire that evening, the only area that became any warmer was the kitchen.

The next day I went to the local realtor who had handled the house rental and I discussed the heating situation with him.

"Well," he said, "it doesn't take that much heat with us over here. Sure, the system is normal. That's the way it operates. You might find it cumbersome to keep the fire going. You know that over here we use paraffin a lot to heat our houses."

"What is paraffin?" I asked him.

"I think you call it kerosene in the United States," he replied. "It is a white kerosene; it doesn't have any odor. You might just go down to the hardware store and you'll find these paraffin heaters."

I went to the store and bought four of the heaters. They could be carried around easily. They kept that big house reasonably comfortable and only occasionally did we need topcoats indoors.

We enrolled Jerry and Debbie in nearby schools, which they enjoyed. Debbie really had wanted a horse for a long time. Not very far away was a riding academy where children were taught to ride. We enrolled both of them. Our son did not care that much for riding, but he stuck with it. Both became skilled riders. Debbie used to spend as much time on Saturdays helping to clean out the stalls and curry the horses as she did riding them.

With the family now settled into English life, my assignment with 7th Air Division at South Ruislip claimed my attention. From its activation on 20 March 1951, this division was responsible for the development of the complex of SAC bomber, fighter and reconnaissance bases in the United Kingdom all of which supported the peacetime rotational program and were manned and equipped to support whatever wartime requirement that might develop. From 1955 the development of aerial refueling tactics and the ability of the B-47 to fly from continental United States to foreign targets meant that in wartime these bases would mostly be used for recovering post-strike aircraft. These bomber wings were stationed at Brize Norton, Lakenheath, Greenham Common, Fairford and Mildenhall. As Director of Plans for the Division, I was responsible for the necessary planning for the use of our resources in England. This required working closely with the RAF (Royal Air Force) and the British government.

The THOR missile was the first intermediate range ballistic missile developed by the United States. Due to its limited range it had to be placed outside the United States in order to be effective against

Soviet targets. England had agreed to have the missiles placed on British soil. I had arrived in England at just the right time to become involved in solving the many problems associated with the THOR's deployment.

The added element in our relationship with Britain and in our use of their bases was the need for nuclear storage facilities and the nuclear weapons themselves at some of these bases. The use of missiles as weapons of war were to both American and British people quite new. The deployment of the THOR onto British bases got a lot of attention and some opposition by British citizens and the government. The THOR with a range of 1,000 to 1,200 miles was very accurate. Deployment of the THOR to the bases was reluctantly accepted by the British but there was concern for safety not only on the bases but in the communities. It was thought that these bases would be targeted by Soviet missiles or bombers. Naturally the local populace were curious and concerned that a weapon system was being placed in their midst that might attract Soviet missiles or bombs.

As a part of my job as Director of Plans, I became involved in meetings and discussions between the United States government and the British government as well as between SAC and the RAF. I understood why the British press reported the furor over the RAF's delay of the announcement of the initial operational capability of THOR on technical grounds as a front to deal with political reservations about the missile on British soil. I think the RAF had to use the technical reason to camouflage the real political concern and to gain more time to resolve the political objections. As ballistic missiles developed and their effective range increased, these shorter-range missiles were no longer needed and they were removed from British soil.

My two years with 7th Air Division in England led to a similar assignment in the Directorate of Plans at SAC Headquarters in Omaha in August 1959 under Gen. Charles B. Westover. At this time SAC was expanding its programs into tests of airborne alert, collaboration with the Federal Aviation Administration to establish low-level bombing training routes, transition to the B-52, and delivery of the

Hound Dog missile by the B-52G. (The Hound Dog missile is a miniature airplane with a nuclear warhead, carried beneath the wings of the B-52 and able to be fired against targets outside the range of enemy defenses).

General Westover was not an easy boss. Not only was he very demanding but was very often totally unrealistic in his demands. SAC was a tough command in those days, and it was recognized as such. The colonels, of which I was one, were carefully selected; they were capable and they worked long and hard hours. They did not need extra demands without merit placed on them. Friday nights were special nights at the Officers Club for these hard-working Headquarter SAC types. It was the one night a week when we tried to leave the office by a little after five and relax and let our hair down at the Club. Also we seemed always to be able to get something accomplished that night at the bar that we had not been able to get done during the week. Our wives would join us about 7:30 for dinner later. It was always a special evening.

General Westover never went to the Club on Friday evenings. Instead he would call a meeting of his key staff members about 4:30 almost every Friday. He would start to talk about some areas he was conceerned about and many other things that we either already knew or cared nothing about. This meeting would go on and on with him during which he would munch raisins or peanuts which he never offered us. We became restless. The meeting would usually end around 6:30 with a requirement for us to have a briefing on one of his subjects complete and ready for presentation to General Power, who was SAC Commander-in-Chief, at 8 a.m. Monday. We accepted this without argument because we wanted to get to the Club.

The next day we had to gather at the office to figure out how to put the briefing together, which we probably did not believe in. Finally by late Sunday afternoon we had it finished, polished and ready to go. Monday morning we arrived early as always. When we did not see General Westover by 8:30 or 9 o'clock, we asked his secretary if he had an appointment with General Power. She would say, "Not that I know of." When we did reach General Westover to ask him about the briefing for General Power, he would say, "Which one was that?"

"It's the one you gave us last Friday to develop for this morning," we reminded him.

"Ah, well," he said, "we are not on his calendar yet."

Sometimes we would never make such a briefing and sometimes it would occur later in the week. We always knew that his extra-work weekends were intentional on his part, but we could never understand why he did it. It indicated to me his total lack of concern for his people.

General Power also had a tough mode of operation for us to cope with. With any audience he tended to be a showman. He selected his wing commanders very carefully and demanded from them complete integrity and honesty. One of the many things wing commanders dreaded was reporting an airplane accident to SAC Headquarters. After the investigation of an aircraft accident was completed and the report had been written, the wing commander had to carry the report to SAC Headquarters and brief General Power. The briefing was done in General Power's office. The wing commander sat in front of General Power's desk, and his key staff would be seated behind the wing commander. And of course, he could not see the general's staff. The staff would be completely knowledgeable of this accident. Having read and analyzed the report, and often having asked questions of different people at the wing commander's base, they knew, or at least thought they knew, all the answers. General Power asked the questions directly of the commander, watching his staff to see if they agreed with what the commander said. Caught between the questioner and the staff, the wing commander had to be very sure he honestly and correctly revealed all the facts of the accident. If a mistake had been made, he had to admit it because in this kind of interrogation he could not hide it.

Such a trip to SAC Headquarters to brief the Commander in Chief of SAC on an accident was a tough and demoralizing event. It was designed to be that way. That was part of the deterrent to having accidents. SAC's wing commanders were senior, experienced and highly qualified individuals. The SAC staff on these accident reporting days made them feel as if they were inexperienced, with no knowledge of their airplane or their crews and certainly with no experience or interest in accident prevention. Many wing commanders did not survive a major accident in their wing. Almost all left SAC Headquarters after one of these experiences and returned to their base expecting to receive transfer orders.

In my second year at SAC Headquarters, Maj. Gen. Bill Martin, Director of Personnel, came into my office one Friday afternoon and said, "Jerry, you know that Dick Allison, my vice director of personnel, is leaving. I am looking for another vice and I have selected you. I want you to come over to my office Monday morning and take Dick's seat."

"Yes, Sir." Despite my feeling about personnel, what else could I say?

Deputy Chiefs of Staff in SAC Headquarters had fairly large offices with a big squawk box beside their desks, an inter-office communication system tied to other directorates and to the Commander in Chief of SAC. The deputy sat on the other side of the office. I arrived at this office by 7 o'clock that Monday. General Martin's secretary arrived about 7:45 a.m. but he had not arrived by 8:30. I asked her what time he usually arrived, and she said usually about 7:30.

"Where is he this morning?" I asked her.

"He is in North Africa. He left yesterday. He will be gone for a week."

I did not know anything about personnel matters at this level, and General Martin had not given me any instructions before he left. I asked her if General Power had been informed of my appointment. She did not know but suggested that I should move over and sit in General Martin's chair while he was in North Africa. I had sat in his chair no more than 10 minutes when the squawk box dinged. I pushed the first button down with some hesitation. "Yes, Sir." General Power said, "Who is this?" I replied, "Sir, this is Colonel Johnson." Then he asked me his question.

I said, "I'm sorry, Sir. I don't have the answer but I will get it right away."

When I had the answer I took it to his office. These calls happened with considerable frequency every day of that week, and I do not recall a single question during that entire week that I knew the answer to. But he never said an unkind word to me. Several times when I took an answer down to his office and his door would be closed, his secretary would tell him I wanted to see him and he would say, "Come in." He laid down the book he was reading, or whatever else he was doing, and I gave him the answer he sought. We talked about it a little bit, and he might make a few comments and usually asked me to look into something else. He was a brilliant man with a very sharp mind, yet he did not have a formal high school education. He developed his keen mind by reading a lot and using a dictionary. On the contrary side, if he had his staff in his office and someone was giving him a briefing, he became a showman, putting on quite a demonstration. He could be pretty cruel to the briefing officer, and he could put his staff officers on the hot seat by pinning them down with questions they could not properly answer. He had a dual personality, but I found him on a one-to-one basis to be a delightful and receptive person to work with.

General LeMay and General Power insisted on standardization throughout SAC. From administrators to operations people to pilots and specialists in the tactical crews, they all did their job in the same way. Everyone did it according to the book. This standardization contributed greatly to SAC's tremendous deterrent power as well as to its ability to respond immediately to any air power need or crisis at home or overseas. Standardization paid off when I commanded the 8th Air Force on Guam during the Vietnam War in the early 1970s. SAC sent people to Guam from every SAC base—maintenance people, supply people, support people, and crew members. I had to fit them into different sections on the base because these new people arrived there TDY. These people were so well standardized that they could leave their base at Barksdale, Louisiana or Wurtsmith, Michigan or any other air base and fly into Guam and go to work the next day. If SAC had not been standardized to that degree, I would have had a hodgepodge of people who did not do the same job the same way. We never could have pulled off the 11-day war in December 1972 successfully without the standardized skills of these TDY people.

Much of the success of the standardization effort was due to the use of assistance teams. These teams put together at SAC Headquarters were composed of administrative, finance, personnel, maintenance, supply and operations personnel, some 25 to 30 people on a team. They would arrive on a base, spread out through the various areas and truly assist in every way to make that wing better. These teams had the best people available in these individual specialities. They were an assistance team, not an inspection team. They wanted to assist the wing commander to carry out SAC directives as specified. And they did.

My assignment with SAC Headquarters gave me another insight into where SAC's best resources lay and how to utilize them. At first I did not think becoming Deputy Chief of Personnel would be interesting and challenging. However, as I learned that job, I realized that people were the greatest asset SAC had. How we treated them, how we assigned them, how we trained them were extremely important. I also discovered that we had some very fine people working in personnel. Often the leaders in the field would refer to them disrespectfully as those SAC personnel wienies. To me they were really hard-working guys who often did not get the recognition they deserved and should have received. But I had felt this way about the people who worked for me in all my assignments.

From July 1957 to August 1962, I had worked in demanding staff assignments, in planning both in England and at SAC Headquarters, and in personnel at SAC Headquarters. After five years of this kind of strenuous duty, it was time for a break. I believed that education was important and one could not get too much. I also knew that attending the National War College was almost a necessity for promotion to general rank. I had been a colonel since 1951 and I was approaching the time for another promotion. When my name came up on the list for the 1962-63 class of the National War College in Washington, I did not resist even though I hated leaving SAC

Headquarters. Despite the long hours I had thoroughly enjoyed the assignments and the responsibility.

My family did have one small problem in moving again. After returning from England with my children who were now accomplished horsepersons, they wanted a horse of their own. At the Fastonia Farm in Missiouri I happened to find a three-year-old five-gaited saddle horse that was for sale at a price I could afford. His name was Fastonia's Chief A. That became a Christmas present in 1959. He was a real beauty and became primarily Debbie's horse. We had a horse trailer for Chief and he and Debbie traveled to small shows around the Omaha area where she won many ribbons riding and showing him. Then in the summer of 1962 he became our problem. We thought we could not part with Chief, but moving him to Washington and finding a place to board him and to provide him with exercise for what would probably be only one year was a problem. I knew I would be very busy for this year and I wanted to devote full time to the National War College assignment. In the end, it turned out Chief had to go but certainly not without considerable tears and not just from Debbie. We had all become very attached to Chief. Debbie's girl friend and her parents liked Chief. I could not bring myself to sell Chief, but I arranged to leave him with this family along with the trailer. He would continue to be Debbie's horse but just living away from his real home for one year. This seemed to be a satisfactory solution for everyone and we went to Washington.

The curriculum of the National War College provided lectures and discussion in the morning, exercise before or after lunch—we had a short nine-hole golf course that was layed out around the building—and afternoons in the library to work on papers, to read and research various topics, and to work toward a thesis on a topic selected by each student and approved by the faculty as significant. Among the students were a few who chose two- to three-hour martini lunches and then went home, but I had a lot of company among those who wanted to get as much out of this experience as possible. Interaction among Army, Navy and Air Force classmates provided opportunity for cross-fertilization with the other services that had untold dividends in our careers. In the early 1960s, military leaders increased requirements for cross-assignments and cross-training in what the other services were doing.

The highilght of the National War College was the field trip covering three weeks and scheduled in April. Students could choose from five areas for the trip: Europe, the Middle East, the Far East, South America and Africa. I chose Africa for several reasons. I knew Europe, the Middle East and the Far East. Although these would be pleasant places to visit, I wanted this trip to be a learning experience. I thought at some time I would undoubtedly visit South America, but Africa except for Libya and Morocco I knew very little about and probably would never visit on my own. I was never sorry with this choice.

In 1963 Africa was almost totally different from what it is today in names of states or countries, boundary locations, foreign influence and local responsibility, to name a few of the differences. We landed first at Dakar in Gambia, proceeded down the west coast to Johannesburg, up the east coast to Kenya, across the rain forest to Ghana and then departed from Senegal. This trip was excellent in every way, very educational, and the other students who had made the trip with me were outstanding.

For my thesis, perhaps because I had come from SAC, a nuclear command, I was particularly interested in nuclear weapons and how they could be controlled and maintained only in the hands of responsible nations. It was necessary to think about how many countries could and probably would acquire nuclear capability. What effect on world stability and on individual nations would nuclear capability have? How difficult would it be to build a nuclear weapon? What were the odds of a significantly wide proliferation? These questions I had to probe in the library more widely and deeply than I had anticipated. No one in my research sources had a satisfactory answer. I had to put forth my own estimates. I stated that the United States policy consistently had one objective, to arrest the proliferation of nuclear powers, and concluded that its present (1963) policy of nuclear sharing and its guarantee of a nuclear deterrent for the European members of

NATO comprised the best arrangement possible then or until "some means [could] be found for developing closer political unity." More than 30 years later, the same questions haunt the world. My thesis titled "An Analysis of U.S. Policy Regarding the Sharing of Nuclear Weapons" was selected among 31 others for special commendation.

I thoroughly enjoyed these nine months at the National War College. Despite the demands of the busy school program I attended night classes at George Washington University to earn a master's degree in international relations. My thesis was accepted as being appropriate for this major. I also enjoyed many interesting lunchtime discussions with other students and most often students from other services at the McNair Officers Club or the Market Inn, a delightful nearby restaurant.

IN BOMBERS AT LAST

Gen. W. G. Kieffer, Deputy for Personnel at SAC Headquarters, had told me shortly after my return from Africa that I would return to SAC and would take command of a B-52G wing in 15th Air Force. General Kieffer and Gen. Archie Old, Commander of 15th Air Force, had feuded on several occasions over the assignment of colonels in 15th Air Force. General Old felt that he and he alone would select his wing commanders. I was caught in the middle of this feud and that was unfortunate for me. General Old would easily have accepted me if it had been his decision, but he was not about to let a two-star SAC Headquarters general tell him who would command his wings. Consequently I went to 15th Air Force but not as a commander. I went to 12th Strategic Aerospace Division at Davis-Monthan Air Force Base, Tucson, Arizona as Director of Operations under newly promoted Brig. Gen. Bill Bacon who I had first met on the deployment to Alaska in 1946. I did absolutely nothing in that position to foster my career, and I groused because my leaving National War College a little early cost me the opportunity to finish my master's degree at George Washington University before going to Tucson. I did fly the B-47 again, but I wanted to fly the B-52 and command a B-52 wing.

By early September I had been at Davis-Monthan almost three months. Davis-Monthan and Tucson were pleasant places and considered choice areas in which to live. I lived in a nice set of quarters on base, and we had started our children in school. However, I was miserable. I could not believe that my career that had been going so well was now finished. Maybe I had arrived at the time that I had always told myself, if my job was not interesting and challenging I would leave the Air Force. However I did not want to leave. I liked the Air Force, and there was so much I still wanted to do.

I did not know General Old very well, but I did know that he was thought of as a difficult person to understand and work for. I could not stand any longer not knowing what was in store for me. Without an appointment to see General Old, I flew a T-33 from Tucson to March Air Force Base at Riverside, California, went to General Old's office hopefully to discuss my future. His secretary told me he was off the base attending a meeting in town and should be back before lunch. It was then about 10 a.m. I waited, I drank coffee, read a magazine, drank more coffee and waited. At 1230 I told his secretary I was going for a quick lunch. I felt as if I needed a couple of martinis before lunch but declined. I hastily devoured a quick sandwich and returned to General Old's office. I did not want to take any chance of missing him. Again I waited. His secretary was not sure when he would return. At 4 p.m. I gave up, went to flight operations, got my T-33 and flew back to Tucson.

I really felt terrible. This unsuccessful effort must be the end. That was on Thursday. On Saturday I was in my office as I always was, at least until noon. At about 1230 the phone rang. I picked it up. The voice said, "General Old here. Jerry, I want you at Castle Air Force Base (that was the training base in California for B-52s and KC-135s) Monday morning when a new B-52 class starts."

"Yes, Sir," I said.

"Well, don't you want to know where you will go after that?" he asked.

"I think that is up to you, Sir. Where do you think I ought to go?" I probably was holding my breath.

"Go to El Paso, Texas. Take that 95th Bomb Wing at Biggs Air Force Base."

The next day I drove our little Volkswagon to Castle and I was in class on Monday morning. I did the B-52 ground school and KC-135 ground school as well as all flight training simultaneously. This concentration of training normally was never done, but I was in a hurry. During the remainder of that September and early October, the weather was beautiful. I was in ground school all of every day. When the flying training started about mid-October, the notorious San Joaquin Valley fog arrived. Almost all of the B-52 and KC-135 transition flights were instrument take-offs and landings. That foggy weather was a real advantage for it greatly increased the quality of training. I found both of these airplanes a pleasure to fly. On 23 November after I had completed my last test standboard check on the KC-135 and returned to my room about 11 o'clock, my roommate Colonel Edwards, said, "Have you heard the news?"

"No, what?"

"The President has been shot." On that sad news, I drove back to Tucson to prepare for taking up my long-awaited assignment with a bomber wing at Biggs Air Force Base.

Taking command of the 95th Bombardment Wing was a major point in my career. I had already commanded two fighter squadrons, one fighter wing, and one reconnaissance wing, but always there had been another commander on the base whom I served under. At Biggs I was the senior commander. The base commander reported to me. Because of all of my experience on other bases, I had observed things and activities that I wanted to try at Biggs. When I arrived, the airman on the gate saluted properly, but on my questioning, he did not know that I was the new wing commander, and he did not know the base commander's name. There was no sign of welcome for me at base headquarters or at my quarters. I called the base commander to inform him of my arrival and the fact that the front gate guard did not know his name. This call really annoyed him. The next day I learned that he had demoted that gate guard. I called the base commander to my office and explained to him that he had made a mistake. It was not the guard's fault that he did not know his base commander's name, I told him, but that was his fault. I assured him that if he would let himself be seen more often and would talk to and work with the troops they would know his name.

I had learned a lot during previous commands where I was not the senior commander and I had noted things I would have done if I had been the senior commander. I had decided I was going to test these things at Biggs, and if I was right the result would be that Biggs would become the finest base with the best B-52 wing in SAC. I wanted from the start to let everyone know that they had a new commander and what his objectives were.

Biggs was not the most attractive air base in 15th Air Force or SAC and our B-52Bs were the oldest B-52s in SAC. The base stood at the edge of the desert northeast of El Paso. Its landscape was mostly sand and had almost no grass, and the sand, blown by the wind, had been permitted to drift against fences, buildings and other obstructions. Many senior people had become complacent and were themselves just drifting. I meant to change this drifting environment and make Biggs and the 95th Bomb Wing the best in 15th Air Force. But I almost missed this opportunity as I will explain later.

When I arrived at an air base and while it was totally new to me, I always carried a scratch pad and pencil with me. As I drove around I noted all those things that did not look good or needed attention. If I did not do this right away, I would become accustomed to what I saw, accept it and not get it corrected.

During the first few weeks at Biggs I spent a lot of time talking with just about everyone and trying to impress them with the importance of their job and how they contributed to the overall mission. We had telphone operators in those days. When outside calls came into the base, the caller would hear a female voice answering. I met with these operators and told them that for many people these calls were the only contact they would ever have with Biggs and maybe with the Air Force. I wanted the callers to be favorably impressed by operators who were courteous, helpful and sincere. The operators understood and responded. I talked with the gate guards using the same theme, i.e., they were the first contact a visitor had with the base and the impression left with the visitor from that first contact would stay with him and not be forgotten. I wanted to put the Air Force's best foot forward in all contacts. After all, the military worked for civilians who paid our way through their taxes, and I wanted them to be proud of their investment. I spent a lot of time with the local community to build a very close relationship between military personnel and civilians that was respected by each.

Not long after I arrived at Biggs I was on the golf course one Saturday afternoon with three El Paso community leaders. It was a pleasant afternoon, and when the golf game was finished, I made a monetary contribution to them because I missed too many of my putts. At the 19th hole they unanimously announced to me that they were very proud and happy to have me as the new 95th commander. They now knew for sure I did not spend all my time on the golf course.

At this time one of SAC's most critical issues was the method of airmen promotions. It seems that on several previous occasions the wrong airman had been promoted. Not only were these mistakes very embarrassing, they also were not good for troop morale. I did not think much about this situation since I could not really believe such mistakes could ever happen if the promotion board was properly handling the promotion procedure. Since I simply did not have time for everything and the promotion boards were time-consuming, I delegated this chore to my vice wing commander, a colonel I had not known before but who seemed knowledgeable and capable. Several weeks later to my utter disbelief I was called from 15th Air Force Headquarters with the information that I had promoted an airman who should not have been promoted. I went to my vice commander to find out what had happened. He did not know, but somehow I got the impression that he also did not much care. This indifference disturbed me. Could this mistake have been intentional? I knew that he had been the vice commander to the previous commander at Biggs that I had replaced and had hoped that he would be assigned as wing commander.

At this time also, SAC approached the time to send its first B-52s to the Far East in support of the Vietnam War. My wing had been selected to provide these initial resources of support. Fifteenth Air Force had set up a trip to the Far East to survey the bases and facilities available in that area. I was to accompany General Old and to be a member of this survey group. I called my friend Col. Frank Nye, who was Director of Operations at 15th Air Force, to check on the trip. Frank was sympathetic but told me he did not think I was scheduled to go. I said, "What the hell has happened?" He told me he was sorry but that airman promotion deal was just something General Old did not tolerate. He was afraid I was finished. This information was a serious blow as I was just getting started at commanding a bomb wing.

A few days later I was told General Old was on his way to my base. I had not seen him since taking command and had only talked with him once by phone. He had not called me after the mistake on the airman promotion.

I met him when he landed and suggested a tour of the base. He agreed. I knew that the nuclear storage site, its appearance and security were one of his top subjects. Of course, I took him there first. Everyone there knew me and security and appearance were perfect. We then drove around the base, stopping at several places. Every time I stopped we were both greeted by name. He said little during that tour, but I knew he was favorably impressed by what he saw. We then went to my office, coffee was brought in, and I then brought up the subject of the airman promotion and told him in detail how it had happened. I also told him I knew how serious this subject was and accepted full responsibility for its happening. I had made a mistake and I knew better than to have given my vice commander, whom I did not know well, the job of running the promotion board. It would not happen again, I assured him. He had not interrupted my comments, but then he said, "I know that vice of yours and should have gotten rid of him a long time ago." He hesitated a little and then said, "But let me tell you, that does not let you off the hook. And by the way, I know about that trip you made to my headquarters last September, and I think I know what it was about." I said nothing, but I thought maybe that trip to his Headquarters had not been in vain. After all, he did call me and sent me to B-52 training two days later.

Although it was now after five o'clock and he showed no interest in leaving my office, I offered more coffee. He said, "Let's go to quarters, change our clothes, and go to Juarez. I haven't been over there for a long time." We had a pleasant evening, the airman promotion was never mentioned again, and he left Biggs the next morning. I went to the Far East with him on the survey, and we became good friends. Many years later and after Archie Old had been retired about a year, I met him at an Air Force get-together. Knowing he had been an enthusiastic golfer, I asked, "Archie, how's your golf?" "Awful," he replied. I asked him why since I knew he was a good golfer. He replied, "Well, for years there at March Air Force Base, if my ball got within six feet of the hole my golfing buddies would say, 'That's good, General, pick it up' and now I can't putt."

I flew the B-52 and KC-135 at every opportunity. As my experience increased I began to feel confident and knew that I was becoming a good big airplane driver. I enjoyed the crews and I got to know the pilots very well. They knew my background and limited experience in big airplanes. We kidded a lot. It was often necessary for one reason or another to transport B-52 crews in the back of a KC-135. I enjoyed being the pilot on these flights because more of the crews would be exposed to my flying ability. To kid the crews I had the crew chief install a light in the back of the KC-135. Before take-off, I pointed out this light to the B-52 crews in the back of the plane and explained that at our destination the landing would probably be so smooth they would not feel it and that this light was designed to come on when we touched down so they would know we were on the ground. They thought this invention was hilarious. I believe the light did actually come on a few times. The pilots and I had a good time, and with this rapport between us they developed an unbelievable "Can do" attitude.

This attitude was soon demonstrated during an ORI (Operational Readiness Inspection). The target for this particular ORI was really tough because the offset radar positions were difficult to identify.

Despite the fact that our airplanes were the oldest B-52s and the new B-52Gs and B-52Hs had far more sophisticated bombing systems, the 95th scored the highest marks in SAC in this ORI. Needless to say, this outcome required me to call my wing's success to the attention of my former roommate at Castle Air Force Base, Colonel Edwards, who had gone to Homestead Air Force Base, Florida and commanded a bomb wing with the latest model, the B-52Hs.

One thing that bothered both the maintenance personnel and the crews were the rather voluminous check lists that had to be followed in order for the maintenance people to accomplish most all maintenance jobs and for the crews to use in all flight operations. Many times they wanted to bypass some of these requirements, and I suspect they did. I was strict about following the check lists, and I insisted that if the check list needed correcting, then we would send the recommendation forward for higher headquarter's approval. In the meantime, I demanded that until the change was approved, we would follow the check list as it was.

By chance, I was provided an insight that helped me in putting across this point on following the check list. A new chaplain for the 95th Wing had recently arrived and during my first interview with him I noticed some inscription on the front of the Bible he carried. It read, "Jesus said it, I believe it, and that settles it." He told me that he had often used this expression to end arguments or discussions in which he could not seem to get his point accepted. I borrowed this expression and his story and used them often when discussing the check list problem. "The check list says it, I believe it, and that settles it." I believe this expression helped in making my point.

Finally a date was set for the next, and my first, 15th Air Force facilities inspection. I had just over a month to prepare Biggs Air Force Base for it. I talked to several other wing commanders in 15th Air Force about this inspection. Most of them had beautiful bases— trees and grass and new buildings. They remarked that I was lucky since no one expected Biggs to even be in the competition. I might as well just relax and coast through the inspection, they advised. This passive acceptance was not my nature, and besides I had other ideas.

I had grown to like Biggs and I did not think the sand was that unattractive.

I called my staff together. We discussed our opportunity and made a list of all those things we could do. I wanted them to take a very positive approach to the forthcoming inspection and to recognize that our efforts in improving the appearance of the base would pay off through improved morale and pride in being a part of a base that looked cared for. I then met with everyone in separate gatherings and explained what we were to do. I told them that we might have very little but sand but our sand would be the best looking sand anyone had ever seen. My enthusiasm caught on and everyone went to work, mostly in their off-duty time. In the short time we had we totally changed that base by painting buildings, painting stones to outline sand areas, removing all the sand from fences, and planting flowers. All the shops were properly arranged to be neat and clean and equipment was polished. The base became beautiful. A few days before the inspection team was to arrive, I invited the mayor of El Paso and a few dignitaries out for lunch and a tour. They were amazed and delighted at Biggs' bright appearance.

When the inspection team arrived, they were almost apologetic at having to bother me with an inspection they felt I had little interest in. When they were ready to leave the base, they told another story. Biggs was chosen as the best maintained base in 15th Air Force. During the next few weeks and not without General Old's encouragement, several wing commanders visited Biggs to see just what had happened there.

In April 1964 we sent the first B-52 nonstop from El Paso to Guam. I had carefully selected the crew. I went along, making the take-off from Biggs and landing at Andersen Air Force Base, Guam. I had had painted on the nose of the B-52 "City of El Paso." The Mayor of El Paso was present at the take-off and he had put aboard several momentos to be delivered to the Governor of Guam, who would be present to meet me when we landed. At take-off that morning we weighed just under a half-million pounds. It took 71 seconds for the B-52 to travel the 10,560 feet and reach take-off speed of 172 MPH.

Seventy-five hundred pounds of jet fuel were pumped through the eight jet engines. After traveling 7,106 miles, refueling in flight twice and consuming 43,344 gallons of fuel, we landed at Andersen Air Force Base, Guam, taxied to the reviewing stand where the Governor waited. On the return flight three days later the Governor of Guam sent momentos to the Mayor of El Paso. Painted on the nose of the B-52 was "Island of Guam." This event was just one of many of my efforts to emphasize and improve relations between the community and the base.

My command of the 95th Bombardment Wing at Biggs (December 63 to July 1965) was the first of my five commands for SAC during the lengthening war in Vietnam. For a year (July 1965 to July 1966) I commanded the 305th Bomb Wing at Bunker Hill, Indiana, flying the B-58 and pinning on my first star in November 1965. In the next two years (July 1966 to June 1968) I commanded the 825th Strategic Aerospace Division at Little Rock, Arkansas. Under this division were both the Little Rock-based B-58 Wing and the Bunker Hill B-58 Wing as well as the Titan II missile wing with missiles deployed around Arkansas. It was during this assignment that I received my second star and was moved to vice commander of 2nd Air Force at Barksdale Air Force Base, Shreveport, Louisiana; and for five months (April to August 1969) I commanded the 1st Strategic Aerospace Division at Vandenberg Air Force Base, Lompoc, California. After all of this command experience in the field, I returned to SAC Headquarters at Omaha as Director of Operations (August 1969 to September 1971). To put this summary of commands in a different way reveals the pattern of commitment expected of those who wanted to move up the promotion ladder in SAC during those years. I left SAC Headquarters in 1962 as a colonel and returned there in 1969 as a two-star general. I made eight moves in those seven years from colonel to major general rank. My individual experience seemed to represent SAC's deterrent principles of mobility, flexibility and preparedness at a moment's notice to fight for one's country and the free world. For each one of these field assignments I provide some details on how those principles were performed.

The 305th Bombardment Wing at Bunker Hill near Peru, Indiana, was a very famous World War II unit led by General LeMay as a colonel. Gen. Jack Ryan, commanding general of SAC, told me that many of the B-58 pilots of the Wing formerly flew fighters with whom I probably would have immediate rapport. Yet I thought this move from command of a B-52 wing to one flying a smaller but faster B-58 bomber that had a lower priority in SAC's inventory was more a lateral than an upward move in my career. Nonetheless, I went through the B-58 training course and then I moved my family from El Paso to Bunker Hill. The B-58 known as the Hustler had a delta wing, a long nose, four engines with air refueling capability and a top speed of just over Mach 2—that is more than 1,500 mph. The pilot's cockpit was much like a fighter airplane's with a stick rather than a yoke and four throttles. Behind him was the navigator and systems operator, each contained in individual capsules which would slam shut sealing in the crew member for ejection if that became necessary. There was no physical contact between crew members; communication took place by interphone.

In view of its sophisticated mission and performance, Mach 2 capability and high approach and landing speeds the B-58 really needed a co-pilot. Most airplanes approach and land at slower air speeds than the B-58's 215 knots on its final approach. That is pretty fast. On a dark night, for instance, when the pilot breaks through a 300-foot ceiling he must quickly transition from instruments to visual and be perfectly lined up with the runway because at that speed, if he was not right on the centerline of the runway, he had very little time to correct. The pod down the underside of the fuselage of the B-58 was designed to carry fuel and a nuclear weapon in its nose. The B-58 was designed to fly to the target on the fuel in the pod and then drop the entire pod with the nuclear weapon in the nose onto the target. Then the airplane was cleanly streamlined for the return back to its base on the fuel in the wings. The B-58 was never very popular with SAC's leaders and staff because they preferred larger planes with a co-pilot and room to walk around inside.

I had not been at Bunker Hill very long, about a month I guess, when on landing one night about midnight, I had just taxied in and was completing the Form 1 for the mission when I saw another B-58 coming in to land. I knew the pilot, a former fighter pilot and a very competent one. I was watching the landing when to my amazement about half way down the runway I began to see some sparks and then some fire. It was obvious that this airplane was in trouble. I quickly climbed from the cockpit and drove my staff car to the site as soon as I could. By that time the crew were out of the airplane, which was just off the side of the runway and burning. I found the pilot and asked him what had happened. He said he didn't know because he had made a normal touchdown and the plane, moving down the runway, started to veer to the right and he could not correct it. He could not keep it on the runway. As it left the runway the right main gear collapsed and the fuel pod ruptured causing the fire.

I was required to report an accident immediately to General Dave Wade, the commanding general of 2nd Air Force at Barksdale Air Force Base, and to the command post at SAC Headquarters. General Wade arrived at Bunker Hill the next morning, wanting to talk with me in my office, and he seemed to have no interest in viewing the crash site.

Without any knowledge at all of the accident, he proceeded to state, "It is pilot error, no question about it. A fighter pilot who doesn't know very much about flying anyhow, and he's got a bomber that he can't handle."

General Wade's remarks disturbed me. They were totally uncalled for and a terrible indictment of a fighter pilot who had flown a tour in Vietnam before coming to B-58s. I was not able to convince him other factors must have entered into the accident. I thought to myself that to have an accident was a disastrous way to get started on my assignment at Bunker Hill. However, two weeks later General Wade called to say that I was on the promotion list for brigadier general. Needless to say, I felt much better. Later the full investigation of the accident revealed that a steering malfunction caused the B-58 to veer off the runway, thus canceling the element of pilot error General Wade had charged.

Flying a mission in a B-58 for me was a satisfying and thrilling experience. My navigator and my systems operator were fine, well-trained young men. A typical mission for us was a night flight because I had more time to fly at night than in the daytime. We arrived at base operations about 4 or 5 o'clock in flight suits and were ready to develop the flight plan. Usually the navigator already knew what the mission was to be, how long we were to fly, and what our objectives on this mission would be. He would have it pretty well laid out by the time I arrived at operations. We went over his plan together and decided exactly what parts were critical and what part each would play in the mission. Since we had no physical contact once we got into the airplane and communicated only by intercom, we wanted to be sure there was no misunderstanding about any part of the mission. Even without any transmission from me, these two crewmen knew from what I was doing where we were in the mission and my reason for making certain turns or maneuvers.

Having our plan worked out, we spent some time in the weather office, reviewing the weather along the route we would fly, the weather at the rendezvous point with the tankers that was a part of each mission, and the weather we could expect on our return to land at Bunker Hill. Then we proceeded to our assigned airplane and did a walk around the plane. The very competent ground crews explained to me any problems the airplane had had over the past two or three flights and what they had done to correct these problems. If the airplane had any deficiency at this time, that was described. Then all three of us climbed into our places, got strapped in, and I proceeded to start the engines. I always felt very comfortable once I got into that airplane. The controls were easy to reach. The stick instead of a yoke had the familiar feel of a fighter plane.

At the take-off end of the runway, I secured clearance from the tower and pushed the throttles up. The four afterburners were always used on take-off and made a bright glow against the night sky. I climbed on up, usually making a few turns, and headed out toward the southern end of Lake Michigan. As we reached the center of the lake, we would be at 30,000 feet or so under Mach 1. Then with full power, we continued to climb and quickly passed through Mach 1. The reason for flying over Lake Michigan was that the B-58 made quite a boom as it passed through the sound barrier. Not only did this disturb the people we were passing over, it could cause damage to buildings. I was very busy at this point of the climb. Many things happened in the cockpit as the plane moved from Mach 1 to Mach 2. Although the engine spikes which controlled the amount of air entering the engines were automatically controlled, I usually had to make some adjustments manually. Engine temperatures were also critical. The B-58 had a system of lights plus voice that told the pilot he had a problem and what it was. A very nice calm female voice kept him informed. I rarely made a flight without that red light coming on, even though the problem was something that I as pilot could correct; I would see a bright red light come on and the voice might say, "No. 1 is overheating." Of course, I would know immediately what was occurring and I took corrective action.

By the time we reached 50,000 feet, I had shot right through Mach 2. I was hardly ever able to get the throttles back soon enough. It did not really matter that the plane might go a little over Mach 2. It was really a thrill to know it could and to experience it. After the mission I always tried to think back to whether I really noticed any change going through Mach 1 or Mach 2. Quite honestly, I never could note a change. I had gone through Mach 1 many times in a fighter, but no fighter took me past Mach 2. It was always very quiet. Above 50,000 feet the sky was very dark. We were in another world, moving miraculously fast.

Having accomplished our Mach 1 and Mach 2 transitions and having arrived at the top end of Lake Michigan, I pulled the power back and started to descend to 40,000 feet. At this point I usually went on to the rendezvous with the tanker or went on a bomb run, depending on how much fuel the airplane had used. Refueling the B-58 was an easy task. The receptacle was in front of the pilot in the nose of the airplane. Lining up with the tanker and letting the tanker insert the boom into the airplane's receptacle was no problem. The bomb run was usually made at low level although high level runs were frequently made. Speeds were at about 400 to 500 knots. I always enjoyed the low-level portion of the mission, especially in the daytime because I enjoyed seeing how fast we passed over the ground. The throttles on the B-58 to maintain that speed would be about half open. Since I sat far ahead of the engines, I did not hear anything except the swoosh of air and very little of that since the B-58 was so well streamlined.

After completing everything in the mission plan and starting back toward Bunker Hill, I received a report on the weather there and hoped the ceiling would not be too low as that condition made landing somewhat of a chore. As I approached the base and slowed the airplane to approach speed, the nose came up high, making it hard to see the field. I had to raise my seat as high as possible. This was limited because the seat was inside the capsule. The instruments were very small, about the same size as those in the T-33. The attitude indicator and the ILS tracking device that showed the alignment of the airplane on the runway centerline, were also gauges only three inches in diameter, and seemed far away as I looked down at them from my raised seat. I had to sit this high in the cockpit so that I could transfer my vision to the runway lights as quickly as possible on the final approach after breaking out of any overcast. Of course by this time, the gear and flaps were down. Coming in at the end of the runway, the airplane had a speed of about 170 knots. After touchdown the nose was held up in order for the big delta wing to cause drag and slow the airplane. Then the drag chute was popped and the brakes applied and the airplane slowed down for the turn-off the runway and taxi in to the parking spot. Low ceiling night landings in the B-58 Hustler were always a great experience. To me they never became routine.

It was unfortunate that the B-58 was designed to do only one thing but to do that very well—to deliver a nuclear weapon and to return home minus the fuel pod. By contrast, the B-52 had a huge bomb bay and although designed to deliver nuclear weapons for use in the Vietnam War, it had been converted to conventional weapon delivery. Since the United States fought that war without any increase in funding, the Air Force took a beating trying to continue SAC's role of deterrence and at the same time to support the war in Southeast Asia. Because the B-58 could not contribute to the Vietnam War, the decision was finally made to eliminate the two B-58 wings. At SAC Headquarters in 1969 as Deputy for Operations, I had many arguments with Gen. Sherm Martin, Deputy for Plans, on this matter because I hated to see the B-58 taken out of service. All the B-58s from the two bases that I commanded—Bunker Hill and Little Rock—were sent to the boneyard at Tucson and chopped up as quickly as they arrived. Only a very few of them are left for historical display around the country.

After pinning on my general's star in November 1965, I gained another type of SAC duty. In the late 1950s when SAC was the United States' major deterrent in the Cold War, the command believed it possible that in time of war it could lose its ground command post and control organization at Omaha. It was determined that an airborne command post was needed, a post to be manned by a general officer 24 hours a day, seven days a week. Some KC-135s were modified to have the equipment necessary to control the B-52 force if the United States had to go to war and the ground control force was lost. These airplanes were known as EC-135s; they served as an airborne command post called Looking Glass. This duty put an extra burden on general officers since each had to go to Omaha to do his tour. For instance, I would be in Omaha about three or four days each month and would fly one eight-hour mission each day. For each 24 hours, three general officers had to be available. The eight-hour mission took about 12 hours, including pre-take-off time and after-landing reports. Sometimes due to some problem that might develop because of weather at Omaha (all EC-135s operated out of Omaha) or maybe we had some other problem, I would have a longer than an eight-hour mission in the air.

On my first airborne command control mission, I flew a T-33 to Omaha and had a problem with this bird on landing. The runway at Offutt Air Force Base at Omaha had been extended to 10,000 feet, an easy runway for a T-33 except that this bird lost its braking capability as I rolled out of my landing. Without brakes, I had to steer the airplane and keep it on the runway with the aileron and rudder. The aileron and rudder became less effective as the speed decreased, and finally I had no directional control at all. By this time I was slow enough that as the airplane left the runway and was stopped by the soft soil, there was no damage to the airplane but a great deal of embarrassment to me. I knew that within a matter of seconds the phone would ring in Gen. Jack Ryan's office and he would be told that a pilot by the name of General Johnson had gone off the runway in a T-33. That was the first of my monthly trips to Omaha to fly the Looking Glass mission that continued for approximately 30 years until the Berlin Wall came down.

At Bunker Hill, I continued my program of involving the community with the air base in many ways. The base formed a triangle with the towns of Peru, Logansport and Kokomo. In The Hustler, a newspaper printed by a person in no way connected with the Department of the Air Force, I wrote a weekly column encouraging base personnel to be as good citizens in the nearby towns as they were expected to be on base. In April 1966, the Kokomo Lions Club chose Bunker Hill Air Force Base to receive its award called "man of the month" because of the base's help in putting out fires in Peru and Logansport.

A BOMBER AND MISSLE COMMANDER

In July 1966, I assumed command of the 825th Strategic Aerospace Division at Little Rock Air Force Base, Arkansas where I was responsible for the 43rd Bombardment Wing (flying B-58s), the 308th Strategic Missile Wing (Titan II ICBM) as well as the 305th Wing at Bunker Hill. The 825th contained all the B-58 supersonic bomber wings and one-third of all Titan II ICBMs. I did not know very much about the Titan II which was deployed around Arkansas. The Division had a few helicopters for transportation to the missile sites. The regular crews of the Titans traveled to and from the sites by motor vehicle. This was my opportunity to fly the helicopter which I flew to the sites whenever I had to inspect or to visit them to observe their work on site. The intricacies of the Titan missile were interesting to learn. To spend a 24-hour span with the crews was difficult because I was busy during the day, and night operations became the best time for me to spend with them.

The missile complex where the crews operated opened up a new and challenging area for me. The tunnels and the different levels on which to view the missiles and the approaches that the maintenance people used to get to the missiles to make adjustments or checks as they went through their check lists when discrepancies showed up and had to be corrected—all of these I had to become familiar with. Of course, the turnkey for the launch of the missile had been established to guarantee absolutely that it could not be inadvertently launched. The turnkey operation required two people responsible for these two keys; they were positioned so as to make it impossible for one person to simultaneously reach them. Later, in March 1967, two of the Titan II crews of Little Rock were selected to compete in the SAC Missile competition at Vandenberg Air Force Base, California. At the same time these two crews also received the 2nd Air Force's Master Crew Award for a certain six-month period from Lt. Gen. A. J. Russell, commanding general of 2nd Air Force.

My moving up from wing commander to division commander took a little adjustment. As a wing commander I was involved in every detail of the wing operation. I worked with the maintenance people, operations people, and the crews. I was very much involved with the ongoing activities of the base. At the division level, I had wing commanders who reported to me. They had the same responsibilities that I used to have. I did not want to interfere with their way of carrying out their duties; I wanted them to have the full latitude to do their job as I had when I had their position. However, I also wanted to know what was going on at their levels of maintenance, operations, supply, and the like. As I had a small division staff, it was difficult for my staff to gain this knowledge and be helpful to the wing commanders when they needed assistance from my staff in different areas. In this position as division commander I had the opportunity to measure my former opinion about the effectiveness of the division in the coordination of duties among the different levels within SAC. The 825th Division monitored and coordinated the equipment and operational readiness of its assigned units for the primary purpose of conducting strategic warfare on a global scale. The motto on the shield of the 825th Aerospace Division was "Watch and Protect." I think that was what I did most of the time.

The friendly competition between the B-58 wings at Little Rock and Bunker Hill continued. At the World Series of Bombing scheduled for October 1966 again at Fairchild Air Force Base, the Little Rock 43rd Bomb Wing offered a challenge to the 305th Wing at Bunker Hill. The 43rd bet a razorback hog that they would win while the Hoosier's 305th bet one bushel of Indiana corn. These sister cities decided to continue their "civic war" with annual gatherings between them despite SAC's cancelation of the competition among the airplanes and crews. Other community relationship activities included my arrangement of a tour of the General Dynamics Corporation at Fort Worth for civic leaders of the Little Rock area and the awarding of the Scroll of Appreciation, the Air Force's second highest civilian award, to Kenneth P. Wilson of Jacksonville, Arkansas for "meritorious achievement or service by a civilian" and for promoting favorable community relationships between the greater Little Rock area and Little Rock Air Force Base.

In the summer 1968, Gen. A. J. Russell, commanding general of 2nd Air Force at Barksdale Air Force Base, under whose command the 825th operated, selected me to be his vice commander. When I had the 508th Fighter Wing at Turner, General Russell commanded a B-47 Wing at Hunter Field near Savannah, Georgia. We would meet often at SAC Headquarters and 2nd Air Force Headquarters. Becoming a deputy commander of an Air Force was not a position that I really enjoyed, even though it could be regarded as a place to learn the responsibilities of a numbered Air Force. I liked to be the commander, the number one. As Vice Commander of 2nd Air Force, I spent a lot of time with the units of 2nd Air Force, visiting them to see how they progressed, meeting their personnel, and the like. I did not make any decisions, but having participated in discussion of problems, I hoped the contributions I offered might assist General Russell to make the final decision. I was at Barksdale for 10 months. In April 1969, I moved to Vandenberg Air Force Base, Lompoc, California to take command of the 1st Strategic Aerospace Division. I approached command of this division with great interest because it promised to challenge me in a totally different way. I was back in command again after being a deputy and I was anxious to get involved in an exciting assignment and at a pleasasnt location. The mission required close coordination among many organizations, including the Navy, the Army, Civil Service, civilians, contractors and the National Air and Space Agency. This interaction presented some challenges, but they were not difficult to handle. A very large base, Vandenberg had originally been an Army area for tank training during World War II. It was the only place where a missile could be launched on a north-south orbit that would not take it over land during launch. From Vandenberg long-range launches of the ICBMs could also be made to some very small islands in the South Pacific.

We worked with many civilians from companies that built or supported Vandenberg's launching activities. My duties brought me many responsibilities that I had not been exposed to before. The manned orbiting laboratory being built at that time and controlled completely out of Washington caught my attention immediately. I had only peripheral responsibility for it in terms of the divison's support to its construction. At this time questions began to be raised about the viability of the concept of an orbiting laboratory in view of some of the cutbacks in budgeting and the extra cost to the Air Force as well as everyone else in waging the war in Vietnam. However, after millions of dollars had been expended on the laboratory, it was canceled.

Sometimes it is useful to listen to Robert Burns' advice "to see ourselves as others see us." E. C. Stevens, managing editor of the Lompoc Record sometime after I arrived at Vandenberg interviewed me (17 April 1969). His article was headlined "Vandenberg's boss puts accent on people." He wrote that it was a pleasant surprise to find in a new commander a soft voice, friendly nature and gentle disposition [that] are slightly alien to the tough disciplined world of the military. [My] easy-going style does not seem to fit the popular personality recipe of the hard-charging World War II ace who shot down 18 enemy planes, flew 88 combat missions, was shot down himself and then booked into a German prison camp for 13 months. But the realization comes quickly that this easy nature is made possible by the strength of strong discipline and self-reliance.

With this article Stevens briefly became my spokesman for promoting the extension of the cooperative spirit on Vandenberg to the surrounding communities and soliciting their support for helping the missile base to achieve its highest potential in technological progress and development. After Stevens's presentation I had to follow through.

I spent many nights at control centers of the missile launches. I observed some fantastic missile launches. SAC's top missile men entered the week-long competition in May 1969. The competition determined the "best of the best" among the men who handled SAC's operational Titan II and Minuteman missile forces at nine different bases scattered across the Midwest. Both maintenance and launch crews went though realistic tests to determine the best of the best. I had some degree of satisfaction that in this exercise my old Titan II wing, the 308th at Little Rock, won the Titan competition. I felt pretty good about that.

Vandenberg had one of the finest golf courses in the Air Force. Since I had been able to play golf very little for many years, I planned to be on the course each Saturday afternoon. One Saturday afternoon about three months after arriving at Vandenberg, my wife Ann received a call from Gen. Bruce Holloway, commanding general of SAC. After she had told him I was on the golf course, he told her to let me finish my game before I returned his call. When I arrived home and telephoned him, he said, "I hate to tell you this but I really do need you back at SAC Headquarters as Deputy Chief of Staff for Operations." There was not much I could say to that message except "Yes, Sir, when would you like to have me there?" Within a week or so I packed my bags and household goods and moved back to Omaha.

In Omaha, working underground where the Deputy Chief of Staff for Operations office was located, about three stories underground,

I used to call up to my friends in their offices above ground to ask them how the weather was. It seemed to me that I always got to work in the morning while it was still dark and it was dark again in the evening when I came up from below ground. Except for meetings or briefing General Holloway or having lunch upstairs, I saw daylight infrequently in the next two years in this position. I had suspected, and now found, that this job was to be extremely demanding. And far more so by our involvement and responsibilities in Vietnam. The number of B-52s kept on continuous alert status along with crews housed in the adjacent alert facility and ready for launch within a very few minutes had remained the same and were frequently exercised. Looking Glass, the airborne Command Post, was still kept in the air 24 hours every day. This was SAC's deterrent role and would not be changed.

SAC's support of the Vietnam War at this time was flown totally from U-Tapao in Thailand with approximately 50 B-52s. The management of this force which required crew rotation every 90 days and rotation of the maintenance personnel that were on TDY status was a tremendous job requiring very careful planning. With these requirements so firm, we also had to continue training and exercising the remaining force to assure that the quality of personnel and their professionalism which was widely known and recognized as the symbol of SAC was maintained. In hindsight, this job prepared me for my next assignment on Guam.

I found myself in the middle of the problems that SAC had in trying to continue to handle the war in Vietnam and maintain an adequate alert force for deterrence. It was decided at this time to deactivate the two B-58 wings that I had commanded because they were more costly to operate than the B-52 and could not be used in a conventional bombing role in Vietnam. Although the B-52s were not originally designed to deliver conventional bombs but were modified to do so, they did an amazing job as a conventional bomber in carrying and dropping 106 500-pound bombs each. Unfortunately even though we were dropping huge numbers of bombs, they were having little effect on the North Vietnamese ability to continue the war. We simply were restrained from using the B-52s effectively. To have used them effectively we would have been hitting strategic targets in North Vietnam. Instead they primarily were being used against interdiction targets which really did little serious damage to North Vietnam. In a very real sense the B-52s were being used as an extension to the Army's field artillery. And it was a terrible waste of air power. Despite this waste, however, the crews flew these missions with typical SAC professionalism and with precision timing.

My job gave me a better understanding of this larger picture. I discovered how to comprehend the real vastness and complexity of SAC, not only physically the most powerful military force in history, but also tightly controlled and very efficiently managed and trained. In addition, it was always changing; the mission, the airplanes, the bomb systems. The only thing that did not change in SAC down through the years and that General LeMay emphasized from the beginning was SAC's dedication to people. People made SAC. SAC acquired the best people and trained them thoroughly. Its mission—maintaining a credible strategic posture that would deter general war—never changed.

The statistical evidence of SAC's effort in Vietnam by 1969 showed me that the command had already flown 40,000 B-52 sorties. We had dropped more than one million tons of bombs. Comparing this to the B-17 capability of World War II, it would require 480,000 B-17 sorties to deliver this bomb tonnage. One B-52 could deliver the equivalent tonnage of 12 B-17s. The KC-135 tankers, operating in Southeast Asia and at this time primarily supporting the tactical operations flown by fighter aircraft, had flown around 100,000 sorties, offloading four billion pounds of fuel. I visited Vietnam several times during this period and traveled to the target area to witness a B-52 bomb drop. The magnitude of these bombs as they descended from a three-ship B-52 cell and the sound as they exploded delivered a deafening swath of destruction on the ground and produced a demoralizing situation for the Viet Cong who were caught in the target area. I could never fail to wonder, however, just how much damage was actually done or even whether there had really been a target there. Bomb damage assessment was very difficult to perform.

On a trip to one of our western bases sometime in August 1971, I had to get up from bed during the night and I hit my right foot against the wooden bed post. I broke a toe. I didn't realize a broken toe could be so painful. A few days later on my return to Omaha, General Holloway told me that he was sending me to Andersen Air Force Base, Guam to take command of the 8th Air Force and to get my third star. I told him that I would appreciate that assignment since with my broken toe I thought duty in the United States was becoming too dangerous. He thought my irony was slightly amusing. As I prepared to move to Guam, General Holloway was very kind to me. My wife Ann had died the previous year, and my daughter Debbie had spent a good bit of time with me during that summer when she was finishing her college work, doing much of her study by correspondence. She had set a date for her marriage in early October, and I wanted her to have a perfect marriage ceremony which was being planned for the same church in which her mother and I had been married and with the same minister Rev. Acker presiding. The reception to follow would be in the newly decorated Officers Club which thanks to Mrs. Holloway's close supervision had turned out beautifully. So with General Holloway's approval I flew to Guam, assumed command of the 8th Air Force on 1 September 1972 and then came back to Omaha in early October for Debbie's wedding. After that I returned to Guam.

Gen. John C. Meyers, CINC SAC, presents to me the outstanding missle trophy award at Vandenberg AFB, CA. in 1969.

Above: *The B-58 hustler that I flew for three years at Bunker Hill, IN and Little Rock, AR. The finest and fastest airplane I ever flew.* **Below:** *The B-58 cockpit was like a fighter plane - stick in right hand and four throttles in your left.*

Above: *My family at Little Rock AFB in 1966. Debbie, Jerry Jr., and my wife Ann.* ***Below*** *Every flight of Strategic Air Commands Airborne Command Post had a General Officer in command. This was one of my many tours - 2nd from right.*

Above: *My B-58 crew at Bunker Hill AFB, IN receiving weather briefing.* ***Below:*** *Col. Hugh B. Robertson (right) deputy commander of operations, presents Col. Gerald W. Johnson, commander of the 305th Bomb Wing, with a Mach II pin. The pin is awarded following the colonel's first supersonic B-58 ride.*

This artwork in simplification depicts the broad background of experiences of General Johnson.

CHAPTER 7
OVER VIETNAM: MY THIRD WAR

It was a cool, crisp early fall morning in Omaha, Nebraska as I proceeded from my quarters to the flight line to join my KC-135 crew for the flight to Andersen Air Force Base on the Island of Guam in the Southwest Pacific. We would need to land at Hickam Air Force Base in Hawaii to refuel, but this would be a minimum time stop. It would be a long day, yet with the change in time I would still land on Guam in late afternoon.

Lt. Gen. Glen Martin, along with many of my staff and friends, met me at the airplane to say farewell and good luck. Glen, the vice commander of SAC, did have a a number of final comments and instructions to give me before I departed. These I appreciated. Even though I was going to a command job, something I knew and appreciated, this one, I felt, would be different and in the coming months I could use all the advice and guidance I could get.

As I taxied out to take-off position I could feel that the airplane was very heavy and carrying a full load of fuel. The take-off roll was long, and the rate of climb after leaving the runway was low as we passed over the neighboring cornfields of Nebraska. My feelings that morning as I left Offutt were very strong and filled with a good bit of nostalgia. I was leaving my second tour of duty at SAC Headquarters, there would not be another one. I had thoroughly enjoyed the long hours and responsibilities of Headquarters duty. I left a part of my self there, too, for I had lost my wife Ann during this tour. There was much to think about. I was alone now and enroute to accept the biggest challenge I had so far been exposed to. At this time, however, I had no idea just how great this challenge would be nor what part I was going to play in finally bringing the horrible Vietnam War to an end.

During this flight I had much time to ponder this war and review in my mind many things concerning it and the United States' involvement that I had never understood. With full knowledge of France's 100-year involvement with Vietnam and particularly during the period subsequent to World War II which finally ended in defeat and withdrawal for the French, I wondered how the United States could have come along so soon thereafter with our own involvement. As the war escalated, the United States never had an objective as to just what we were trying to accomplish. And certainly at no time did it every appear that winning the war was an objective.

The B-52D, the airplane being used in Vietnam, was a wonderful, reliable and very large airplane weighing almost 500,000 pounds at take-off. It was a nuclear bomb delivery airplane, designed to fly high and fast although at subsonic speed and to deliver massive destruction deep inside the Soviet Union. It had been modified by making the bomb bay slightly larger and installing connecting points under the wings where external bomb racks were mounted. It could then carry 106 500-pound bombs. The crews that flew the B-52 were the best available within the USAF. They were trained to deliver nuclear weapons. They were mature professional pilots with most having accumulated several thousand flying hours. The B-52s and their crews had been flying daily missions in Vietnam for almost six years, carrying bombs designed for use in World War II and dropping them with precision on spots in the jungle that were identified by the Army and were thought to be a point on the North Vietnamese north-south supply route or some stockpiled military supplies. Because these B-52 crews were professionals and highly trained in their specialities, they flew these missions with the same precise timing and accurate delivery as if they were delivering a nuclear weapon. All the Commanding General of MACV (Military Assistance Command Vietnam) had to do was to ask for a strike of B-52s. He would get them in whatever number he asked for, and delivery would be exactly to the designated target spot and exactly at the desired time. Gen. Abrahms was commanding general of MACV when I arrived on Guam and during my first visit to him at Saigon, he spent a good deal of time discussing the B-52s and the great job they were doing. It was obvious that he was very proud of them and appreciated their flexibility in mission and target planning, precision in timing and accuracy.

This was the kind of war I was walking into in September 1971. I didn't like it when I was Deputy Chief of Staff for Operations at SAC Headquarters, and I certainly didn't like it now that I would be the commander of these crews and would have to defend the policies of my superiors in the conduct of this ridiculous no-win war. What could I say to the crews in justification of all the temporary duty they had spent in Southeast Asia, living away from their families and daily flying missions and dropping bombs that they knew were hurting the enemy in only a very minor way.

Immediately after the United States destroyers Turner Joy and Maddox were attacked in international waters by North Vietnamese torpedo boats in the Gulf of Tonkin in 1964, the Joint Chiefs of Staff proposed to quickly end the aggressive actions of North Vietnam with decisive airstrikes dubbed the "94 Target Plan," which had been developed by the Strategic Air Command. This plan called for massive air strikes against the 94 most significant military targets in North Vietnam. This plan was rejected. One year later it was again proposed and rejected. Despite the fact that the plan was proposed and rejected twice, it was not forgotten. These 94 strategic targets that SAC had identified remained the key industrial and transportation centers in North Vietnam that supported the war in South Vietnam and which could not be hit by United States air power. Had this plan been accepted and implemented in 1964, the war could have been brought to an end with the saving of untold numbers of young Americans.

By this time Americans had become totally disillusioned with the performance of the military. They were being told that air power was totally ineffective, and it was. The ineffectiveness of air power occurred only because of the way it was used and because of decisions made by civilian leaders, not military leaders. Everyone was frustrated with the conduct of this war. Jane Fonda and former Attorney General Ramsay Clark visited Hanoi and sympathized with the enemy. The news media seemed to have forgotten which side they were on. The Army began to pull out of South Vietnam. Peace efforts and talks were undertaken, but Hanoi was confident that time was on its side and these talks were largely ineffective.

As I reviewed in my mind these things on my way to Guam, I seemed to conclude that if this war were to be brought to an end, it must be done primarily by the use of air power. I believed the 94 Target Plan was still a viable option if only approval to implement it could be obtained.

Although on the map Guam appears to be an isolated island in the South Pacific, it is, in fact, a major crossroad for travelers through the area. Because of the change in time by the crossing of the International Date Line, Guam was also frequently used as a stopover point for the traveler to reset his biorythmic clock. This phenomenon just might provide a chance for me to discuss and stress with a United States leader the fact that our air power had been and was being misused. It was not that the United States did not have the capability to end the war, it was the fact that the effective use of our military air capability had been so restricted that it was largely ineffective. Just maybe some of my forthcoming visitors might accept and understand this fact and attempt to cause some change in Washington's policies. My plan would be worth a try.

All of these thoughts ran through my mind. This was the biggest challenge the Air Force had given me. Quite honestly, the commander of the 8th Air Force was so far down the line of command that influence with the military and civilian leaders above me would be minimal, and decisions with respect to how the B-52s were to be employed and decisions as to what targets were to be hit really did not rest at all with the commander in the field. Certainly I could express my opinions and I could add my recommendations to what was going on, but the decisions to act I knew came right out of Washington, quite often with the approval of the President before they were put into effect. As I landed on Guam in September 1971, I wondered both if and how I could affect the war that had been dragging on to become eventually America's longest war.

I began my responsibilities as commanding general of 8th Air Force, directing all SAC operations in the western Pacific and Southeast Asia. One of my first tasks was to become acquainted with the commanders and men of the wings and squadrons under my command at Andersen, U-Tapao and Kadena. Col. Glen W. Dunlap commanded the 43rd Strategic Bomb Wing at Andersen, and Col. Dudley G. Kavanaugh commanded the 376th Air Refuelling Wing at Kadena. Commanding the the 307th Strategic Bomb Wing at U-Tapao was Brig. Gen. Frank W. Elliott. I spent as much time at U-Tapao and Kadena with the troops as I could. I also often flew to Saigon in South Vietnam to confer with Gen. John W. Vogt Jr. (another flying school classmate of mine), commanding general of 7th Air Force, and with General Abrahms and his staff with whom I worked to coordinate Arc Light and Linebacker missions.

As it was important to gain support for the air base by Guamanians, a Civilian Advisory Council was formed and their effort contributed a great deal to the success of 8th Air Force's purpose on Guam. We also organized a Guam chapter of the Air Force Association, a national group that had chapters in each state to promote the interests of air power.

In November 1971 Dr. Henry Kissinger, Secretary of State, stopped overnight on his way to China to set up advance plans for President Nixon's forthcoming trip to Beijing. He was suffering from a cold and his watch had stopped. More important to me, he had never been inside a B-52. Here was my first chance to explain the B-52 and what it was really capable of accomplishing with strategic targets. First, I took him by the dispensary to get something for his cold, then to the Base Exchange where he very carefully selected a replacement watch from the selection of relatively inexpensive ones available. Then to a B-52. I wanted this stop to be the last one so he would not be thinking of anything else he needed to do.

Secretary Kissinger was very impressed by the B-52 and the crew whom I had arranged to be there when he arrived. I wanted him to see firsthand what the airplane looked like and how the crew appeared and sounded as they explained a typical mission, how the target was received, how the strike was planned, what the air refueling required, and where the rendezvous with the KC-135 tanker would take place. He spent a lot of time outside the airplane and inside where he was amazed by the very small space available to the different crew members.

Andersen had a nice set of VIP quarters where Mr. Kissinger would stay, and I arranged to have dinner served there where I would join him. In the relative quiet of these quarters over dinner I undertook to explain how badly I felt the Vietnam War had been managed and how particularly unfortunate it was that air power had not been effectively used. Before undertaking the discussion of this subject I was concerned about bringing it up and had no way of knowing how it would be received. I expected his attitude would be defensive. I was, therefore, surprised to find that he did not interrupt me, but asked several questions and was especially attentive as I explained the 94 Target Plan. Dr. Kissinger again stopped at Andersen in June 1972, and I was surprised to find how much detail he remembered concerning his previous visit in November 1971.

In the meantime President Nixon had stopped overnight in late February 1972 on his way to Beijing. It was difficult for me to have private time with President Nixon since the Navy, the Coast Guard, the Governor, and leading political figures of Guam were on hand for his arrival. I did manage, however, before his departure the next day to bring our conversation around to SAC, my mission, and the B-52s, and I emphasized the vast capability I had available with the B-52s, stressing that this capability had not yet been used in all the years the United States had been in the Vietnam War. He appeared to want to pick up on this point, but unfortunately we were interrupted by one of his aides and I never had another opportunity to continue the discussion.

I felt that I had used these opportunities as best as I could, and as events later developed I wondered if I might have contributed to the decision ultimately made by President Nixon regarding the use of air power against North Vietnam—Code name Linebacker II.

During the first four to five months I was on Guam the situation in Vietnam had changed little. We were still bombing targets in South Vietnam identified by MAVC. The Army was operating very little and was slowly pulling out of South Vietnam. The peace talks in Paris were on and off with apparently no progress being made. I had visited MACV Headquarters in Saigon on several occasions but was never able to get any feel that the war was nearing the end. Rather, it seemed the commanders and staff were reconciled to the status quo and were just "doing their jobs" until their tour was finished. I felt this attitude was understandable. After all, how long can highly trained, well-qualified and effective military officers maintain their enthusiasm and initiative in the face of guidance that came down for seven years from the highest levels that indicated no objectives, no will or desire to win and no acceptance of recommendations from the field commanders. This situation of status quo was very demoralizing, and it was not helped by the news media whose reports seemed to favor the United States to "get out at any cost."

I was called back to SAC Headquarters in Omaha in late January 1972 for some detailed briefings and discussion concerning the possibility of a rather massive increase in the B-52 effort in Vietnam that was being considered. On my way back to Guam the next day, I stopped in Honolulu to brief CINCPAC (Commander in Chief Pacific Area Command) on this potential build-up and the impact it would have on CINCPAC facilities. SAC's plan at the outset seemed almost insurmountable. The plan called for 200 B-52s to be under my command, and I had only two bases that were capable of supporting the huge B-52. Approximately 180 KC-135 tankers were also to be placed under my command to support the B-52 operations from Andersen and the increased fighter operations in Vietnam. I was now using Andersen, U-Tapao and Kadena for flying missions. Since the increase in B-52s would have to go to U-Tapao and Andersen, the KC-135s would have to be moved to other bases. But where? I had worked out this problem as I flew from Omaha to Honolulu and had decided on Clark Field in the Philippines and the Ching Chuan Kang base in Taiwan. CINCPAC agreed and authorized me to work directly with the Government of Taiwan and the commander of Clark Field.

As I flew from Hickam to Guam I realized that the build-up in all its magnitude was mind-boggling. In addition to the increased numbers of aircraft I thought of the increased numbers of crew members and support personnel. Where would I put them all? There simply wasn't any space.

I will try to convey the "vastness, complexity and the implication" of 8th Air Force's mission in Southeast Asia from its early start-up to the last year of the Vietnam War—1972—and Linebacker II, the 11-day war from 18 December to 29 December. To explain the magnitude of this operation and the test of men's ability to assimilate and effectively manage the size of the force we had at Andersen and U-Tapao reveals an accomplishment unparalleled in the history of air power.

Strategic Air Command's involvement in Southeast Asia began in the spring of 1964 when I was Commander of the 95th Bomb Wing at El Paso, Texas and flew the first B-52 to Andersen Air Force Base on Guam. Airborne refueling tanker operations utilizing the KC-135 commenced in 1964 to support the tactical fighters operating in Thailand and South Vietnam. These developments were followed by B-52 strikes from Guam starting in 1965.

As the demand for B-52 strikes increased during the following years, U-Tapao Air Base, Thailand, which was being built, became the second base for B-52 operations. As the demand for air refueling sorties increased Kadena Air Base, Okinawa became the primary KC-135 base. However, the KC-135s used almost every available runway including those at Guam, U-Tapao, the Philippines, Taiwan and Kadena.

The major build-up of the B-52 force in Southeast Asia started on 10 February 1972. Up to that time we had delivered 21 sorties per day. Then we slowly built them up and by June 1972 we were flying 105 B-52 sorties per day, 66 of them from Guam and 39 from U-Tapao seven days a week. Sixty-six sorties from Andersen in one day equaled the total number of training sorties a B-52 wing in the United States would fly in one month. We flew almost 2,000 combat sorties from one base each month. The code name for these operations was Bullet Shot I, II, III and IV. This operation deployed B-52Ds and Gs and their crews on TDY from SAC bases in the United States to build up operations on Guam and at U-Tapao in Thailand. Aircraft from as far away as the state of Maine were flown nonstop to Guam, a trip of some 10,000 miles.

Only by enlarging and renovating existing parking spaces and building new ones were we able to accept this huge force. Parking hardstands, equivalent to a runway 10,000 feet long and 200 feet wide was constructed in just 57 days. By the end of May there were 200 B-52s and approximately 275 six-man crews within 8th Air Force and on only two bases. This contingent was about 50 percent of SAC's total bomber force and 75 percent of all combat-ready crews. This force was the equivalent of more than 13 stateside bomber bases. Only by these changes were we able to fly 105 B-52 sorties per day, 66 from Guam and 39 from U-Tapao.

Concurrent with the bomber build-up was the KC-135 tanker build-up to provide aerial refueling for the Guam bombers and the increased tactical fighter forces. From our previous posture of three tanker bases I added Bangkok, Takhli, and Korst in Thailand, Clark in the Philippines, and Ching Chuan Kang in Taiwan. I spent a lot of my time negotiating for these bases and arranging for the necessary support, i.e., parking, housing, fuel, transportation and food.

Andersen Air Force Base was built to accommodate approximately 3,000 personnel. As the number of B-52s increased, so did the support people. More than 12,000 military personnel including 216 complete six-man bomber crews crowded the base. Billets were saturated. We had to improvise, using first the old "tin city" that had been built during World War II and then expanding into tents that had been put in place. Despite my best effort to house 1,000 people in tents on base, there were still 250 people in downtown hotels, which with their travel time further expanded their 12-hour duty day.

The people being sent to me came primarily from SAC units. However, when SAC began to run out of resources, then other commands and overseas units were required to fill our needs. We were a melting pot for people from all over the Air Force. From the beginning I demanded that the senior man in a shop or section was to be the boss regardless of whether he was permanently assigned to the base, or was on temporary duty from SAC or some other command. This plan really worked.

The bombers and crews had been in Southeast Asia since 1965

and always in a temporary duty status, which meant about five months in Southeast Asia, then one month at home., then back to Southeast Asia for another five months. Many individuals had spent more than three years in Southeast Asia in temporary duty status.

This rapid buildup in numbers of personnel, airplanes and sortie rate required the movement of a great many people from where they lived to where they ate and then to where they worked. We needed many buses. The only airplane we had at that time that could carry a large military bus was the C-5. This airplane had been controversial during its early design and production phase. It did at this time, however, prove its worth. Without this airplane our sortie rate build-up would have been delayed until surface transportation could deliver the buses. I mentioned this situation on several occasions to visiting Congressmen. One Congressman asked, "General, were those buses being flown over by C-5s filled with troops?" How nice it would be if all Congressmen were equally efficiency-minded.

The management problem of instant readiness was gigantic. To meet the sortie requirements, planes were refueled and pre-flighted and bombs loaded in four hours—half the normal time. Phase inspections of the bombers, i.e., periodic tests of systems, airframes, tires and the like, were done in eight hours—five times faster than normal. On one occasion a tire change on a B-52 which usually required two-and-one-half hours was accomplished in 18 minutes on the taxiway, the airplane being fully bomb-loaded and all eight engines running. The men's muscles and minds had to be concentrated on the job with such time constraints. Many times a maintenance person, who went aboard the aircraft to repair an electronic or radio problem while the airplane taxied for take-off and was unable to complete the work, would then stay aboard and complete the work enroute to the target with no regard for his personal safety and no knowledge of where the mission would take him. Such was the dedication of these fine young men who made up my maintenance force.

The ground control operation that we developed for these sorties and that worked effectively started with the Deputy Commander of Operations. Under his command were two Charlies, one B-52D and one B-52G. These were manned by the best instructor pilots we had. They could help the crews solve many of their airplane and operational problems which arose after engine start and before take-off. Uncle Ned was Charlie's maintenance counterpart; Uncle Tom directed all airplane taxiing and towing operations.

It took about two hours to refuel a B-52. We had 10 times more B-52s than refueling pits. In addition, many airplanes needed ground engine run-ups to 100 percent for test purposes, and there were few on-base places at which to accomplish this task. Cousin Fred had a pool of 12 taxi crews just to move the aircraft to the sites where they needed to be for a special purpose. He worked directly for Uncle Tom in keeping the wizardy of airplane maintenance and support needs moving and flowing throughout the airfield. All of these control centers were manned by SAC's best people, and they were superb at their jobs—intelligent, knowledgeable, dedicated.

This tremendous build-up and continuing operation did have its problems. One of these was typhoons. We were forced to evacuate Andersen only once and that was in October 1972. We managed to accomplish the evacuation without a major problem. However, the second typhoon that passed through the area caused gigantic complications in completing the missions. Just getting through the refueling areas and to the targets and back was often a difficult effort. In July 1972 one of our B-52 crews was forced to abandon their aircraft due to insurmountable problems and they spent 30 hours in life rafts as Typhoon Rita passed over them. The seas were too rough for surface vessels to rescue them. They were finally picked up by a submarine operating from Guam. I was returning to Guam from U-Tapao the night they were taken aboard the submarine and was able to observe on my KC-135 radar the surfaced submarine in the eye of the storm. It was an eerie feeling to realize what was taking place down there on that very rough ocean. Five of the six crew members were rescued.

As we worked through the summer and fall of 1972, the missions became more hazardous because we flew farther north in South Vietnam. It was inevitable that we would have our first combat loss of a B-52. That happened 22 November 1972, the first B-52 of the war to be a victim of enemy action—a SAM, the surface-to-air missile that Russia supplied to North Vietnam. A B-52D from U-Tapao suffered hits from a SAM that had exploded 150 feet off the wing, causing fires in both wings and the fuselage. The crew managed to fly the crippled aircraft over a hundred miles before its engines flamed out only five miles to the Thai border. Their airplane was a flaming torch without power, but the crew chose to remain on board and to attempt to glide across the border. Just as the B-52 crossed the Mekong River, the right wing tip broke off and the airplane started an uncontrollable spiral downward. The crew managed to eject near the U.S. Marine base at Nakhon Phanom. This was the first B-52 lost to enemy ground fire in seven-and-a-half years of B-52 combat operations in Southeast Asia.

This level of activity comprised our situation and posture in October 1972 when Dr. Henry Kissinger announced to the public that "Peace is at hand." Not quite, he discovered, because the North Vietnamese again walked out from negotiations that had been underway in Paris. Several weeks later President Nixon made the decision that would allow our B-52s to be utilized for the first time as they should have been used in the beginning, strategically against the major industrial targets in North Vietnam that supported the enemy's war effort. These targets were primarily the same ones selected in the 94 Target Plan.

Late in the afternoon of 15 December 1972, I was advised to prepare for maximum effort bombing operations on targets in the Hanoi and Haiphong areas of North Vietnam. This operation would be known as Linebacker II and would commence on 18 December. A three-day maximum effort was specified in this message, but it also stated that it might be extended. We continued to fly sorties at a reduced rate on the 16th and 17th of December.

On the first night of Linebacker II, we launched 87 B-52s from Guam in 90 minutes and 42 from U-Tapao, 129 aircraft in all. As we approached 18 December, the impact of the support required became even more gigantic. Under the earlier Bullet Shot operations, we had launched three airplanes and recovered three airplanes about every hour, 44 launches and recoveries every 24 hours. This operation normally required six crew buses to transport the crew members. For this first night launch, we needed 87 buses to take crews to each of the 87 B-52s. We had only 50. The inflight kitchen, which normally prepared 18 inflight lunches each hour, this night needed more than 500 lunches at one time. All other support of this mission—bomb loading, refueling, dining hall meals and the like—was equally impacted. Mission folders and crew data regarding tanker rendezvous points, refueling tracks, compression points, rendezvous with the 42 aircraft from U-Tapao, initial points (IPs), egress routes, SAM sites, enemy airplanes expected, had to be prepared for the crews. Many times during the days that followed, due to delays in receiving target approvals, mission information was put aboard the aircraft just prior to departure and the information had to be sorted, assimilated and understood by each crew member while enroute to the target.

During my tenure as Deputy for Operations at SAC prior to my arriving at Guam, we had studied the use of B-52s in North Vietnam in great detail, exploring the pros and cons of high versus low altitude, night versus day sorties. We had concluded that high altitude night missions would be most effective and would result in fewest losses. Estimating losses was difficult, however, since we had no experience with SAMs nor with the effectiveness of ECM, the electronic countermeasure aboard each plane. The ECM equipment was designed to jam the enemy radar in such a way that the enemy could determine neither the exact aircraft range nor bearing. Some estimates of B-52 aircraft losses if they were used in combat missions over North Vietnam were as high as 30 percent.

To record the myriad of details of a complex operation such as Linebacker II requires a collective memory of its many participants at different levels of responsibility and action. In my command position I saw the big picture of intricate plans, the necessary coordination among many military units, precise timing over the selected targets, and a host of other elements. During these days I spent as much time as I possibly could with the crews both before the mission and after they returned. I talked with them at the briefings and individually. I wanted them to know of my concern for their safety and my awareness of the dangers involved. Mostly I wanted them to know that they were participating in the use of their B-52s for the first time in an effective manner; that these missions and targets they were to hit were the ones we had wanted to strike since 1966; and that for the first time in all these long years of war they were bringing it to an end. Through these close contacts I was able to know the feelings and attitudes of the crews. I could not have been prouder of this group of true professionals. I was also able to know if some of the details of our plans worked in the actual combat conditions they met. Intelligence officers debriefed the crews more fully, and airplane commanders wrote reports of their missions.

The B-52D carried a crew of six. The pilot and co-pilot sat in the top forward position. The EW (Electronic Warfare Officer) was seated on the same level facing the rear several yards behind the pilots. The navigator and the radar navigator were seated side by side on the lower level facing forward. The gunner was in the tail of the airplane facing to the rear with a 270-degree visual view which was very helpful as a rear observer. The crew placement of the B-52G was the same except the gunner's position was beside the EW and therefore the G-model had no visual observation to the rear of the aircraft except by radar. This was the aircraft crews' environment as they flew these long missions, 12 to 14 hours plus. It was the environment in which they experienced the most violent attacks the North Vietnamese could make with Soviet-built MIG fighters and Soviet-built surface-to-air missiles (SAMs).

The B-52D did not have power-boosted controls as the later G and H models had. It took a lot of plain muscle power to manhandle these 400,000 pound airplanes at night in close formation with SAM missiles streaking up from the ground and coming from many directions. The fact that these crews could fly through this environment and make their rendezvous points and time with air-refueling tankers, turning points and target time with precise timing is a tribute to their professionalism and motivation.

The pilots were authorized to maneuver as much as possible to try to avoid direct hits by the SAMS except just prior to bomb release. At this time the pilot must fly straight and level to permit the bomb computer gyros to stabilize. One crew while in this stabilizing position and only a few seconds from the bomb release point saw a SAM coming that would obviously hit the airplane if the pilot did not maneuver. The co-pilot calmly announced to the crew by interphone that the SAM would strike in moments. The pilot held his course. The bombs were released on the target and almost instantly the SAM struck the aircraft. Such was the dedication of these crews.

To pave the way for the bomber missions, other aircraft carried out a pattern of activity designed to reduce the North Vietnam defensive effort. Air Force fighters of Tacair roared off their bases to attack North Vietnam MIG bases and other defenses. Marine F-4s orbited to protect the tanker and EC-121 forces (early warning, fighter control and reconnaissance aircraft) from MIGs; F-111 fighter-bombers delivered surprise hits on MIG air bases. At the right time, EB-66 jammers provided additional ECM protection for the strike forces, and chaff corridors were laid down to confuse enemy defenses on the ground. Unfortunately due to winds at altitude the chaff drifted from the flight route and was often ineffective.

Linebacker II was a combined and carefully planned and executed operation. All of the players demonstrated their expertise in performing their specific part. After this preparation, three waves of B-52s from Guam and U-Tapao would begin their separate attacks on the targets selected for the night. Certain details of the first Linebacker II mission on 18 December convey the magnitude and complexity of the mission.

At 1945 Hanoi time, Wave One of B-52s from U-Tapao began their attack on the Kinh No complex, Yen Vien complex and three airfields north of Hanoi. Unfortunately, the prevailing 100-knot northwest winds blew the chaff clouds out of the planned corridors, and the B-52s had to count on their own ECM (electronic countermeasures) to cope with the threat of SAMs. For the first time a B-52 gunner shot down an enemy aircraft, a MIG, in combat. Meanwhile, B-52s from Guam attacked vehicle repair yards at Kinh No and the rail yards at Yen Vien. By this time 50 SAMs had been fired at the attacking force. A B-52D Lilac 3 was damaged by a SAM as it tried to make its post-target turn (PTT) after releasing its bombs over the Kinh No complex. The pilot of Lilac 3 was able to coax his aircraft to U-Tapao and landed successfully.

After midnight, Wave Two consisting of B-52s from Guam approached similar targets plus Hanoi rail yards. Peach 2 of this wave was hit on the left wing as the wave turned from the target after bomb release. The crew reported that when they were hit there was a deafening noise, everything was very bright for a second, then totally dark. The external fuel tank and two outboard engines under the left wing were missing along with part of the wing tip. Fuel was coming from many holes along the left wing and fire was streaming from the huge hole where the two engines had been. Most of the flight instruments were not working. Cabin pressurization was lost and the oxygen system had been hit and the oxygen gauges were rapidly falling. The seventh crew member and the gunner had been hit but were not seriously wounded. Two F-4 fighters joined the bomber to provide protection from MIG fighters and to assess the damage. It was serious but the pilot was trying to reach the safety of Thailand before abandoning the airplane. They were descending rapidly and by then the entire left wing was engulfed in flames and there was no possibility of saving the airplane. Soon after crossing the border into Thailand the pilot hit the switch turning on the red abandon light. The six crew members ejected and the seventh bailed out through the hole where the navigator had ejected. They were all rescued and flown to U-Tapao.

Wave Three, the largest and last wave of Day One, consisted of B-52s from Guam and from U-Tapao. They hit the Hanoi radio station and Hanoi rail yards and attacked the Kinh No complex for the third time that night. The B-52s targeted against Hanoi Radio came up against the heaviest SAM attack of the night when at least 50 SAMs were fired against them. Not until the last cell passed the target did a SAM score. The airplane pilot and three crew members ejected and were taken prisoner soon after landing. Wave Three received the heaviest opposition of the campaign, 154 SAM firings and heavy AAA (anti-aircraft artillery). That first night we lost three B-52s plus extensive battle damage to several more.

A review of Day One attacks revealed weaknesses in planning and execution that needed immediate adjustment. Unfortunately as Day Two missions were already planned and briefed and crews were prepared for take-off before the last of Day One aircraft landed, there was little opportunity to apply lessons learned on Day One to Day Two. The need for wider chaff corridors, shorter periods between waves that would not allow the enemy time to reload SAM launchers, the disadvantage of the steeply banked post-target turns, the repetition of the same altitudes and air speeds by each wave—all of these had to be examined and altered.

Wave One of Day Two sent 21 bombers out of Guam against Kinh No again. A large number of SAMs were sighted, but no B-52s were lost or damaged. Wave Two's 21 bombers from Guam and 15 from U-Tapao attacked the Bac Giang transshipment point and the Hanoi Radio station. Several of the SAMs scored hits. The cell Hazel 3 laid itself open to a hit when it was nine miles off its inbound track; it lost its cell integrity for mutual ECM support, and had a problem with several inoperative jamming transmitters. The airplane, however, was not forced down. Wave Three hit the Yen Vien complex and a thermal power plant without any damage to the airplanes. Because of the light damage and no losses of Day Two and due to the long lead time from mission planning to execution, it was decided to use the same attack plan on Day Three.

On Day Three, 20 December, Wave One, attacking a repair facility, rail yards and a warehouse area, did not encounter SAM firings until the last of this Wave's planes approached the targets. It appeared that the North Vietnamese defense allowed the initial cells of aircraft to pass through in order for their defense to recognize the route of the wave. Many of the B-52Gs had problems on this day because of their unmodified ECMs which could not protect them from the SAMs. Day Three is remembered as the day with the greatest number of losses in the Linebacker II campaign four B-52Gs and two

B-52Ds shot down, a third D model sustaining serious damage. Over 200 SAMs were fired at the bombers causing the greatest single day loss in the whole campaign.

The third night was a significant one for me. As always during these 11 days I was up most of every night following the action and analyzing the reports coming in from the crews. This night was no different. As the reports from the first wave started to come in, it was obvious that the North Vietnamese were very determined this night. Two 52Gs and one 52D from the first wave went down. This loss could have occurred because the North Vietnamese were aware of the original message which called for a three-day maximum effort. This was the third day, and if North Vietnam could repulse this last attack it would have benefited their cause tremendously. I was greatly concerned. While these thoughts were going through my mind, I received a call from General Vogt in Saigon, commanding general of 7th Air Force. He was also greatly concerned about our losses from the first wave. He said he had no idea what was happening but strongly recommended that I recall the remaining two waves and permit him to analyze the North Vietnam (NVN) defenses and try to determine changes in their defense plans before we launched another mission.

I still had time to recall the remaining two waves. However, I said to General Vogt, "I can't do that, John. This is the 8th Air Force which has never in all the years since 1942 turned back from their target. These are SAC B-52s and SAC is the deterrent force for the free world. We cannot set such a precedent. The next two waves must continue."

General Vogt reluctantly accepted my decision. I then called Gen. John C. Meyer, Commander in Chief SAC, to relay this conversation and my decision. He agreed with my decision. We then discussed the B-52Gs that with unmodified ECM were bearing the brunt of the losses and we agreed to recall two cells of these aircraft.

Starting on Day Four, 21 December, the waves were compressed to put all bombs on target in 15 minutes instead of 30; post-target turns were changed to allow an overwater exit from North Vietnam; altitude separations of the waves were increased; and only B-52Gs with modified ECM equipment were sent against the most heavily SAM-defended areas. In addition, chaff was dispersed to create multiple corridors to confuse the enemy or to devise a block of chaff. The latter would eliminate the stereotyped corridors, thus overcoming the wind's effect on chaff's position and corridor placement.

On Day Four all B-52Ds striking targets in North Vietnam were flown from U-Tapao. Because of their shorter distance to targets, they needed less fuel and could then carry greater bomb loads, and they did not need aerial refueling. On this night SAM storage depots were also hit. The Guam aircraft were scheduled against targets in South Vietnam. This was to let the North Vietnamese know we had the capability to strike both North and South Vietnam simultaneously and therefore any forces they had in the South were not safe from attack. On Day Five, F-111s flew airfield suppression sorties just prior to the arrival of the B-52s approaching from a westerly direction on six different tracks to attack targets in the Haiphong area. The North Vietnamese were unable to respond effectively as only 43 SAMs were fired, and no B-52 was downed. Day Six's different scenario scheduled targets not even close to the Hanoi-Haiphong area. B-52s from Guam rejoined the attack with 12 B-52Ds along with 18 Ds from U-Tapao. Their targets, the Lang Dang rail yards and three nearby SAM sites, lay about 18 miles from the Chinese border. Their approach took them over the Gulf of Tonkin until they turned northwesterly and then inland toward their targets. Leaving their targets, they would turn back on a south heading to withdraw over the Gulf. To deceive the enemy's defense, each aircraft descended 2,000 feet 180 seconds prior to bomb release. After release, they changed altitudes again. Only four or five SAMs were fired at the B-52s that hit the Lang Dang rail yards within a 16-minute period. Apparently the North Vietnamese were not alerted because the target area had not been "prepared" ahead of time by the Tacair forces.

On Day Seven, the day before Christmas, the 30 B-52s from U-Tapao again surprised the enemy defense forces as they split up their forces at varied altitudes to attack railroad yards. Nineteen SAMs, a few MIGs and intense AAA fire were able to damage only one B-52.

President Nixon ordered a 36-hour Christmas Day stand down in North and South Vietnam. Air crews rested. Planners organized the next maximum effort. Maintenance personnel performed needed maintenance on airplanes. North Vietnam got a break to rebuild its defenses. As it turned out the Christmas break benefited our forces more since they restored our ability to strongly restrike the North on 26 December.

This 36-hour break in the war was the first time we really had the opportunity to carefully review all that had been accomplished during the previous seven days of continuing strikes with next night aircraft taking off as the previous night's aircraft were landing. As I thought back over those last seven days it seemed amazing to me that we could have adjusted to this operation and ironed out so many problems so quickly, not only in the air but on the ground. The support problems we encountered on Day One that seemed so insurmountable had been largely eliminated. We had a smoothly running operation. One concern I had was with the very limited rest the hardworking ground crews were getting. After putting in such long hours in their work shifts they simply didn't want to go home for rest. They wanted to see their aircraft launch, to watch the result of their efforts. It seemed also that we had been fairly successful in implementing changes in formation, tactics and routing to and from the targets. There was a good deal of lag, however, due to many of these changes requiring the approval of SAC Headquarters and sometimes of Washington. The reports from the crews and their recommendations were particularly important and were acted upon as quickly as possible. This 36-hour stand down provided much needed time for sorting out and obtaining approval of many more important concepts of the operation.

Day Eight, 26 December 1972, was to be a maximum effort and planning for it started on 25 December. Although this was Christmas and our flight crews were enjoying a stand down and a badly needed rest, it didn't mean that all were resting. For myself, my commanders, the planners and certainly the support and maintenance people, it was a busy period. In June when our activities had increased to 105 sorties daily, I had had a telephone scrambler machine installed in the bedroom of my quarters. Due to the difference in time between Omaha and Guam I found that I was being called by CINCSAC or members of his staff at all hours of the night. Since the calls almost always involved discussion of classified material, before putting this machine in my bedroom I had to go to my office to take the call; hence I was getting very little sleep. During Linebacker II this bedside phone proved extremely valuable. It meant that on a 24-hour basis I was always immediately available for discussion with Omaha, CINCPAC or Washington. I spent very little time in my quarters during these days, and when there, rarely was I able to get more than one hour of sleep without interruption. This had been the situation during these 36 hours.

Day Eight was to be the largest single launch of B-52s in the history of SAC, tactics had been drastically changed. The plan for this day was to strike Hanoi targets with four bomber waves coming from different directions, and the lead aircraft from each wave would release bombs at exactly the same time. The remaining three waves making up the total force would approach in similar fashion to hit the Thai Nguyen railroad yards and the Haiphong railroad yards and transformer station. This meant that 72 B-52s would converge on a small area around Hanoi to effect simultaneous concentrated bombing. Timing was critical, and the tactics had not been tested or flown before. This was a true test at night in close formation of the flying ability and professionalism of these B-52 pilots and navigators. The Soviet trawler, which was always near Guam and could observe what was happening at Andersen, had obviously alerted North Vietnam that this massive force was enroute and their defenses were ready. There were many MIGs flying and the SAMs came up in great numbers. The B-52s' new tactics, however, were largely effective and the concentrated attack saturated and overloaded the enemy's defenses. We suffered only two losses. But they were tragic. Ebony 2, a B-52D, had taken a direct hit and exploded in mid-aiir. Miraculously four of the crew survived the explosion and became POWs. Ash 1 had also been hit with severe damage to the aircraft. The pilot attempted to get to U-Tapao and almost made it. He crashed just short of the runway with only the co-pilot and tail gunner surviving.

In this Day Eight attack, the B-52s dropped 9,932 bombs, totaling over 2,100 tons in less than 22 minutes. The North Vietnamese fired up to 68 SAMs but with the Tacair support of chaff corridors, bombed MIG airfields, and ECM support, their effectiveness dropped. By Days Nine and Ten the U.S. had gained superiority. SAMs were fired with poor accuracy, evidence that the enemy command and control network was breaking down. On Day Eleven, 29 December, 30 B-52s from Guam and U-Tapao bombed rail yards, support facilities, storage areas, and SAM sites. The 23 SAMs fired were ineffective. The 11-day strategic use of B-52 air power was vindicated. Washington acted immediately.

The Commander-in-Chief of the Pacific received instructions from the Joint Chiefs of Staff that all military operations in North Vietnam north of the 20th parallel would cease at 0659 hours Hanoi time 30 December. Shortly after noon on 29 December, the last B-52G touched down at Guam. The North Vietnamese had decided it was time to return to the peace table again. Linebacker II was over.

At the end of this awesome 11-day effort, I wanted to commend thousands of people and hundreds of B-52 crews for their courageous effort. The B-52s which first flew in 1949 were an aging aircraft yet they had successfully penetrated a highly sophisticated air defense system with a loss rate of less than two percent. The pilots and crews, the maintenance and support people, deserved the highest commendation for their diligence and dedication. Those who stayed at home while their men flew and worked deserved acclaim for their courage during the 11-day war. Linebacker II was without question among the finest military operations ever undertaken and nothing before or since equals it in terms of magnitude, precision and results. It was successful because of the professionalism, courage and dedication of the men and women of the United States Air Force. Twenty-six days after the halt of Linebacker II bombing, the peace accords were signed in Paris and our prisoners of war were on their way home.

I think the greatest tribute to Linebacker II was paid by Col. David Winn, who was a prisoner of the NVN for six years. As his airplane passed over Guam on his way home after being released from prison in NVN, he radioed the following message to me "I cannot overfly Guam enroute home without expressing to you and all members of your command my appreciation and that of all POWs for effecting our release. On the night of 18 December 1972 when we heard the bomb explosions we immediately realized that in those quantities they had to be coming from B-52s and for the first time we realized that finally the doors of our cells were being unlocked."

Air power when properly used can be the decisive force. On 10 April 1988 on NBC's "Meet the Press" program, former President Nixon was asked what he considered to be his biggest mistake while in office. Without any hesitation he replied, "My biggest mistake was not to bomb Hanoi and Haiphong in 1969." He referred directly to SAC's Linebacker II operation in December 1972 and credited these raids with ending the war. One cannot help pondering the question, "Why wasn't air power such as employed during the mining of Haiphong Harbor in May 1972 and the massive Linebacker II strikes of December 1972 carried out sooner?" And, in grim rhetoric, this question can be imagined arising from national and private burial grounds throughout America and unmarked graves in Southeast Asia where some 58,000 Americans lay buried. How many lives could have been saved?

During the last three days of the Linebacker II action we flew with relative impunity over North Vietnam. The enemy had run out of SAMs, and our varied tactics outwitted their defenses that earlier had caused 15 B-52s to go down with 92 crew members, 10 of the 15 aircraft being destroyed over Vietnam with 62 crew members. Fourteen of them were killed in action, 33 became POWs and were subsequently repatriated, and 14 remained missing in action. Had we continued the bombardment for a few more days, it is believed that North Vietnam would have sued for peace on our terms. Instead we stopped, the war ended, our prisoners were released. Yet we left the North Vietnamese free to effect the cruelest of retaliation against the people of South Vietnam, Cambodia and Laos.

At this time President Nixon attempted to settle matters in Cambodia. With the war having ended in Vietnam and our adversaries having formed a new respect for us, probably as a result of pressure applied by strategic air power, I believe total resolution of Communist aggression in Southeast Asia would soon have been reached. However, America retreated and in so doing, signed death warrants for millions of Cambodians.

Congresswoman Bella Abzug was mong the leaders in Congress whose strident voices successfully cut off all funds for continued bombing operations against the enemy in Cambodia and Laos. When the B-52 from the last mission over Cambodia landed at Guam, Congresswoman Abzug and her husband were on the tarmac to meet the crew. Later as one of my commanders gave an assessment of Linebacker II to Congresswoman Abzug and her party, her husband interrupted and said triumphantly, "You may have been the Linebacker, Colonel, but we were the quarterback." And he was right. The great tragedy of the No-Win policy war in Vietnam was that it cost the lives of 58,000 of America's flowering youth, scarred our national conscience and left our nation in shame.

Other avenues of assessment of the U.S. effort in Vietnam give credit to military foresight and planning. When Linebacker II was terminated on 29 December 1972, we had flown 729 B-52 Stratofortress sorties, dropping 15,000 tons of ordnance on strategic targets in North Vietnam with a loss rate of two percent. The North Vietnamese had fired approximately 1,000 SAMs at our B-52s. The exact number is not known but best estimates have varied from 884 to 1,242. Regardless of the number fired only 24 achieved hits, and of these 24 only 15 resulted in a downed B-52. This is truly remarkable when one considers that these missiles represented state-of-the-art technology and were the best that the Soviet Union had at that time. Furthermore, that they were fired against an airplane designed in 1949 and first flown in 1952 also speaks highly of the United States' capability to keep military systems abreast of new and changing challenges as the systems age.

During the Linebacker II campaign the United States news media openly and violently condemned the bombing of North Vietnam and referred to it as carpet bombing with no regard for North Vietnamese civilian losses. On the contrary, the military and industrial targets selected and hit were very carefully executed. Crews were briefed and they followed their instructions that if there was ever any doubt as to the identification of the target they were not to release their bombs. These instructions were effective. By North Vietnam's account and report, only 1,300 North Vietnam civilians were killed, and of these no differentiation was ever made as to how many of those killed resulted from North Vietnam's defensive efforts rather than U.S. bombs. The U.S. news media never made any attempt to correct their untruthful charges of mass carpet bombing.

With the end of Linebacker II most of the commanders and certainly the crews had thought the war was over and our many long years of Southeast Asia involvement were finished. This was not the case. Since the North Vietnamese had been extremely unpredictable, we continued to hit targets in both South and North Vietnam until the signing of the Peace Accords in Paris, which provided for a Vietnam-wide cease fire effective 27 January 1973.

Because of increased pressure for bombing in Laos and Cambodia both Guam and U-Tapao, despite some draw down in forces, remained very active. The last B-52 mission in Southeast Asia was finally flown on 15 August 1973.

Eighth Air Force received the Collier Trophy, sharing it with 7th Air Force and Navy Task Force 77, "for the greatest achievement in aeronautics in America" in 1972. Subsequent to the end of Linebacker II, the pressure and activities at Andersen were reduced to some extent. One of the most rewarding postwar events was taking 10 B-52 crew members, SAC personnel from throughout Southeast Asia and the Continental U.S. to Clark Air Base, Philippines, to welcome home returning POWs. Many visitors continued to come to Andersen, including Republic of Vietnam President Thieu, who was enroute to the United States on 31 March 1973. Several times I visited the troops at U-Tapao and Kadena. On a trip to Brisbane, Australia on 9 May, I had an an unusual arrival. Because Amberley Air Base personnel had not realized that my KC-135 needed mobile stairs for proper exit, on arrival I was stranded in my airplane. Since all of the troops had been assembled in formation in the hot sun and the official party on the dais was waiting, I exited by the emergency stairs of the airplane. I then presented the USAF's Outstanding Unit Award to No. 2 (Canberra) Squadron for exceptionally meritorious service in Vietnam. The Squadron won the award while serving with the USAF from 1967 to 1971, the award making No. 2 Squadron unique in the history of the Royal Australian Air Force as the only squadron to be granted three unit awards from foreign governments.

As my two-year assignment was coming to an end, I realized it was time to leave. The great and many challenges of the past two years were now gone and with them, I think, my interest in this command. It was now time to move on. I was scheduled to become Inspector General of the United States Air Force stationed at the Pentagon in Washington, D.C. It was gratifying to hear my military personnel and civilian supporters say in a variety of ways that they would miss me. Guam's Governor Carlos G. Camacho and Mrs. Camacho hosted one of many farewell parties for me.

I took my family to Washington, D.C. before the formal change of command ceremony took place a month later. That trip to Washington gave me one more chance to fly the KC-135. My household goods were loaded aboard the slightly modified KC-135 that I had used for my travels while at Guam. The day of our departure from Guam was a somewhat sad day for me. Moving to Washington and undertaking the responsibility of the USAF Inspector General I knew would be an interesting challenge and I looked forward to it. On the other hand, I had only three more years before mandatory retirement. I really felt at home in command positions. I had had nine commands during my military career, and I knew I was a good commander. I was leaving what I knew was my last command. The job I was going to would be my last. And I did not want to leave this job that had produced so many challenges and which had ended so well. However, I do not want to look back, that is not my nature. I want always to look forward and prepare myself for the challenge that may lie ahead.

I knew my crew was already at the airplane and everything ready to make our scheduled take-off time. My wife, three small girls and our cat were ready to leave our quarters and go to the airplane. When we arrived we were surprised to find a rather large group of my people, officers and airmen and their wives plus a delegation from Agana to bid us a farewell complete with leis. It was a rather emotional time just before getting aboard. I must admit I had some difficulty saying goodbye to the wonderful people who had helped and supported me so well.

Finally I climbed aboard, started the engines, taxied out and took off. The KC-135 was very heavy, and it climbed slowly on our easterly course, destination Hickam Air Force Base, Honolulu. I had flown back to Omaha several times during these past two years. Each time we landed at Hickam, refueled and then flew nonstop to Offutt Air Force Base, Omaha. Today we would stay overnight at Hickam and the next day would fly to Andrews Air Force Base in Maryland, just outside Washington, D.C. Normally I made the take-offs and landings when I traveled by KC-135 but enroute I would go back and work on the many papers and memos that I somehow never seemed able to stay abreast of. On this flight, however, I was reluctant to leave the cockpit. I knew the three take-offs and three landings on this trip would probably be the last I would ever make in a KC-135. I was going to really miss this experience in my new assignment. I loved flying, and it never became boring. I was determined on this flight to make three absolutely perfect landings.

It was necessary to go through customs at Hickam and a customs team came aboard and thoroughly searched the airplane. On each of the times I had flown back to Omaha my crew had purchased excellent United States steaks from our commissary on Guam. After take-off from Hickam, our plan always was to climb to cruising altitude and around 11 p.m. we would have a very delicious steak dinner. On two of these previous stops customs had confiscated the steaks even though they were U.S. meat. This was really annoying and more so particularly on the next trip when one of the customs officials told my crew how good those steaks were and how he hoped we had some more this night. There was nothing we could do. On this homebound trip we did not have any steaks; we would have dinner on the ground at Hickam.

We arrived at Andrews Air Force Base after refueling at Fort Worth, Texas, in late afternoon and found good weather except for turbulence and a cross wind equivalent to 20 knots. The KC-135 did not handle cross winds very well and this cross wind rate approached its maximum. I had flown KC-135s a lot from Bunker Hill, Indiana. There were always cross winds there and I knew how to handle them. My aide sat in the jump seat (a small seat just behind and between the pilot and co-pilot). He knew how badly I wanted to really grease this one in. As I came down the final approach, with air speed at 10 knots above normal, the air was turbulent. The wings were moving up and down which was o.k., but as I flared for touch down I wanted that up-wind wing slightly low and I wanted the up-wind main wheel to touch first and ever so softly. I thought this is not going to be easy. It was no problem to land with these conditions, I told myself, it just might be a little bumpy. I wanted this one to be perfect.

To my considerable relief as I approached flare speed over the end of the runway, I was holding that left wing slightly low and it was steady, the left wheel touched, then the right. That landing had hardly been felt and there was a wild cheer from all the crew. My wife in the back heard this cheering and later asked me why only because she did not know we were on the ground. And that was my last landing in a KC-135.

The change of command ceremony which took place after my taking the family to Washington was an event I have never forgotten. My reporting date to take over the Inspector General job was 1 September 1973, with the understanding that I would return to Guam for the change of Command. Gen. John C. Meyer, CINC SAC, had asked me to accompany him in his airplane for my return to Guam. He did not mention that others would be aboard on this flight. Therefore, to my utter surprise, I found when I arrived at Andrews Air Force Base to board General Meyer's airplane that Gen. Ira Eaker, Commanding General of 8th Air Force when I joined it in England as a 1st Lieutenant in January 1943 was going with us to Guam for this ceremony. I then learned that there were more on board—Gen. William E. Kepner, Commanding General of 8th Fighter Command when I arrived in England; Lt. Gen. Dave Wade, Commanding General of 2nd Air Force when I served under him as Commander of the 305th Bomb Wing and when I received my first star; and Maj. Gen. J. B. Montgomery, my good friend and former Commander of the 8th Air Force. What a great honor to me that I was to travel with all of these people from Washington to Guam. They would attend my change of command ceremony and the reception that followed and then travel back to Washington with me. General Meyer, my friend since World War II and SAC Commander, had set up this special honor as his way of showing appreciation to me for my part as Commander of 8th Air Force in bringing the Vietnam War to an end.

As the change of Command Ceremony neared the end and I took my position to review the troops for the last time as they passed in review, I suddenly thought of General Eaker who was seated behind me. I turned around, walked to him and asked that he take the review with me. As he stood beside me and the troops passed by, I wondered how many times he might have reviewed 8th Air Force troops some 30 years before and how long it had been since he had been so honored. After the ceremony he thanked me profusely for this honor. He wrote me later that he was glad that I had been selected as the Inspector General of the Air Force. "This is a very critical assignment," he said, "and your main mission is the efficiency of the Air Force. . . . Since you have had personal experience in command of many organizations and have a battle combat record behind you, I am certain that the tactical units will feel they have a friend in you and one who understands their problems."

Once again, a reporter, this time from the <u>Pacific Daily News</u>, provided a public view of the impressive change of command ceremony at Andersen on 1 October during which Lt. Gen. George H. McKee succeeded me as commander of 8th Air Force. The reporter wrote:

> The 45-minute change of command ceremony...
> was remarkable not so much for its thousand-man
> ceremonial brigade, its marching band, and an impres-
> sive cast of dignitaries as it was for the almost surreal

silence which surrounded the event. For an hour yesterday afternoon, the entire 11,000 acre base fell silent in tribute to its departing commander. No planes landed. None took off. The usually bustling terminal at Andersen was so still that spectators gathered along its fences could hear ceremonial flags snapping in the wind 100 yards away. The only sounds to be heard near the raised reviewing stand were the soft whirring of movie cameras and an occasional hum as a gust of wind buffeted the microphones. It was a startling contrast to the tempo of operations [Lt. Gen.] Johnson presided over during his two years on Guam. During that time the 8th Air Force—in support of allied forces in Southeast Asia—carried out some of the most awesome and extensive campaigns in military history, a mission SAC Gen. John C. Meyer termed "a grand legacy of courage and dedication."

General Meyer praised the "raw courage and consummate conviction" of the air crews and the "determination and sense of duty" of the thousands of support personnel. He credited the 8th's efforts under Johnson—particularly the blitz—with bringing the United States prisoners home, and with bringing the North Vietnamese to the bargaining table.

After General Meyer's address, I thanked the men and women of my command for their hard work during my tenure at Andersen. General McKee and I exchanged salutes, and we watched ten 80-man squadrons pass in review, led by the 30-piece SAC marching band. As the newspaper headline proclaimed, this was "a moment in time, as power passes. All Quiet on Andersen Front."

Above: B-52 landing, drag chute out, in the congestion that was Anderson AFB in 1972. *Below:* Anderson AFB, Guam was saturated with B-52s shown are some of the 152 aircraft that operated from Anderson in 1972.

*Above: Just prior to departure from Offutt AFB, NE to Guam to take command of the 8th Air Force. Lt. Gen. Martin, on left and Brig. Gen. Larry Steinkraus, on right. September 1971. **Below:** Bob Hope was my guest at Guam.*

I asked retired General Ira Eaker, who commanded the 8th Air Force in England when I was there as a Lieutenant, to review the troops with me at the change of command ceremony, at Guam in October 1973.

598

Just before climbing into the cockpit of this B-52 to take-off for a bombing mission over Vietnam.

CHAPTER 8
INSPECTOR GENERAL: CLIMAX OF A 33-YEAR CAREER

The Inspector General of the United States Air Force is a respected and honorable job, but to me it was a real letdown from commanding an Air Force with more than half of the Strategic Air Command my responsibility. I liked command, I liked being my own boss, making decisions and being responsible for their outcome. The Pentagon was a different operation. Of all the key positions in the Air Staff, the Inspector General was much more on his own than others but still he was a staff officer. Despite my feelings I was determined to make the most of this assignment, probably my last in the USAF.

The Secretary of the Air Force requires the assistance of the Inspector General, and I really worked with him almost as much as with the Chief of Staff of the Air Force. The Secretary at this time was John L. McLucas, a fine man and dedicated to the Air Force. We spent a lot of time in discussion of some of the major problems such as integration, the promotion system, the relationship with other services, image and always leadership and money.

I was surprised when I arrived in the new job to find that no one had anything to say about Southeast Asia. After all that terrible war was finished, the last mission had only been flown six weeks before and I had been there during the last years and had been at Hickam in Hawaii to greet the prisoners of war upon their return. I had expected many would want to learn details of just what happened. I guess it was finally the morning of 18 December 1973 before I learned that apparently no one in the Pentagon really cared about how the war ended or who was responsible. At each morning meeting with the Chief of Staff, he would go around the table obtaining the latest information from each staff member. When on that December morning General Brown reached me, I said, "I would just like to mention that this is the first anniversary of the beginning of the 11-day war that ended the war in Vietnam." It was quiet. General Brown then said, "The first anniversary of the beginning of the 11-day war." (Pause)

"Oh, that. Next." General Brown had been in Vietnam as Command-ing General of the 7th Air Division during the late 60s and I had visited him on one of my trips from HQ SAC when I was Deputy Chief of Staff for operations. As Air Force Chief of Staff he had been deeply involved in every aspect of providing support to the Vietnam War. With this in mind it was easy to understand his remark. For too many years, we had to deal daily with this horrible thing called the Vietnam War, it was now behind us so let's move forward.

When I began visiting the Air Force bases during the following months I found the subject of Vietnam to be paramount in the minds of many. Because so many people throughout the Air Force had served in Southeast Asia and on Guam, on every base I visited officers and airmen would recognize me and come up with some comments about those Vietnam years and the great job done during Linebacker II. Their comments made me feel better. During my career I had had a series of commands of fighter squadron and wings, bomber wings, aerospace divisions and an Air Force. This breadth of experience and my involvement in three wars and with every weapon system of the Air Force may have contributed to my being selected as Inspector General. I do not know of any of my contemporaries who had this range of assignments. People express a wide range of attitudes toward the purpose of the Inspector General. Some say a person can not find the dirt under the rug unless he has swept some of it under there himself. And I certainly had had that opportunity and would know where to look. It is also often said that the two biggest lies that are told occur when the Inspector General arrives on a base and he is met by the wing commander.

"It's good to be here," the IG says, greeting the commander. "I want you to know that I am here just to help you."

"Yes, Sir, General," the wing commander replies, "it is good to have you here."

During the year I served as Inspector General, I looked upon my job as one of assistance rather than one of finding fault. From my experience as commander in the field and from the people who worked for me I found that by and large most tried to do their best.

The wing commander was selected for that position not by sheer accident because someone liked his name or the way he hit the golf ball. He was selected because he was thought capable of running that wing and commanding that organization. If I knew before a visit to a wing that something in this organization was not going too well, I always had the feeling that the wing commander had for some reason not become aware of the problem or had not found the answer. It was my job to find which was the case. Because the answer would tell me a lot about this commander, I spent a lot of time with the wing commander when I was on his base and got to know him during my visit. I hoped and believed that through these discussions I caused him to be a stronger commander.

Of course, now and then my inspection team and I found some fairly serious situations in a wing. We generally knew what was going on before we arrived, and our inspection visit verified that prior knowledge. We did not encounter specific kinds of problems, just very different ones. I have observed that in military commands as well as in other institutions in our country things tend to move in cycles. People put emphasis on one thing in their area of command for awhile and they get that fixed, and while they emphasize it, something else comes up. It rarely happens that everything in an organization goes well all the time. Some of the problems had to do with shortages of personnel, changes in aircraft, new systems of weapons or administration, and a few racial problems from time to time.

Looking back on four decades, I believe that I can say truthfully we have come a long way in handling integration in the military units and in the services overall. The 1960s was a period of turmoil, lots of demonstrations taking place partly because of the anti-Vietnam War attitude and partly because of the vocal unrest on college campuses. The 1970s was a major time of transition as the question and concern of how to integrate women and minority groups in the military and other areas of the society were being addressed. In the 1970 decade we started to settle down a bit and to put some programs of integration into practice. By and large the 1980s ran a little more smoothly. We needed two decades, a generation at least, to work through some of the main sticky points of integration. These issues in American society were reflected in the Air Force, and as Inspector General I sometimes had to deal with evidence of them.

On beginning a visit to a base, some of my staff used to remark, perhaps facetiously, "Well, we found everything all right when we arrived. We took a tour around the base first. We found the golf course was filled with wives. We found the nursery school and the other schools filled with kids of military personnel. We did not see any military people so we assumed all of them were working." Their comments described the normal scene seen from the outside. I always felt that to some degree I had left the air base a little better than I had found it. After I had visited a base and when I returned to my office, I invariably picked up the phone and called the major commander of the bases I had visited, telling him that I had been at one of his bases the previous week. I reported what I had found and what my thoughts were about some of his key people. These commanders were most appreciative to have this opportunity for firsthand information. After all they were commanders and wanted their units to do well, and they were personally concerned that if things were not going well it was a reflection on them.

The Inspector General's job carried many other responsibilities. I was involved in a number of activities such as security and air safety. At that time all the safety operations were conducted at Norton Air Force Base, California. Chuck Yeager, famous for breaking the sound barrier in 1947, ran that operation for me. I spent a lot of time probing aircraft accidents and the problems of accidents. As security personnel came under the IG's responsibility, I spent a good deal of time with the problems of security throughout the Air Force. This was an important function that quite often didn't get the attention locally that it deserved. In addition, I was always brought into the policy sessions in the Pentagon when change in tactics, in personnel rating systems, and in maintenance procedures were being considered. On my staff were some of the most highly qualified people in the Air Force in each speciality area. Therefore, an input in these discussions was valuable and sought after. Moreover, we were regularly in the field and knew at the lowest levels the effects of Air Force policy. Therefore, as IG, I was expected to lend some good advice on questions of what effect any changes in these areas would have on outfits and commanders in the field. After any change went into effect, I had to know very quickly how it was received and was it as effective as it was intended to be.

The nature of my job caused me to be away from Washington a lot. Since we made inspections in Europe and the Pacific, I had far flung responsibilities. When I was in Washington the social life was active and interesting. With all the embassies and their many parties we could accept only a few of the many invitations received. I was part of a small group of 12 people who enjoyed golf. Most of us worked at least part of every Saturday so from among the 12 golfers we hoped that on every Saturday there would be eight players or two foursomes who could play. Weather conditions were not an excuse. If we weren't working we must report to the Andrews Air Force Base golf course regardless of weather. We followed this right through the winter in rain, snow, cold or sunshine and had a great time. I think I probably played about twice a month.

So the time passed very quickly during my year in Washington. Then the summer of 1974 approached. Summer is the period when changes in assignments are made in the Air Force and people are moved. This summer meant a change in the Air Force Chief of Staff. Knowing the new Chief I was quite sure he would effect a number of changes in his key staff. It was time for me to start thinking about my life beyond the Air Force. If I were to leave, what would I do, where would I go? I was not particularly concerned as to whether I could find something to do, rather it would be my decision and my choice. After 33 years of going where I was told to go and undertaking the job I was assigned to do, this change would take a bit of getting used to. I also could not forget the thoughts and comments of General Power (former CINCSAC) concerning early retirement. Why would anyone want to leave the Air Force where his contemporaries and associates were well-educated, physically fit, dedicated and possessed with high integrity to go into the civilian world where you would have no control or ideas as to what kind of person you might be working with? General Power made a good point, but I was not that young anymore, and I had given to the Air Force my very best effort.

In any case, retirement would come soon. It was not likely that I would again be presented with a real challenge. After long and careful thought and consultation with some of my best friends, both military and civilian, I decided to retire on 1 September 1974.

After making this decision I thought a lot about what I was leaving—the many changes that had taken place since 1941, the great challenges I had faced, and the many, many wonderful people I had known and worked with. For me, the Air Force had been more than a job or profession. It had been, in a sense, a family, a much deeper relathionship I believe than one would have found in civilian business, industry or laboratory. This feeling of belonging, of esprit, had been extremely rewarding.

I couldn't help remembering some of the remarks my commandant had made at my graduation and commissioning ceremony at Ellington Field, Texas so long ago. I had just had my 2nd Lieutenant bars and wings pinned on, and as I stood in the hot sun, I listened to words to this effect "A great and unprecedented opportunity is offered to you with your commission. It is a tremendous honor and sincere tribute to your ability and potential as a leader. You will make mistakes and you will make incorrect decisions. But your correct decisions will by far outnumber your errors. The personal qualities that have brought you to this point in your life and marked you for selection as a military officer virtually guarantee that you will most often have the good judgement to do the right thing. Keep an open mind, pursue knowledge and be honest with yourself and others. The future belongs to you."

That message stayed with me down through the years, and I believe I lived it to the best of my ability. I had no regrets. My career had been an interesting one during a challenging and changing period—World War II, Korea, Vietnam, fighters, bombers, reconnaissance and missiles. It was now time to leave to start a new career and to see what I could accomplish in the civilian world. So on 1

September 1974 I retired from the Air Force in an appropriate ceremony with many friends and contemporaries present and was presented for the second time the Distinguished Service Medal.

L to R: Gabby Gabreski, Jerry Johnson and Bud Mahurin in Oshkosh, WI., 1993.

With my boss, Governor David Pryor, and two members of the Crime Commission Board of Directors in Little Rock, AR 1975.

EPILOGUE

After retiring from the Air Force, I moved to Little Rock, Arkansas for several reasons. I knew most of the leaders in the area, the climate was acceptable, the area offered excellent recreational opportunities, and I had been offered a job that appealed to me. Before leaving Washington, however, I had accepted an offer to become a consultant with a small but rapidly growing professional services company named after the three founding members, Braddock, Dunn and MacDonald. This was later changed to the BDM Corporation. This position would not interfere with my work in Little Rock.

It happened that my retirement occurred during the rather severe economic recession following the oil embargo of 1973. Therefore, the Little Rock job did not materialize as I had expected it would. David Pryor was Governor of Arkansas at this time and invited me to join him for lunch one day. I accepted and during lunch he asked if I would be interested in becoming involved with state government. Of course, I wanted to know what kind of involvement. He explained that he would like me to become the Executive Director of the Arkansas Crime Commission. He explained his great concern for this area of his responsibilities and felt that it needed some strong leadership and direction. I thanked him but said I would need to think about it. After much serious thought I decided to accept his offer. I would be working with the Law Enforcement and Assistance Administration (LEAA) in Washington, would travel quite a bit and would be my own boss reporting to Governor Pryor as needed. I continued with my consulting job with BDM.

This job with state government turned out to be a challenge in many ways and I learned a lot. Bill Clinton was active in Arkansas politics at this time and I saw him often. In the 1978 election he became Governor and David Pryor became a United States Senator. Since I was a governor's appointee, I immediately submitted my resignation to Governor Clinton. A few months later he accepted it.

BDM for some time had been interested in opening a market in the Middle East. I was now free to spend more time in this endeavor. In the spring of 1980 through competitive bidding BDM won a contract with the Royal Saudi Air Force. There was a stipulation, however, that I would be the on-site contract manager. I was promoted to vice president of BDM and on 1 July 1980 I arrived in Ryadh to undertake what would be another major challenge.

I had read a lot about the Saudis and particularly about their customs and attitudes toward women, crime and alcohol. I had visited and worked with them on three occasions during contract negotiations and had flown a B-47 into Dahrein in the fall of 1957. I had thought I knew them pretty well. I soon found out, however, that I didn't know them well at all. The ensuing period proved to be a real test of my best skills and diplomatic training. I was fortunate in finding a really first-class young Saudi to act as my interpreter whom I found to be highly respected by other Saudis.

Eventually things got sorted out and the contract ran smoothly. I returned to BDM Headquarters in Washington quite often and time passed quickly. My contract had been set for only two years, but I stayed for more than three, The original contract had been increased in scope and value plus I had successfully negotiated two additional contracts. BDM was doing well. I felt it was time to go back to the home office in Washington. There I would be responsible for expanding our market into other Middle East countries.

After returning to Washington I was very busy with a great amount of travel to the Middle East. Suddenly in August 1985 I found myself in Georgetown University Hospital undergoing triple by-pass surgery. Shortly after this event I was divorced.

As I thought back over my Air Force career and the recent eleven years with the many things I had been involved with and the resulting stress and pressure that I had survived, I began to realize that maybe it was time to start living a less stressful life.

I had visited Sarasota on the west coast of Florida and thought the cultural environment of this town with its interest in the arts and live theater just might be a desirable location. I moved to Sarasota and am now married to an absolutely charming and wonderful lady. We are leading a full and interesting life which includes much travel and a small house in the mountains of western North Carolina. In addition, we each have our own interests and pursuits which keep us busy. But we do have time for golf which we both enjoy.

Despite the many changes that I have witnessed in our society and the problems our country faces I have great confidence in this great country and its people and believe the good far exceeds the bad. I often visit Air Force Bases both here and abroad. It is always a pleasure to meet and talk with the young Air Force people of today. It always renews my confidence in the future and my firm belief that this country has not yet reached the heights it is capable of achieving.

Jerry and Mardi Johnson - Sarasota, FL, 1995.

INDEX
Groups

B-29 91, 93, 103, 116
B-47 133, 146, 149, 150, 161
B-50 91
B-52 153, 161, 162, 167, 169, 182, 183, 190, 192, 196, 199, 201, 204, 207, 209
B-52B 164
B-52D 198, 199, 202, 205
B-52G 153, 161, 167, 198, 202, 205
B-52H 167
B-57 134, 143, 144
B-58 170, 171, 173, 182
B-58 Hustler 175
Bacon, Brig. Gen. Bill 93, 161
Baltimore, Sgt. George 32, 33, 36, 64, 65
Barksdale Air Force Base 170, 172, 179
Barksdale, Martha 12, 13
Basic Trainer 17
BDM Corporation 230
Biggin Hill 44
Biggs Air Force Base 162, 168
Bill, Col. Hudnell 111
Black Knight Squadron 139, 143, 144
Blanchard, Maj. Gen. William G. 145
Boeing Aircraft Company 91, 112, 149
Bovington 28
Braddock, Dunn and MacDonald 230
Bradley Field 22
Bradley, Gen. Omar 46
Brewer, Lt. 17
Brickner, Cpl. 65
British Broadcasting Company 82
British Broadcasting Corporation 45
Brize Norton 152
Brown, General 224
Bryant and Stratton Business School 11
BT-14 17
Bunker Hill Air Force Base, IN 177, 185, 187
Burtonwood Depot 28
Byerly, Col. Jean 81

C

C-46 84
C-47 105

C-5 198
C-54 103
C-61 45
C-97 121, 122, 124
Cagney, James 57
Camacho, Carlos G. 214
Camp Kilmer 23
Castle Air Force Base 162, 167
Chickasha, Oklahoma 8, 14
Ching Chuan Kang base 195
Chrysler, Warrant Officer 130
Clark Air Base 213
Clark Field 195
Clark, Ramsay 191
Class 42-D 19
Clough, Lt. Col. Bill 109
Cohen, Oscar 54
Cold War 176
Collier Trophy 213
Command and Staff School 90
Conger, Lt. [Paul] 42
Cope, John 7, 9
Corrigan, Wrong-way 9
Curtis, Joe 20

D

Danish Air Defense Command 124
Davis-Monthan Air Force Base 161
Deane, Wing Commander 44
Department of Defense 138
Devers, Lt. Gen. Jacob L. 47
Distinguished Flying Cross 67
Distinguished Service Cross 67
Dixon, Major 105
Doolittle, Gen. Jimmy 55, 80, 88
Dulag Luft 69
Dulles, John Foster 138
Dunham, Lt. Col. Dinghy 111
Dunkerque 78
Dunlap, Col. Glen W. 192
Duxford, England 65

E

Eaker, Gen. Ira 47, 88, 216, 221

Printed in the USA
CPSIA information can be obtained
at www.ICGtesting.com
JSHW022324140824
68134JS00019B/1278